German
verb handbook

Joy Saunders

Berlitz Publishing /
APA Publications GmbH & Co. Verlag KG,
Singapore Branch, Singapore

German Verb Handbook

CONTACTING THE EDITORS
Every effort has been made to provide accurate information in this publication, but changes are inevitable. The publisher cannot be responsible for any resulting loss, inconvenience, or injury. We would appreciate it if readers would call our attention to any errors or outdated information by contacting Berlitz Publishing, 95 Progress Street, Union, NJ 07083, USA. Fax: 1-908-206-1103. email: comments@berlitzbooks.com

All rights reserved.
Published by Apa Publications GmbH & Co. Verlag KG, Singapore Branch, Singapore. Printed by Insight Print Services (pte) Ltd. May 2005

Berlitz Trademark Reg. U.S. Patent Office and other countries. Marca Registrada.
Used under license from Berlitz Investment Corporation.

Cover Photo © Andy Sitt / Alamy; inset photo © Photo Alto

The Author:

Written by **Joy Saunders**, an experienced teacher, schools inspector and educational consultant.

The Series Editor:

Christopher Wightwick was formerly principal inspector of Modern Languages for England and UK representative on the Council of Europe Modern Languages Project.

CONTENTS

B The model verbs

How to use this handbook

This handbook aims to provide a full description of the German verb system for all learners and users of the German language. It provides the following information:

• a chapter on the verb system
• the conjugation in full of ninety-two common verbs, grouped to show the common patterns underlying the system
• a full subject index
• a verb index containing over 2,300 verbs with their English meanings

An important feature of the handbook is that examples, showing many of the verbs in use, are given in the model verb pages.

THE VERB SYSTEM IN GERMAN

This section describes the functions of verbs in general. Information is given on word order, the use of tenses, the way verbs govern different cases and prepositions and the way they are formed.

THE MODEL VERBS

This section gives the conjugation in full of every tense of a verb in the active and the passive. The two reflexive verb forms are also illustrated. Ninety-two common verbs are then set out as models.

A selection of verbs that follow the same pattern as each individual verb is listed underneath. For each model, separable and inseparable verbs are also given. Examples are then provided of these verbs in use, to illustrate different tenses and a wide range of different meanings and idiomatic constructions.

THE SUBJECT INDEX

The subject index gives page references for all the main grammatical terms used.

THE VERB INDEX

For each verb, information is given on whether it is transitive or intransitive, the auxiliary it takes in the past tenses, the case and/or prepositions that it governs and its English meaning. Common secondary meanings are illustrated in a brief phrase. The most important and up-to-date forms of verbs with inseparable prefixes and separable particles are listed.

HOW TO FIND THE INFORMATION YOU WANT

If you want to check on the form, meaning or use of a verb, first look it up in the index. This gives a range of information:

- A hairline in the middle of the verb shows that the verb is separable. The first part is the separable particle and is stressed.
- Any preposition that normally follows the verb. The preposition takes its normal case, but where there is a choice, this is indicated.
- The case that the verb governs, unless it is the accusative (direct object) or dative (indirect object).
- Whether the verb is transitive, intransitive, reflexive or impersonal, and whether it takes the auxiliary **sein** in the compound past tenses. If no auxiliary is shown, the verb takes **haben**.
- The English meaning of the verb. Only the basic meaning is shown for most verbs.
- A number indicating at which entry or entries you will find further information about the verb or others like it.
- A short phrase or sentence following some verbs, giving important subsidiary meanings.

If you want further information on the form or use of the verb, turn to the entry reference given. At this entry you will find:

- the full conjugation of the present and simple past (imperfect tenses) of each model verb
- the first person singular form of other tenses, including the **Konjunktiv** (subjunctive)
- a list of other verbs following the same pattern
- notes indicating any exceptions to this pattern
- short dialogs and sentences illustrating usages of these verbs and some of the different tenses

Where two entry references are given, the first refers you to a verb with a similar stem. The second indicates a separable or inseparable verb that is similar.

If you want to know the full form of other tenses, you should note that they are always regular. They can easily be checked by looking up the full tense of the auxiliary verb indicated, **sein** [➤1] or **haben** [➤2] for the past tenses, and **werden** [➤3] for the future.

For further information on how the verb system works, refer to Part A The Verb System in German.

A
THE VERB SYSTEM IN GERMAN

1

The verb system

1a Simple and compound verbs

(i) All verbs can either stand alone as a simple verb or be combined with other verbs to form compound tenses. A small group of verbs is commonly used to form the compound tenses. When used like this, they are called auxiliary verbs.

(ii) The main auxiliary verbs are **sein, haben,** and **werden. Sein** and **haben** are used to form compound past tenses. [➤2i(i)]. **Werden** is used to form the future [➤2h(vii)].

(iii) A group of verbs called *modal auxiliaries* is used to give an indication of a mood. Although some can take a direct object, they are more usually followed by an infinitive, without **zu.** They are **können,** (be able, can), **wollen** (want to, will), **mögen** (like, may), **müssen** (must, have to), **dürfen** (may), and **sollen** (shall, am to, be obliged to). **Lassen** (let, have done) can also be included in this group.

Ich will gehen.	I want to go.

[➤model verbs 4-10]

1b Transitive and intransitive verbs

(i) Verbs are said to "govern" other parts of the sentence. A verb is said to be *transitive* if it governs a direct object, which may be a word or phrase; in German, the direct object is in the accusative case.

Wir bauen einen neuen Wohnblock.	We are building a new block of apartments.

(ii) A clause can also be used as direct object.

Er sagt, dass er kommen wollte.	He says he wanted to come.

(iii)   A verb is said to be *intransitive* if it stands alone without an object, or is followed by an indirect object or preposition. Although many verbs can be used in both ways, many more cannot, and this must be checked in the index.

Er glaubt *mir*.	He believes *me*.

Note that in this case the English verb governs a direct object and the German verb an indirect object.

Note: that **bitten** (to ask/request), **fragen** (to ask/inquire), and **sprechen mit** (to speak to) take a direct accusative object.

Ich habe *ihn* gefragt.	I asked *him*.
Ich werde *ihn* sprechen.	I will talk *to him*.

(iv)   Some verbs govern two objects, a direct and an indirect: these are still transitive. Verbs of saying, showing, giving, and taking from are in this group.

Ich gab *ihm* das Buch.	I gave *him* the book.

The **ihm** here refers to the person *to whom* the book is given and is the indirect object. The indirect object is in the dative case.

(v)   The indirect object can also show the person affected by an action. This usage is common in German.

Er hat *mir* das Auto repariert.	He repaired the car *for me*.

(vi)   A very few verbs take two objects in the accusative. The most common are **kosten** (to cost), **lehren** (to teach), **nennen/ heißen** (to call/name) and **angehen** (to concern).

Das kostet *mich ein Vermögen*.	That is going to cost *me a fortune*.

(vii)   A very few German verbs, mainly used in formal writing, take an object in the genitive case.

Ich kann mich *seines* *Namens* **nicht entsinnen.**	I cannot remember *his name*.

(viii) A few verbs are used to link two phrases in the nominative, which refer to the same thing. The most common are **sein, werden, heißen,** and **bleiben**.

Er *ist/bleibt* **mein bester Freund.**	He *is/remains* my best friend.

Note Transitive verbs are indicated in the index by (tr.). Intransitive verbs are indicated by (intr.). Where a verb can be used both transitively and intransitively, it is indicated by (tr. & intr.). If a verb is marked as transitive in the index, it takes a direct object in the accusative. The normal use of the direct and indirect object is not specially indicated for each verb. The case governed by a verb is only shown where usage is different from what you might expect from the English.

1c Reflexive verbs [➤Model verbs sich setzen]

(i) Many verbs can be used reflexively as in English, to show:

 • that the action is done by the subject of the verb to him/her/itself

Ich wasche mich.	I wash myself.

 • that the action is reciprocal, that is, people are doing it to each other

Wir küssten uns.	We kissed (one another).

(ii) Some verbs are frequently used reflexively with a change of meaning or an English passive meaning.

Ich interessiere mich für...	I am interested in...

(iii) A dative reflexive (indirect object) pronoun is often used if the verb already has a direct object, to make it clear that the action is being done to, or affects, the subject.

Ich habe mir den Arm gebrochen.   I have broken my arm.

(iv)   A few verbs are always used with a dative reflexive pronoun.

Ich bilde mir etwas ein.   I am imagining something.

Note   Reflexive forms are indicated in the index by (refl.) or (dat. refl.). They are only shown if the verb is always used in the reflexive, or if there is a significant change of meaning.

1d   *Impersonal verbs*

(i)   A number of verbs are commonly used impersonally, i.e., with **es** as their subject. Some verbs are almost always found in this form.

Es regnet.   It's raining.

(ii)   Some verbs have a different meaning when they are used impersonally.

Er kommt an.	He arrives.
Es kommt darauf an, ob ...	It depends on whether ...
Er gibt mir das Buch.	He gives me the book.
Es gibt hier viele Kneipen.	There are many bars here.

(iii)   Verbs are sometimes used impersonally when it is not clear who is performing the action.

Es klopft.   Someone is knocking.

(iv)   The **es** subject is commonly used in certain idioms in a caretaker role and not as a true subject.

Es tut mir leid.	I am sorry.
Mir ist kalt.	I am cold.

Note   Impersonal use is shown in the index as (impers.).

THE VERB SYSTEM IN GERMAN

1e   *Verbs governing a preposition*

(i)   Many verbs are commonly followed by a preposition.

Er besteht auf einer Antwort.   He insists on an answer.

(ii)   The prepositions take the same case as usual. It is worth
         noting that where the case can be either accusative or dative,
         the accusative case is most common with **auf** and **über**, and
         the dative with **an**.

Sie denkt an mich.   She is thinking of me.

Note   The preposition is only shown in the index where the usage differs
         from the English. The case is shown where there is a possible choice.

1f   *Separable and inseparable verbs*

(i)   Inseparable prefixes and separable verbal particles are an
         important feature of the German verb system. They modify the
         meaning of the simple verb and give greater precision of
         meaning [➤2l]. All the common simple verbs have a wide
         range of compounds formed in this way.

2 The formation of the tenses

2a Tenses

(i) Verbs are used in tenses, which indicate when the action takes place, i.e., in the past, present, or future.

(ii) Verb forms can also be said to be either *indicative* or *subjunctive*, which we shall call by its German name **Konjunktiv** [➤2k]. The indicative is the most common form.

(iii) Tenses that are formed of more than one element are called compound tenses.

Ich bin nach Hause gegangen.	I have gone home.
Wir werden später essen.	We will eat later.

2b The stem of the verb

(i) The stem is the basic unit of the verb without prefixes, verbal particles, or endings. The ending of a verb is determined by the person (first, second, third) and number (singular/plural) of its subject, e.g., **komm** is the stem of **kommen**, and **-en** is the ending.

2c The infinitive

(i) This is the stem of the verb plus the ending **-en**, e.g., **kommen** (to come). It is the part listed in dictionaries. In English it is usually preceded by "to." In German it is sometimes preceded by **zu**.

2d The present participle

(i) The present participle is the form that corresponds to the English form in "-ing." All German verbs form it by adding the ending **-d** to the infinitive, e.g., **schreibend** (writing). The only exceptions are **sein** and **tun**, which have the forms **seiend** and **tuend**.

(ii)   German uses its **-end** form far less than English uses its "-ing" form. An infinitive or relative clause is often used instead.

2e   The past participle

(i)   The past participle is the form that combines with auxiliary verbs to form the compound past tenses and the passive.

(ii)   It ends in **-t** or **-et** in weak verbs and **-en** in strong verbs [➤2f].

(iii)   If the prefix of a verb is unstressed and the verb is inseparable, the past participle is formed without **ge-**, e.g., **erklärt** (explained). A few verbs appear in both separable and inseparable forms, but with different meanings.

(iv)   If a modal auxiliary [➤1a (iii)] is followed by an infinitive, the past participle is the same as the infinitive; if there is no infinitive, it takes the weak form in **ge...t.**

Ich habe nichts hören können.	I could not hear anything.
Ich habe es nicht gekonnt.	I could not do it.

2f   The verb endings used to form the tenses

Pronoun	Present tense	Past tense (weak)	Konjunktiv (subjunctive)	Past tense (strong)
ich	-e	-(e)te	-e	–
du	-(e)st	-(e)test	-est	-(e)st
er/sie/es	-(e)t	-(e)te	-e	–
wir	-en	-ten	-en	-en
ihr	-(e)t	-tet	-et	-(e)t
sie	-en	-ten	-en	-en
Sie	-en	-ten	-en	-en

Note   The endings are set out in this way to show that the endings of the different tenses are very similar. The simple past of weak verbs also adds **-t-** or **-et-** to the stem [➤3a, **machen** 11 and **arbeiten** 12].

2g The imperative

(i) The imperative, or command form, is regular in all verbs except
sein [➤**sein** 1]. It is formed as follows:

• **du** form
– infinitive stem, which is the most common pattern:
   Geh! (Go!); **Fang an!** (Begin!);
   Lauf! (Run!); **Setz dich!** (Sit down!).

– verbs that change the stem-vowel to **-i-** or **-ie-** in the
present also change in the imperative:
   Gib es mir! (Give it to me!); **Lies!** (Read!).

• **ihr** form
As in the present tense:
   Kommt! (Come!); **Setzt euch!** (Sit down!).

• **Sie** form
The **Sie** form, inverted:
   Gehen Sie! (Go!); **Hören Sie zu!** (Listen!)

• First person plural
The **wir** form, inverted:
   Gehen wir! (Let's go!). **Essen wir!** (Let's eat!)

There is an alternative form: **Wir wollen gehen!** (Let's go!).
The **wir** form is not listed in the model verb pages.

2h The active tenses

(i) A verb in the active form is a verb in its most usual form, i.e.,
when the subject performs the action. Active tenses (indicative)
are formed as shown below. [For **Konjunktiv** forms ➤2k.]

(ii) The present tense is formed from the stem of the verb with
present tense endings.

Ich komme.	I come.	**Er geht.**	He goes.

(iii) The simple past tense of weak verbs is formed from the stem
of the verb, plus **-t-** or **-et-** and the weak past tense endings.

Ich kaufte...	I bought...	**Sie arbeiteten.**	They worked.

THE VERB SYSTEM IN GERMAN

(iv) The simple past tense of strong verbs is formed from the stem of the verb, modified as shown in the model verb pages, and the strong past tense endings.

Sie ging.	She went.	**Sie schrieben.**	They wrote.

(v) The present perfect tense is formed from the present of either **sein** or **haben** with the past participle.

Er ist gefahren. He has driven.
Ich habe geschlafen. I have slept.

(vi) The past perfect (pluperfect) is formed from the simple past of **sein** or **haben** and the past participle.

Sie hatten sich gesetzt. They had sat down.
Wir waren angekommen. We had arrived.

(vii) The future tense is formed from the present tense of **werden** and the infinitive.

Sie werden reisen. They will travel.

(viii) The future perfect is formed from the future of **haben** or **sein** and the past participle.

Er wird gefahren sein. He will have driven.
Sie werden geschrieben haben. They will have written.

2i *The auxiliary verbs* sein *and* haben

(i) Compound past tenses are formed from the past participle plus an auxiliary, as in English.

Ich habe geschrieben. I have written.

In German, two auxiliaries are used, **haben** and **sein**.

(ii) If the verb is used transitively or as a reflexive verb, it takes **haben**.

(iii) If the verb is intransitive, it may take **sein** or **haben**. It must use **sein** if it indicates a change of place or a change of state.

Ich bin gelaufen.	I have walked.	**Er ist gegangen.**	He has gone.

(iv) A few verbs can take either **sein** or **haben,** depending on how they are used.

Ich bin nach Frankreich gefahren.	I have driven to France. (change of place)
Ich habe das neue Auto gefahren.	I have driven the new car. (transitive use)

(v) Verbs with prefixes or verbal particles listed as following a certain model do not necessarily take the same auxiliary as the simple verb. Each verb has to be checked separately.

2j The passive

(i) A verb is used in the passive to show that the action is done to the subject of the sentence.

(ii) All active tenses are mirrored by passive forms. These are formed from the appropriate tense of the auxiliary **werden** and the past participle of the verb.

Ich wurde befördert.	I was promoted.

(iii) The past participle of **werden** is shortened to **worden** in the passive.

Ich bin befördert worden.	I was/have been promoted.
Er war angerufen worden.	He had been called on the phone.

THE VERB SYSTEM IN GERMAN

(iv)   The future perfect is rarely found and is replaced by a different construction, e.g., using **man**.

Man wird ihn gefunden haben.	He will have been found.

(v)   Note that an indirect object cannot become the subject when a verb becomes passive: **man sagte mir** (they told me) becomes **es wurde mir gesagt** or **mir wurde gesagt** (I was told) in the passive.

(vi)   Note the distinction between the true passive, which focuses on an action, and the use of the past participle to describe a state. In this case **sein** is used, not **werden**.

Der Tisch wird gedeckt.	The table is being set.
Der Tisch ist gedeckt.	The table is (already) set.

2k   Tenses in the *Konjunktiv (subjunctive) mood*

(i)   These are the tenses used in indirect speech, in conditional sentences, or to indicate uncertainty. All indicative tenses, active and passive, have their "mirror" **Konjunktiv** tenses. They are formed as shown below. All tenses have the same endings [➤2f].

(ii)   The names often given to the different tenses can be confusing, since their use and meaning differ from the English. In particular, the terms *present subjunctive, past subjunctive,* and *conditional* are misleading. We prefer to use the terms given below, but the terminology used in older grammars is given in parentheses (brackets).

(iii)   **Konjunktiv I,** simple, (present subjunctive) is formed from the stem of the verb with **Konjunktiv** endings. The present tense of all verbs (except **sein**) is regular: **er gehe, du laufest, ich sei.**

(iv)   **Konjunktiv I**, future, (future subjunctive) is formed from the **Konjunktiv I,** simple, of **werden** and the infinitive: **er werde schreiben.**

(v)   **Konjunktiv I**, perfect, (perfect subjunctive) is formed from the **Konjunktiv I,** simple, of **haben** or **sein** with the past participle: **er sei gegangen, er habe gesehen.**

(vi)   **Konjunktiv II**, simple conditional, (past or imperfect subjunctive) of almost all weak verbs is identical with the indicative simple past tense. Strong verbs add the **Konjunktiv** endings to the simple past tense, but the vowel is often modified by an *umlaut*. There are several irregular forms, and the most common are given. The simple conditional of verbs is often avoided, especially in speech, by using the compound conditional tense instead. This occurs particularly with weak verbs which have no distinct **Konjunktiv** form, and with the irregular strong forms: **er kaufte** or **er würde kaufen**; **er schriebe** or **er würde schreiben**.

(vii)   **Konjunktiv II**, compound conditional, (conditional) is formed from the **Konjunktiv II**, simple, of **werden** and the infinitive: **er würde gehen.**

(viii)   **Konjunktiv II**, past conditional, (conditional perfect) is formed from the **Konjunktiv II**, simple, of **sein** or **haben** and the past participle: **er hätte gewartet, sie wäre gekommen.**

Note   In the model verb pages, the terms have been shortened for the sake of simplicity: **Konjunktiv I**, simple, is called **Konjunktiv I**; **Konjunktiv II**, simple, is called **Konjunktiv II**, and the reference to **Konjunktiv I** or **II** has been omitted in the other tenses.

2l   *Inseparable prefixes and separable particles*

(i)   Inseparable prefixes are:

  • always written as one word with the main verb
  • never stressed

(ii)   Separable particles are:

  • semi-independent words that are always placed at or near the end of the clause: **er kommt heute** *an*; **ich fahre** *los*
  • attached to the main verb only when this is at the end of a clause: **... wenn ich morgen** *an*komme
  • always attached to the infinitive and the participles: **ich bin** *an*gekommen; **ich werde** *los*fahren
  • always stressed: **ich bin** *an*gekommen

(iii)   It is important to check whether verbal prefixes and particles are separable or inseparable.

  • **be-, ent-, er-, ge-, ver-,** and **zer-** are always inseparable prefixes. The past participle is formed without **ge-**, e.g., **bestellt.**

- **ab-, an-, auf-, aus-, ein-, mit-**, and **zu-** are always separable particles. The past participle is formed with **ge-**, e.g., **abgestellt, ausgegangen.**
- **hin-, her-**, and their compounds **hinab-, heraus-**, etc. are separable.
- **durch-, hinter-, miss-, über-, unter-, voll-, wider-, wieder-**, and **um-** are sometimes separable.

(iv) If there are two prefixes or a combination of prefixes and particles, follow these examples:

- two separables, e.g., **ich ging hinaus, ich bin hinausgegangen**
- two inseparables ,e.g., **er missversteht, er hat missverstanden**
- separable plus inseparable, e.g., **er bestellt ... ab, er hat ... abbestellt**
- inseparable plus separable, e.g., **er beauftragt, er hat beauftragt**

(v) There are a large number of double verbal particles formed with **hin-** and **her-**. They are formed fairly freely and added to verbs of movement to show direction. **Hin-** indicates movement away from the speaker or onlooker; **her-** indicates movement toward the speaker. The most common forms are given in the index, but not all can be included.

2m *Word order*

(i) German word order is often the same as in English, i.e., the verb follows the subject.

Ich gehe nach Hause.	I *am going* home.

(ii)   In main clauses, the main verb is always the second idea (although not necessarily the second word). This means the verb precedes the subject when another word, phrase, or clause comes before it.

Bald *gehe ich* **nach Hause.**	Soon I *am going* home.
Wenn ich fertig bin, *gehe ich* **nach Hause.**	When I am ready, I *will go* home.

(iii)   In compound tenses, the past participle and the infinitive always go at the end of the clause. In Part B, which lists model verbs, the words following the three dots are those which go to the end of the clause, e.g., **ich werde ... getan haben** (I will have done ...) could be used as follows: **Ich werde die Arbeit bis Montag getan haben** (I will have done the work by Monday).

(iv)   In subordinate clauses, the main verb goes to the end. If it is an auxiliary, it usually follows the past participle or infinitive.

Er konnte mich nicht treffen, weil ich nach Berlin gefahren *war.*	He could not meet me, because I *had* gone to Berlin.

The main categories of verbs

3a   Weak and strong verbs

(i)   There are two main categories of verbs, called *weak* and *strong*.

(ii)   *Weak verbs:*

- add **-t-** or **-et-** to the stem in the simple past before the endings
- add **-t** or **-et** to the stem to form the past participle (with or without the prefix **ge-** [➤2e])

(iii)   *Strong verbs:*

- change the stem-vowel in the simple past
- usually change the stem-vowel in the past participle
- often change the stem-vowel of the **du** and **er/sie/es** forms of the present tense
- add **-en** to the modified stem to form the past participle (with or without the prefix **ge-** [➤2e])

(iv)   A few verbs can be either strong or weak. In some of these verbs, the strong and weak forms have different meanings, e.g., **schaffen, schaffte, geschafft** (to do, achieve); **schaffen, schuf, geschaffen** (to create) [➤schaffen 74].

(v)   Some verbs have both forms in use, with one form predominating, e.g., **schmelzen** (to melt).

Note   Some verbs have very rare strong forms. These are not given. For further details see the model verb pages.

3b   Classes of verbs

(i)   You can predict the forms of most verbs by knowing which class or group they fall into.

(ii)   Weak verbs are nearly all regular, [for minor spelling changes ➤3c]. For the full conjugation of a weak verb, of a similar verb with an inseparable prefix, and for one with a separable verbal particle, see the model verb section. The irregular weak verbs are listed separately.

(iii)   Strong verbs fall into seven major classes. Each class has a distinctive pattern of vowel changes, although there are variations of stem-vowel in the infinitive. The main classes are:

Class I

infinitive in **-ei-**
(occasionally **-e-** or **-au-**)
past stem in **-ie-** or **-i-**
past participle in **-ie-** or **-i-**

Class V

infinitive in **-e-**
(occasionally in **-i-/-ie-**)
past stem in **-a-**
past participle in **-e-**

Class II

infinitive in **-ie-**
past stem in **-o-**
past participle in **-o-**

Class VI

infinitive in **-a-**
past stem in **-u-**
past participle in **-a-**

Class III

infinitive stem in **-ind-, -ing-** or **-ink-**
past stem in **-a-**
past participle in **-u-**

Class VII

infinitive in **-a-**
(but also many other vowels)
past stem in **-ie-**
past participle in **-a-**

Class IV

infinitive in **-e-** or **-i-**
(except for **kommen**)
past stem in **-a-**
past participle in **-o-**

other verbs: **stehen** and **tun**

For each class, a model is given of a simple verb without a prefix, of a compound verb with an inseparable prefix, and of one with a separable verbal particle. There are some sub-groups, and models of the most important ones are also given in full. A few verbs with small irregularities that could cause problems are given in full.

3c   *Spelling variations*

(i)   There are some common spelling changes. These are not shown for every verb if they follow common rules.

(ii)   Many verbs add or omit an **-e-** in their different forms, and the rules are set out below. However, a common-sense rule is that the **-e-** should be added or omitted when this makes it easier to pronounce the word.

THE VERB SYSTEM IN GERMAN

(iii) If the stem of a verb ends in **-d** or **-t,** it is always followed by an **-e-**, e.g., **er/sie/es antwortet, du leitest, ich arbeitete, er/sie/es findet.**
There are the following exceptions:

- vowel change in the **du** form of the present tense, e.g., **du hältst, du rätst**
- vowel change in the **er/sie/es** form of the present tense when the **-t** is not usually added, e.g., **er hält, er rät** (*but* **er lädt**)
- **du** form simple past of strong verbs, e.g., **du fandst, du batst.**

(iv) If the verb ends in **-eln**:

- take off the **-n** of the infinitive before adding endings (not **-en** as with most verbs), e.g., **er behandelt**
- form the **ich** form of the present tense and the **du** form of the imperative by omitting the **-e** of the stem, e.g., **ich lächle, lächle!**

(v) Verbs ending in **-ern** sometimes drop the **-e-** of the stem in speech, e.g., **ich wandre.**

(vi) The stem of weak verbs ending in a consonant + **m** or **n** usually adds an **-e-** to make it easier to pronounce (not if the consonant is **l** or **r**), e.g., **du atmest, er segnet, ihr rechnet** *but* **es qualmt, er warnt, es wärmt.**

(vii) If the stem of a strong or weak verb ends in: **-s, -ß, -z, -tz, -x:**

- the **du** form of the present ends in **-t** (not **-est**), e.g., **du heißt** (The full form **heißest** is now archaic.)
- the **du** form of the simple past ends in **-est** (not **-st**), e.g., **du hießest**

(viii) If the verb stem ends in **-ß** or **-ss**, use **ß** after a long vowel or a dipthong, e.g. **beißen, vergaß**; use **-ss** after a short vowel, e.g. **vergessen, gebissen.**

Personal pronouns

English subject	Nominative	Accusative	Dative	Reflexive accusative/ dative	English object/ reflexive
Singular					
I	**ich**	**mich**	**mir**	**mich/mir**	me/myself
you	**du**	**dich**	**dir**	**dich/dir**	you/yourself
he	**er**	**ihn**	**ihm**	**sich**	him/himself
she	**sie**	**sie**	**ihr**	**sich**	her/herself
it	**es**	**es**	**ihm**	**sich**	it/itself
Plural					
we	**wir**	**uns**	**uns**	**uns**	us/ourselves
you	**ihr**	**euch**	**euch**	**euch**	you/ yourselves
they	**sie**	**sie**	**ihnen**	**sich**	them/ themselves
you (formal)	**Sie**	**Sie**	**Ihnen**	**sich**	you/yourself/ yourselves

Scheme of German tenses and their usual English meanings

Note   Of the **Konjunktiv** tenses, only the **Konjunktiv** II, compound conditional and past conditional, are shown in this scheme. It is misleading to give English meanings for the other **Konjunktiv** tenses because of their range of use and meaning.

5a   Active

Present
ich werfe

I throw
I am throwing
I do throw

Imperative
wirf!   throw! (informal, singular)
werft!   throw! (informal, plural)
werfen Sie!   throw! (formal, singular and plural)
werfen wir!   let's throw!

Simple past
ich warf

I threw
I was throwing

Present perfect
ich habe geworfen

I threw
I have thrown
I did throw

Past perfect
ich hatte geworfen   I had thrown

Future
ich werde werfen

I shall throw
I shall be throwing

Future perfect
ich werde geworfen haben   I shall have thrown

Konjunktiv II, compound conditional
ich würde werfen   I would throw
                                      (I would be throwing)

Konjunktiv II, past conditional
ich hätte geworfen   I would have thrown

5b Passive

Present
ich werde gelobt   I am praised
                                      I am being praised

Imperative (rare)
sei gelobt!   be praised!
seid gelobt!   be praised!
seien Sie gelobt!   be praised!

Simple past
ich wurde gelobt   I was praised
                                      I was being praised

Present perfect
ich bin gelobt worden   I was praised
                                      I have been praised

Past perfect
ich war gelobt worden   I had been praised

Future
ich werde gelobt werden   I shall be praised

Future perfect
man wird mich gelobt haben   I shall have been praised

Konjunktiv II, compound conditional
ich würde gelobt (werden)   I would be praised

Konjunktiv II, past conditional
ich wäre gelobt worden   I would have been praised

List of abbreviations and conventions used in this handbook

acc.	accusative	**+s./h.**	the verb takes the auxiliary **sein** or **haben**
dat.	dative		
dat. refl.	dative reflexive	**( )**	the verb is normally followed by the case or preposition indicated
gen.	genitive		
impers.	impersonal		
intr.	intransitive		
pers.	person	**&**	the verb can be used in both ways with the same meaning
pl.	plural		
pres.	present		
refl.	reflexive	**/**	indicates an alternative, e.g., **s/h** – **sein** or **haben**
sing.	singular		
so.	someone		
sth.	something	**|**	a hairline shows that the first part of the verb is a stressed, separable particle
tr.	transitive		
+s.	the verb takes the auxiliary **sein**		

Notes

(i) Parentheses (brackets) in both the German and English columns relate to each other, e.g., "**verhandeln (über** + acc.) (tr. & intr.) negotiate (about)" indicates that **verhandeln** may be used with **über** to mean "negotiate about."

(ii) If used with verbs, prepositions govern the same case as they usually would. The case is only indicated where prepositions govern two possible cases, e.g., **weisen (auf** + acc.) shows that **auf** is followed by the accusative.

(iii) Reflexive use is not indicated where usage is very similar to the English, e.g., **er wäscht sich** (he washes himself) is not shown separately.

Reflexive use is only shown where the verb is used reflexively in German but not in the corresponding English expression, or where the verb has an extended meaning when it is used reflexively, e.g., **vor|stellen** (tr.) (introduce), and (dat. refl.) **ich stelle mir vor** (I imagine).

(iv)   Many verbs can be used both transitively and intransitively. Where the meaning is identical, this is shown in the parentheses.

Where the meaning changes, it is shown separately, e.g., **halten** (tr.) (hold), (intr.) **er hält** (he stops).

(v)   The most important English meanings are listed for each verb. Many German verbs have a great range of shades of meaning, and not all of these can be shown. For further information, a dictionary should be consulted.

B
THE MODEL VERBS

Index of model verbs

Full tenses

Auxiliary verbs

Modal auxiliary verbs

Weak verbs

Strong verbs

Index of model verbs

Full tenses

Active tenses – weak	**wohnen**
Active tenses – strong	**fallen**
Reflexive verbs	**sich setzen/sich vorstellen**
Passive tenses	**gelobt werden**

Auxiliary verbs   *number*   *number*

sein	1	**werden**	3
haben	2		

Modal auxiliary verbs

können	4	**dürfen**	8
wollen	5	**sollen**	9
mögen	6	**lassen**	10
müssen	7		

Weak verbs

machen	11	**wenden**	19
arbeiten	12	**verwenden**	20
probieren	13	**anwenden**	21
verkaufen	14	**denken**	22
abstellen	15	**verbringen**	23
kennen	16	**nachdenken**	24
erkennen	17	**wissen**	25
niederbrennen	18		

Strong verbs

Class I strong verbs

schreiben	26	**leiden**	29
erscheinen	27	**zerreißen**	30
aussteigen	28	**angreifen**	31

Class II strong verbs

biegen	32	**anbieten**	35
ziehen	33	**heben**	36
verlieren	34	**erwägen**	37

wohnen (live)

Wohnen also serves as an example of a verb with the auxiliary **haben.**

PRESENT PARTICIPLE	PAST PARTICIPLE
wohnend	gewohnt

PRESENT
ich wohne
du wohnst
er/sie/es wohnt
wir wohnen
ihr wohnt
sie/Sie wohnen

SIMPLE PAST
ich wohnte
du wohntest
er/sie/es wohnte
wir wohnten
ihr wohntet
sie/Sie wohnten

KONJUNKTIV I, SIMPLE CONDITIONAL
ich wohne
du wohnest
er/sie/es wohne
wir wohnen
ihr wohnet
sie/Sie wohnen

KONJUNKTIV II, SIMPLE
ich wohnte
du wohntest
er/sie/es wohnte
wir wohnten
ihr wohntet
sie/Sie wohnten

PRESENT PERFECT
ich habe ... gewohnt
du hast ... gewohnt
er/sie/es hat ... gewohnt
wir haben ... gewohnt
ihr habt ... gewohnt
sie/Sie haben ... gewohnt

PAST PERFECT (PLUPERFECT)
ich hatte ... gewohnt
du hattest ... gewohnt
er/sie/es hatte ... gewohnt
wir hatten ... gewohnt
ihr hattet ... gewohnt
sie/Sie hatten ... gewohnt

IMPERATIVE (rare)

wohne! (du)   wohnen Sie!   (ihr) wohnt!

FUTURE

ich werde ... wohnen
du wirst ... wohnen
er/sie/es wird... wohnen
wir werden ... wohnen
ihr werdet ... wohnen
sie/Sie werden ... wohnen

FUTURE PERFECT

ich werde ... gewohnt haben
du wirst ... gewohnt haben
er/sie/es wird ... gewohnt haben
wir werden ... gewohnt haben
ihr werdet ... gewohnt haben
sie/Sie werden ... gewohnt haben

KONJUNKTIV II, COMPOUND CONDITIONAL

ich würde ... wohnen
du würdest ... wohnen
er/sie/es würde ... wohnen
wir würden ... wohnen
ihr würdet ... wohnen
sie/Sie würden ... wohnen

KONJUNKTIV II, PAST CONDITIONAL

ich hätte ... gewohnt
du hättest ... gewohnt
er/sie/es hätte ... gewohnt
wir hätten ... gewohnt
ihr hättet ... gewohnt
sie/Sie hätten ... gewohnt

KONJUNKTIV I, PERFECT

ich habe ... gewohnt
du habest ... gewohnt
er/sie/es habe ... gewohnt
wir haben ... gewohnt
ihr habet ... gewohnt
sie/Sie haben ... gewohnt

KONJUNKTIV I, FUTURE

ich werde ... wohnen
du werdest ... wohnen
er/sie/es werde ... wohnen
wir werden ... wohnen
ihr werdet ... wohnen
sie/Sie werden ... wohnen

Fallen also serves as an example of a verb with the auxiliary **sein**.

PRESENT PARTICIPLE	PAST PARTICIPLE
fallend	gefallen

PRESENT	SIMPLE PAST
ich falle	ich fiel
du fällst	du fielst
er/sie/es fällt	er/sie/es fiel
wir fallen	wir fielen
ihr fallt	ihr fielt
sie/Sie fallen	sie/Sie fielen

KONJUNKTIV I, SIMPLE	KONJUNKTIV II, SIMPLE CONDITIONAL
ich falle	ich fiele
du fallest	du fielest
er/sie/es falle	er/sie/es fiele
wir fallen	wir fielen
ihr fallet	ihr fielet
sie/Sie fallen	sie/Sie fielen

PRESENT PERFECT	PAST PERFECT (PLUPERFECT)
ich bin ... gefallen	ich war ... gefallen
du bist ... gefallen	du warst ... gefallen
er/sie/es ist ... gefallen	er/sie/es war ... gefallen
wir sind ... gefallen	wir waren ... gefallen
ihr seid ... gefallen	ihr wart ... gefallen
sie/Sie sind ... gefallen	sie/Sie waren ... gefallen

IMPERATIVE
falle! (du)   fallen Sie!   fallt! (ihr)

FUTURE
ich werde ... fallen
du wirst ... fallen
er/sie/es wird ... fallen
wir werden ... fallen
ihr werdet ... fallen
sie/Sie werden ... fallen

FUTURE PERFECT
ich werde ... gefallen sein
du wirst ... gefallen sein
er/sie/es wird ... gefallen sein
wir werden ... gefallen sein
ihr werdet ... gefallen sein
sie/Sie werden ... gefallen sein

KONJUNKTIV II, COMPOUND CONDITIONAL
ich würde ... fallen
du würdest ... fallen
er/sie/es würde ... fallen
wir würden ... fallen
ihr würdet ... fallen
sie/Sie würden ... fallen

KONJUNKTIV II, PAST CONDITIONAL
ich wäre ... gefallen
du wärest ... gefallen
er/sie/es wäre ... gefallen
wir wären ... gefallen
ihr wäret ... gefallen
sie/Sie wären ... gefallen

KONJUNKTIV I, PERFECT
ich sei ... gefallen
du seist ... gefallen
er/sie/es sei ... gefallen
wir seien ... gefallen
ihr seiet ... gefallen
sie/Sie seien ... gefallen

KONJUNKTIV I, FUTURE
ich werde ... fallen
du werdest ... fallen
er/sie/es werde ... fallen
wir werden ... fallen
ihr werdet ... fallen
sie/Sie werden ... fallen

Reflexive pronoun as direct object

PRESENT PARTICIPLE	**PAST PARTICIPLE**
sich setzend	sich gesetzt

IMPERATIVE
setz(e) dich! (du)   setzen Sie sich!   setzt euch! (ihr)

PRESENT	**SIMPLE PAST**
ich setze mich	ich setzte mich
du setzt dich	du setztest dich
er/sie/es setzt sich	er/sie/es setzte sich
wir setzen uns	wir setzten uns
ihr setzt euch	ihr setztet euch
sie/Sie setzen sich	sie/Sie setzten sich

KONJUNKTIV I	**KONJUNKTIV II**
ich setze mich	ich setzte mich

PRESENT PERFECT	**PAST PERFECT (PLUPERFECT)**
ich habe mich ... gesetzt	ich hatte mich ... gesetzt

FUTURE	**FUTURE PERFECT**
ich werde mich ... setzen	ich werde mich ... gesetzt haben

CONDITIONAL	**CONDITIONAL PERFECT**
ich würde mich ... setzen	ich hätte mich ... gesetzt

sich vorstellen (imagine)

Reflexive pronoun as indirect object

PRESENT PARTICIPLE
sich vorstellend

PAST PARTICIPLE
sich vorgestellt

IMPERATIVE
stell(e) dir vor!   stellen Sie sich vor!   stellt euch vor!

PRESENT
ich stelle mir vor
du stellst dir vor
er/sie/es stellt sich vor
wir stellen uns vor
ihr stellt euch vor
sie/Sie stellen sich vor

SIMPLE PAST
ich stellte mir vor
du stelltest dir vor
er/sie/es stellte sich vor
wir stellten uns vor
ihr stelltet euch vor
sie/Sie stellten sich vor

KONJUNKTIV I
ich stelle mir vor

KONJUNKTIV II
ich stellte mir vor

PRESENT PERFECT
ich habe mir ... vorgestellt

PAST PERFECT (PLUPERFECT)
ich hatte mir ... vorgestellt

FUTURE
ich werde mir ... vorstellen

FUTURE PERFECT
ich werde mir ... vorgestellt haben

CONDITIONAL
ich würde mir ... vorstellen

CONDITIONAL PERFECT
ich hätte mir ... vorgestellt

PRESENT PARTICIPLE	PAST PARTICIPLE
(gelobt werdend)	gelobt worden

PRESENT
ich werde ... gelobt
du wirst ... gelobt
er/sie/es wird ... gelobt
wir werden ... gelobt
ihr werdet ... gelobt
sie/Sie werden ... gelobt

SIMPLE PAST
ich wurde ... gelobt
du wurdest ... gelobt
er/sie/es wurde ... gelobt
wir wurden ... gelobt
ihr wurdet ... gelobt
sie/Sie wurden ... gelobt

KONJUNKTIV I
ich werde ... gelobt
du werdest ... gelobt
er/sie/es werde ... gelobt
wir werden ... gelobt
ihr werdet ... gelobt
sie/Sie werden ... gelobt

KONJUNKTIV II
ich würde ... gelobt
du würdest ... gelobt
er/sie/es würde ... gelobt
wir würden ... gelobt
ihr würdet ... gelobt
sie/Sie würden ... gelobt

PRESENT PERFECT
ich bin ... gelobt worden
du bist ... gelobt worden
er/sie/es ist ... gelobt worden
wir sind ... gelobt worden
ihr seid ... gelobt worden
sie/Sie sind ... gelobt worden

PAST PERFECT (PLUPERFECT)
ich war ... gelobt worden
du warst ... gelobt worden
er/sie/es war ... gelobt worden
wir waren ... gelobt worden
ihr wart ... gelobt worden
sie/Sie waren ... gelobt worden

FULL TENSES

IMPERATIVE

sei gelobt! (du)   seien Sie gelobt!   seid gelobt! (ihr)

FUTURE

ich werde ... gelobt werden
du wirst ... gelobt werden
er/sie/es wird ... gelobt werden
wir werden ... gelobt werden
ihr werdet ... gelobt werden
sie/Sie werden ... gelobt werden

FUTURE PERFECT

(ich werde ... gelobt worden sein)
etc or
(man wird mich/dich etc gelobt haben)

KONJUNKTIV II, COMPOUND CONDITIONAL

ich würde ... gelobt werden
du würdest ... gelobt werden
er/sie/es würde ... gelobt werden
wir würden ... gelobt werden
ihr würdet ... gelobt werden
sie/Sie würden ... gelobt werden

KONJUNKTIV II, PAST CONDITIONAL

ich wäre ... gelobt worden
du wärst ... gelobt worden
er/sie/es wäre ... gelobt worden
wir wären ... gelobt worden
ihr wäret ... gelobt worden
sie/Sie wären ... gelobt worden

KONJUNKTIV I, PERFECT

ich sei ... gelobt worden
du seist ... gelobt worden
er/sie/es sei ... gelobt worden
wir seien ... gelobt worden
ihr seiet ... gelobt worden
sie/Sie seien ... gelobt worden

KONJUNKTIV I, FUTURE

ich werde ... gelobt werden
du werdest ... gelobt werden
er/sie/es werde ... gelobt werden
wir werden ... gelobt werden
ihr werdet ... gelobt werden
sie/Sie werden ... gelobt werden

Note   The future perfect is rarely used and is normally replaced by an active construction with **man**.

1 sein   be

Auxiliary verb, irregular strong, stress on stem **sei-**

PRESENT PARTICIPLE	PAST PARTICIPLE
seiend (wesend)	gewesen

PRESENT	SIMPLE PAST
ich bin	ich war
du bist	du warst
er/sie/es ist	er/sie/es war
wir sind	wir waren
ihr seid	ihr wart
sie/Sie sind	sie/Sie waren

KONJUNKTIV I	KONJUNKTIV II
ich sei	ich wäre
du seist	du wärst
er/sie/es sei	er/sie/es wäre
wir seien	wir wären
ihr seiet	ihr wäret
sie/Sie seien	sie/Sie wären

Similar forms

an sein	be on	**aus sein**	be out, have
auf sein	be up, open		finished
		los sein	be the matter

Note **-wesend** is used as the present participle in forms used as adjectives,
e.g., **anwesend**.

Ist Jochen immer noch *auf*? Das Licht in seinem Zimmer *ist* noch *an*.	*Is* Jochen still *up*? The light in his room *is* still *on*.
Was *ist los*, Jochen? Warum *bist* du so früh zu Hause?	What *is the matter*, Jochen? Why *are* you home so early?
Die Schule *war* heute um ein Uhr *aus*.	School *was out* at one o'clock.
Unsere Lehrerin *war* krank.	Our teacher *was* sick.

IMPERATIVE

sei! (du)   seien Sie!   seid! (ihr)

PRESENT PERFECT	**PAST PERFECT (PLUPERFECT)**
ich bin ... gewesen	ich war ... gewesen

FUTURE	**FUTURE PERFECT**
ich werde ... sein	ich werde ... gewesen sein

COMPOUND CONDITIONAL	**PAST CONDITIONAL**
ich würde ... sein	ich wäre ... gewesen

Das *ist* mein Freund, Jürgen.	This *is* my friend, Jürgen.
Er *ist* Programmierer.	He *is* a computer programmer.
Wir *waren* zusammen auf der Computerausstellung.	We *were* at the computer exhibition together.
Die *ist* jetzt zu Ende.	It *is* over now.
Unser Kollege Hans *war* auch dabei.	Our colleague Hans *was* also there.
Es *war* gestern schrecklich kalt.	It *was* terribly cold yesterday.
Wenn bloß die Heizung *angewesen wäre*!	If only the heating *had been on*!
Morgen *werden* wir um 12 Uhr in Bremen *sein*.	Tomorrow we *will be* in Bremen at 12 pm.
Ich wollte *sicher sein*, dass wir rechtzeitig ankommen.	I wanted to *ensure* that we get there on time.
Wären Sie auch *dafür*, dass wir heute Abend im Hotel essen?	*Would* you also *be in favor of eating* in the hotel this evening?

Auxiliary verb, irregular weak, stress on stem **hab-**

PRESENT PARTICIPLE	PAST PARTICIPLE
habend	gehabt

PRESENT	SIMPLE PAST
ich habe	ich hatte
du hast	du hattest
er/sie/es hat	er/sie/es hatte
wir haben	wir hatten
ihr habt	ihr hattet
sie/Sie haben	sie/Sie hatten

KONJUNKTIV I	KONJUNKTIV II
ich habe	ich hätte

Similar forms

- with separable particle

anhaben	have on (clothes)
zuhaben	be closed
vorhaben	intend (to have sth. planned)

Die Kinder *haben* heute *frei.*	The children *have* the day *off today.*
Wir *hatten vor*, zusammen ins Museum zu gehen.	We *had planned* to go to the museum together.
Aber das Museum *hatte zu.*	But the museum *was closed.*
Ich *fahre* in die Stadt.	I *am going* to the city.
Wollen Sie *mitfahren*?	*Do* you *want to go with me*?
Herr Scholz *hat* einen neuen Anzug *an.*	Mr. Scholz *has* a new suit *on.*

IMPERATIVE
hab(e)! (du)   haben Sie!   habt! (ihr)

PRESENT PERFECT	*PAST PERFECT (PLUPERFECT)*
ich habe ... gehabt	ich hatte ... gehabt

FUTURE	*FUTURE PERFECT*
ich werde ... haben	ich werde ... gehabt haben

COMPOUND CONDITIONAL	*PAST CONDITIONAL*
ich würde ... haben	ich hätte ... gehabt

Haben Sie ein Zimmer?	*Do* you *have* a room?
Ich *hätte gern* ein Zimmer mit Dusche.	I *would like* a room with a shower.
Wir *haben* das Anmeldeformular ausgefüllt.	We *have* filled out the registration form.
Ich *habe* keinen Kugelschreiber bei mir.	I don't *have* a ballpoint pen on me.
Den Wievielten *haben* wir heute?	*What's* the date today?
Habt ihr alle *Spaß gehabt*?	*Did* all of you *have fun*?
Warum seid ihr so hungrig?	Why are you so hungry?
Wir *haben* den ganzen Tag nichts zu essen *gehabt*, weil wir kein Geld dabei *hatten*.	We *have had* nothing to eat all day. because we *had* no money with us.
Kennen Sie Familie Krüger?	Do you know the Krüger family?
Nein, ich *habe* bisher keine Gelegenheit *gehabt*, sie kennen zu lernen.	No, I *have* not yet *had* a chance to meet them.
Montag gehen wir mit Krügers ins Kino.	On Monday we are going to the cinema with the Krügers.
Haben Sie *Lust* mitzukommen?	Do you *want* to come with us?

3 werden   become

Irregular strong verb, stress on stem **werd-**
Auxiliary verb used to form future and passive

PRESENT PARTICIPLE	*PAST PARTICIPLE*
werdend	geworden

PRESENT	*SIMPLE PAST*
ich werde	ich wurde
du wirst	du wurdest
er/sie/es wird	er/sie/es wurde
wir werden	wir wurden
ihr werdet	ihr wurdet
sie/Sie werden	sie/Sie wurden

KONJUNKTIV I	*KONJUNKTIV II*
ich werde	ich würde

Similar verbs

- with separable particle

fertig werden	cope	**loswerden**	get rid of

Note   **loswerden** takes a direct object in the accusative.

Wir *werden* nächste Woche nach Frankfurt *fahren*.	We *will go* to Frankfurt next week.
Ich *kann* meine Erkältung nicht *loswerden*.	I *can*not *get rid of* my cold.
Hoffentlich *werde* ich bald wieder *gesund*.	Hopefully I *will get well* soon.
Ich *würde mich* sehr *freuen*, wenn Sie an dem Projekt *mitwirken würden*.	I *would be delighted* if you *would work with us* on the project.
Die neue Software *wird* ein großer Erfolg *werden*.	The new software *will be* a great success.
Es wurde viel *gelacht*.	*There was* a lot of *laughing*.

IMPERATIVE
werde! (du)   werden Sie!   werdet! (ihr)

PRESENT PERFECT
ich bin ... geworden
      worden

FUTURE
ich werde ... werden

COMPOUND CONDITIONAL
ich würde ... werden

PAST PERFECT (PLUPERFECT)
ich war ... geworden
      worden

FUTURE PERFECT
ich werde ... geworden sein

PAST CONDITIONAL
ich wäre ... geworden
      worden

Es *ist* gestern sehr spät *geworden.*	It *got* very late yesterday.
Wann *wurde* das Schloss *erbaut?*	When *was* the castle *built?*
Es *wurde* 1805 *erbaut.*	It *was built* in 1805.
Jetzt *wird* das Dach *repariert.*	Now the roof *is being repaired.*
Letztes Jahr *ist* der Garten neu angelegt worden.	Last year the garden *was redesigned.*
Nächstes Jahr *wird* der große Saal *restauriert werden.*	Next year the big hall *will be restored.*
Mein Großvater *wäre* heute 95 Jahre alt *geworden.*	My grandfather *would have turned* 95 today.
Viele Kollegen *würden* zu der Party *eingeladen werden.*	Many colleagues *would be invited* to the party.
Der Architekt *wurde* 1953 *geboren.*	The architect *was born* in 1953.
Werden Sie *gesund!*	*Get well!*

4 können

be able (can)

Modal verb, irregular weak, stress on stem **könn-**

PRESENT PARTICIPLE	PAST PARTICIPLE
(könnend)	gekonnt/können

PRESENT	SIMPLE PAST
ich kann	ich konnte
du kannst	du konntest
er/sie/es kann	er/sie/es konnte
wir können	wir konnten
ihr könnt	ihr konntet
sie/Sie können	sie/Sie konnten

KONJUNKTIV I	KONJUNKTIV II
ich könne	ich könnte

Meine Kinder *können* alle *schwimmen* und *Rad fahren*.	All my children *can swim* and *cycle*.
Meine Mutter *kann* immer das Kreuzworträtsel in der Zeitung *lösen*.	My mother *can* always *solve* the crossword puzzle in the newspaper.
Ich *habe* das nie *gekonnt*.	I *have* never *been able to do* it.
Er rief so laut er *konnte*.	He screamed as loud as he *could*.
Können Sie Italienisch?	*Do* you *know* Italian?
Es *kann sein*, dass wir einen Vertreter in Rom brauchen.	It *may be* that we will need a representative in Rome.
Ich weiß nicht, ob ich dieses Jahr werde in Urlaub fahren *können*.	I don't know if I *will be able to go* on vacation this year.

IMPERATIVE

— — —

PRESENT PERFECT	PAST PERFECT (PLUPERFECT)
ich habe ... gekonnt/können	ich hatte ... gekonnt/können

FUTURE	FUTURE PERFECT
ich werde ... können	ich werde ... gekonnt haben
	ich werde ... haben können

COMPOUND CONDITIONAL	PAST CONDITIONAL
ich würde ... können	ich hätte ... gekonnt/können

Kann ich Ihnen *helfen*?	*Can I help you?*
Ja, danke, *könnten* Sie mir *sagen*, wo man hier *parken* kann?	*Yes, thank you, could you tell me where one can park around here?*
***Es könnte sein*, dass Sie vor dem Bahnhof einen Parkplatz finden.**	*It could be that you will find a parking space in front of the train station.*
Leider *habe* ich Ihre Waschmaschine nicht *reparieren können*.	Unfortunately I *have* not *been able to repair* your washing machine.
Wenn ich von dem Konzert *gewusst hätte*, *hätte* ich Karten *kaufen können*.	*Had I known* about the concert, I *could have bought* tickets.
Kannst du mir *sagen*, wer das *gewesen sein kann*?	*Can you tell me who that could have been?*

5 wollen

want to (will)

Modal verb, irregular weak, stress on stem **woll-**

PRESENT PARTICIPLE	PAST PARTICIPLE
wollend	gewollt/wollen

PRESENT	SIMPLE PAST
ich will	ich wollte
du willst	du wolltest
er/sie/es will	er/sie/es wollte
wir wollen	wir wollten
ihr wollt	ihr wolltet
sie/Sie wollen	sie/Sie wollten

KONJUNKTIV I	KONJUNKTIV II
ich wolle	ich wollte

Willst du mit *schwimmen gehen*?	Do you *want to go swimming*?
Nein, ich *will lieber* zu Hause bleiben.	No, I *would rather* stay at home.
Wollen Sie jetzt schon nach Hause?	Do you *want to go* home already?
Unsere Freunde *wollen*, dass wir sie nach Spanien *begleiten*. Wir *wollten* schon lange einmal dorthin *fahren*.	Our friends *want* us *to accompany* them to Spain. We *have wanted to go* there for a long time.
Als Kind *wollte* ich Fußballspieler *werden*.	As a child I *wanted to be* a soccer player.
Ich *wollte*, Sabine wäre schon da, aber sie *will* erst morgen *kommen*.	I do *wish* Sabine was here already, but she *does* not *want to come* until tomorrow.
Heinz *will* seinen Chef gestern in der Stadt *gesehen haben*.	Heinz *claims to have seen* his boss in town yesterday.

IMPERATIVE
wolle (du)!   wollen Sie!   wollt! (ihr)

PRESENT PERFECT
ich habe ... gewollt/wollen

PAST PERFECT (PLUPERFECT)
ich hatte ... gewollt/wollen

FUTURE
ich werde ... wollen

FUTURE PERFECT
ich werde ... gewollt haben

COMPOUND CONDITIONAL
ich würde ... wollen

PAST CONDITIONAL
ich hätte ... gewollt/wollen

6 mögen   like (may)

Modal verb, irregular weak, stress on stem **mög-**

PRESENT PARTICIPLE	**PAST PARTICIPLE**
mögend	gemocht/mögen

PRESENT	**SIMPLE PAST**
ich mag/möchte	ich mochte
du magst/möchtest	du mochtest
er/sie/es mag/möchte	er/sie/es mochte
wir mögen/möchten	wir mochten
ihr mögt/möchtet	ihr mochtet
sie/Sie mögen/möchten	sie/Sie mochten

KONJUNKTIV I	**KONJUNKTIV II**
ich möge	ich möchte

Ich *mag* das Buch sehr.	*I like* the book very much.
Mögen Sie lieber Kaffee oder Tee?	*Do* you *like* coffee better or tea?
Ich *mag* keinen Kaffee, ich *möchte lieber* Tee.	I *do* not *like* coffee, I *would prefer* tea.
Ich *möchte* wissen, wozu die Kinder *Lust haben*.	I *would like* to know, what the children *would like to do*.
***Möchten* sie lieber *schwimmen gehen* oder *fernsehen*?**	Would they *like to go swimming* or *watch television*?
Meine Mutter *mag* es *gern*, wenn die ganze Familie da ist.	My mother *likes* it when the whole family is there.

IMPERATIVE

—   —   —

PRESENT PERFECT
ich habe ... gemocht/mögen

PAST PERFECT (PLUPERFECT)
ich hatte ... gemocht/mögen

FUTURE
ich werde ... mögen

FUTURE PERFECT
ich werde ... gemocht haben
ich werde ... haben mögen

COMPOUND CONDITIONAL
ich würde ... mögen

PAST CONDITIONAL
ich hätte ... gemocht/mögen

Wen *möchten* Sie bitte
sprechen?
Ich *möchte* Frau Arendt
sprechen.

Whom do you want/would you *like*
to speak *to*?
I *would like* to talk to Mrs. Arendt.

Ulrich sagt, er *möchte* nicht in
die Kneipe kommen.

Ulrich says he *does* not *want* to
come to the pub.

Was immer du auch sagst, ich
habe den Film nicht *gemocht*.

No matter what you say, I *did* not
like the movie.

7 müssen   have to

Modal verb, irregular weak, stress on stem **müss-**

PRESENT PARTICIPLE	PAST PARTICIPLE
müssend	gemusst/müssen

PRESENT	SIMPLE PAST
ich muss	ich musste
du musst	du musstest
er/sie/es muss	er/sie/es musste
wir müssen	wir mussten
ihr müsst	ihr musstet
sie/Sie müssen	sie/Sie mussten

KONJUNKTIV I	KONJUNKTIV II
ich müsse	ich müsste

Muss ich schon um 6 Uhr *losfahren*?	*Must* I *leave* at 6 o'clock?
Nein, das *müssen* Sie nicht.	No, you don't *have to.*
Wann *muss* ich am Flughafen *sein*?	When *do* I *have to be* at the airport?
Wir *müssten uns* an der Information *erkundigen*.	We *ought to ask* at the information desk.
Ich weiß, Sie *mussten* letztes Jahr nach Washington.	I know you *had to go* to Washington last year.
Leider *muss* ich Ihnen *mitteilen*, dass Sie auch dieses Jahr *werden hinfahren müssen*.	I am sorry *to have to tell* you, that you *will have to go there* this year as well.

IMPERATIVE

—   —   —

PRESENT PERFECT
ich habe ... gemusst/müssen

PAST PERFECT (PLUPERFECT)
ich hatte ... gemusst/müssen

FUTURE
ich werde ... müssen

FUTURE PERFECT
ich werde ... gemusst haben
ich werde ... haben müssen

COMPOUND CONDITIONAL
ich würde ... müssen

PAST CONDITIONAL
ich hätte ... gemusst/müssen

Du *musst* dich *umziehen.*	You *must get changed.*
Wir *mussten* um 6 Uhr *aufstehen.*	We *had to get up* at 6 am.
Er *hat* den Computer heute *bestellen müssen.*	He *needed to order* the computer today.
Das *muss* man *gesehen haben.*	You've got *to have seen* that.
Wir *mussten* alle *lachen,* als Ute von ihrem Urlaub erzählte.	We all *had to laugh* when Ute told us about her vacation.
Es *muss* stark *geregnet haben.*	It *must have rained* heavily.
Wir *hätten* unsere Einkäufe gestern *erledigen müssen.*	We *should have taken care of* our shopping yesterday.

8 dürfen   be allowed to

Modal verb, irregular weak, stress on stem **dürf-**

PRESENT PARTICIPLE	PAST PARTICIPLE
dürfend	gedurft/dürfen

PRESENT	SIMPLE PAST
ich darf	ich durfte
du darfst	du durftest
er/sie/es darf	er/sie/es durfte
wir dürfen	wir durften
ihr dürft	ihr durftet
sie/Sie dürfen	sie/Sie durften

KONJUNKTIV I	KONJUNKTIV II
ich dürfe	ich dürfte

Was *darf* es *sein*?
Ein Glas Bier bitte, aber die
Kinder *dürfen* keinen Alkohol
***trinken*.**
***Dürfte* ich Sie um ein Glas**
Wasser *bitten*?

Die Kinder *durften* nicht im
Wasser *spielen*, aber sie haben
es trotzdem getan.
Das *hätten* sie nicht *tun dürfen*.
Sie *dürfen* aber im Garten
***spielen*.**

What *would* you *like*?
A glass of beer, please, but the
children *are* not *allowed to drink*
alcohol.
Might I *ask* you for a glass of
water?

The children *were* not *allowed to*
play in the water, but they did it
anyway.
They *should* not *have done* that.
But they *are allowed to play* in the
garden.

IMPERATIVE

—   —   —

PRESENT PERFECT
ich habe ... gedurft/dürfen

PAST PERFECT (PLUPERFECT)
ich hatte ... gedurft/dürfen

FUTURE
ich werde ... dürfen

FUTURE PERFECT
ich werde ... gedurft haben
ich werde ... haben dürfen

COMPOUND CONDITIONAL
ich würde ... dürfen

PAST CONDITIONAL
ich hätte ... gedurft/dürfen

Darf ich ins Kino?

May I *go* to the movies?

Darf ich Sie *bitten*, um 9 Uhr in meinem Büro zu sein?

May I *ask* you to be in my office at nine o'clock?

Die Besprechung *dürfte* nicht so lange dauern.

The meeting *should* not take too long.

Ich *habe* mit 18 meinen Führerschein *machen dürfen.*

I *was allowed to get* my driver's license at 18.

In Zukunft *wird* man hier nicht mehr *rauchen dürfen.*

In the future, one *will not be allowed to smoke* here anymore.

9 sollen   be obliged to (shall, should)

Modal verb, irregular weak, stress on stem **soll-**

PRESENT PARTICIPLE	PAST PARTICIPLE
sollend	gesollt/sollen

PRESENT	SIMPLE PAST
ich soll	ich sollte
du sollst	du solltest
er/sie/es soll	er/sie/es sollte
wir sollen	wir sollten
ihr sollt	ihr solltet
sie/Sie sollen	sie/Sie sollten

KONJUNKTIV I	KONJUNKTIV II
ich solle	ich sollte

Unser Büro *sollte* nach Frankfurt *verlegt werden.* *Sollten* wir hier *bleiben*, werden wir ein neues Büro mieten müssen.	Our office *was to be moved* to Frankfurt. *Should* we *stay* here, we will have to rent a new office.
Der Chef hat gesagt, ich *solle* mich nach einer Wohnung in Frankfurt *umsehen.*	My boss told me I *should look around* for an apartment in Frankfurt.
Du *solltest* dein Zimmer öfter *aufräumen*!	*You should clean up* your room more often!
Was *soll* ich *tun*?	What *should* I *do*?

IMPERATIVE

—   —   —

PRESENT PERFECT   *PAST PERFECT (PLUPERFECT)*
ich habe ... sollen   ich hatte ... sollen

FUTURE   *PAST CONDITIONAL*
ich werde ... sollen   ich hätte ... sollen

Der Techniker *sollte* letzte Woche *kommen*.

The technician *was supposed to come* last week.

Er *hätte* uns nicht *warten lassen sollen*.

He *shouldn't have kept* us *waiting*.

Wir hätten eine andere Firma *anrufen sollen*.

We *should have called* another company.

Hätten Sie nicht früher an die Bestellungen *denken sollen*?

S*houldn't* you *have thought* of the orders sooner?

Class VII strong verb, stress on stem **lass**-

PRESENT PARTICIPLE	*PAST PARTICIPLE*
lassend	gelassen

PRESENT	*SIMPLE PAST*
ich lasse	ich ließ
du lässt	du ließest
er/sie/es lässt	er/sie/es ließ
wir lassen	wir ließen
ihr lasst	ihr ließt
sie/Sie lassen	sie/Sie ließen

KONJUNKTIV I	*KONJUNKTIV II*
ich lasse	ich ließe

Similar verbs

[With an inseparable prefix]

entlassen	dismiss	hinterlassen	bequeath, leave
erlassen	pass (law)	verlassen	leave, desert

[With a separable particle]

ablassen	let out (water,air)	hereinlassen	admit, let in
anlassen	start (car)	loslassen	let loose
auslassen	omit, leave out	nachlassen	decrease
durchlassen	let in, let through	sich niederlassen	settle (somewhere)
freilassen	free, release	zulassen	allow, authorize
herablassen	lower, deign to	zurücklassen	leave behind

Note   *lassen* is included with the modal auxiliaries, as it functions in a very
         similar way. It belongs strictly with the Class VII group of verbs.

Er *verlässt* um sechs das Büro.	He *leaves* the office at six.
Gestern *ließ* er mich *warten*, weil er den Bus verpasst hatte.	He *kept* me *waiting* yesterday because he had missed the bus.
Ich *ließ* den Teller *fallen*.	I *dropped* the plate.
Lass das!	*Stop* that!

IMPERATIVE

lass(e)! (du) lassen Sie! lasst! (ihr)

PRESENT PERFECT	*PAST PERFECT (PLUPERFECT)*
ich habe ... gelassen/lassen	ich hatte ... gelassen/lassen

FUTURE	*FUTURE PERFECT*
ich werde ... lassen	ich werde ... gelassen haben
	ich werde ... haben lassen

COMPOUND CONDITIONAL	*PAST CONDITIONAL*
ich würde ... lassen	ich hätte ... gelassen/lassen

Wir *haben* uns mit dem Taxi zum Bahnhof *fahren lassen.*	We *had* a taxi *take* us to the train station.
Das Fenster *lässt sich* nicht leicht öffnen.	The window *can't be opened* easily.
Wir *werden* den Handwerker *kommen lassen.*	We *will have* the repairman *come.*
Ich *hatte* meinen Hund Maxi zu Hause *gelassen.*	I *had left* my dog Maxi at home.
Man *kann sich* auf dich *verlassen.*	One *can rely* on you.
Ich *würde* den Hund ja *rauslassen,* aber es regnet.	I *would let* the dog *out,* but it is raining.
Meine Großmutter *hinterließ* ein Vermögen.	My grandmother *left* a fortune.
Wir *hatten* vor zwei Jahren unser Haus *renovieren lassen.*	We *had* our house *renovated* two years ago.
Frank *kann* das Rauchen einfach nicht *lassen.*	Frank simply *cannot stop* smoking.

Regular weak verb, stress on stem **mach-**

PRESENT PARTICIPLE	PAST PARTICIPLE
machend	gemacht

PRESENT	SIMPLE PAST
ich mache	ich machte
du machst	du machtest
er/sie/es macht	er/sie/es machte
wir machen	wir machten
ihr macht	ihr machtet
sie/Sie machen	sie/Sie machten

KONJUNKTIV I	KONJUNKTIV II
ich mache	ich machte

Note Regular weak verbs of this type form a large group.

Was *macht* dein Italienisch?	How *is* your Italian *coming along*?
Wollen wir jetzt mit der Besprechung Schluss *machen*?	*Should* we *finish* our meeting now?
Ich *will mich frisch machen*, bevor wir *uns auf den Weg* ins Konzert *machen*.	I *want to freshen up* before we *get on our way* to the concert.
Wir *machen* jetzt *Feierabend*.	We *quit working* now.
Die Arbeit *drängt*, und wir *hoffen* auf eine baldige Antwort auf unsere Frage.	The work *is pressing* and we *are hoping* for a quick answer to our query.
Bitte *fassen* Sie sich *kurz*! Es *wird* sicher nicht lange *dauern*.	Please *be brief*! It *will* certainly not *take* long.
Er *dankte* mir aufs herzlichste für meine Arbeit.	He *thanked* me warmly for my work.
Er *sagte*, er *hätte* nicht *geglaubt*, dass ich es rechtzeitig *schaffen* *würde*.	He *said* he *had* not *believed* that I *would get* it *done* in time.

IMPERATIVE
mach(e)! (du)   machen Sie!   macht! (ihr)

PRESENT PERFECT
ich habe ... gemacht

PAST PERFECT (PLUPERFECT)
ich hatte ... gemacht

FUTURE
ich werde ... machen

FUTURE PERFECT
ich werde ... gemacht haben

COMPOUND CONDITIONAL
ich würde ... machen

PAST CONDITIONAL
ich hätte ... gemacht

Ich *habe* gute *Fortschritte* mit meinem Italienisch *gemacht*.

I *have made* good progress with my Italian.

Jochen *hat gefehlt*.

Jochen *was absent*.

Gestern *haben* wir *uns* sehr *gelangweilt*.

Yesterday we *were* very *bored*.

Wir *reisen* morgen mit dem Zug in die Schweiz.

Tomorrow we *will travel* to Switzerland by train.

Haben Sie die Fahrscheine schon *gelöst*?

Have you already *bought* the tickets?

Ich *freue mich* schon darauf.

I *am looking forward* to it.

Ich *kann* es nicht *fassen*!

I *cannot believe* it!

Ich *muss mich* jetzt um das neue Projekt *kümmern*.

I *have to take care* of the new project now.

Sigrid *wird* nächste Woche ihren *Führerschein machen*.

Sigrid *will get* her *driver's license* next week.

Wir *hätten* Tennis *gespielt*, wenn es nicht *geregnet hätte*.

We *would have played* tennis if it had not *rained*.

12 arbeiten   work

Regular weak verb, stress on stem **arbeit-**, stem ending in **-t**

PRESENT PARTICIPLE	PAST PARTICIPLE
arbeitend	gearbeitet

PRESENT	SIMPLE PAST
ich arbeite	ich arbeitete
du arbeitest	du arbeitetest
er/sie/es arbeitet	er/sie/es arbeitete
wir arbeiten	wir arbeiteten
ihr arbeitet	ihr arbeitetet
sie/Sie arbeiten	sie/Sie arbeiteten

KONJUNKTIV I	KONJUNKTIV II
ich arbeite	ich arbeitete

Note   Regular weak verbs of this type form a large group.

Das Flugzeug *startete* um zehn Uhr, und wir *werden* um zwölf *landen*.	The plane *took off* at ten o'clock, and we *will land* at twelve.
Die Wohnung *hat* zu viel *gekostet*.	The apartment *cost* too much money.
Wir *mieten* jetzt eine kleinere Wohnung.	We *are renting* a smaller apartment now.
Wer *hat* die Tür *geöffnet?*	Who *opened* the door?
Es *zieht*.	It *is drafty*.

IMPERATIVE
arbeite! (du)   arbeiten Sie!   arbeitet! (ihr)

PRESENT PERFECT
ich habe ... gearbeitet

PAST PERFECT (PLUPERFECT)
ich hatte ... gearbeitet

FUTURE
ich werde ... arbeiten

FUTURE PERFECT
ich werde ... gearbeitet haben

COMPOUND CONDITIONAL
ich würde ... arbeiten

PAST CONDITIONAL
ich hätte ... gearbeitet

Wir *hätten* die Arbeit früher *geleistet*, aber die Papiere *mussten* erst *geordnet werden.*

We *would have done* the work sooner, but the papers *had to be organized* first.

Ich *habe mir* ein neues Auto *geleistet.*

I *have treated myself to* a new car.

Als wir auf dem Land *zelteten*, *badeten* wir jeden Tag im Fluss.

When we *were camping* in the country, we *bathed* every day in the river.

Die Produkte *werden* immer sorgfältig *getestet.*

The products *are* always carefully *tested.*

Ich *habe* die ganze Woche auf seinen Anruf *gewartet.*

I *waited* the whole week for his call.

13 probieren   try, try out

Regular weak verb ending in **-ieren**, stress on **-ier-**

PRESENT PARTICIPLE	PAST PARTICIPLE
probierend	probiert

PRESENT	SIMPLE PAST
ich probiere	ich probierte
du probierst	du probiertest
er/sie/es probiert	er/sie/es probierte
wir probieren	wir probierten
ihr probiert	ihr probiertet
sie/Sie probieren	sie/Sie probierten

KONJUNKTIV I	KONJUNKTIV II
ich probiere	ich probierte

Note   Regular weak verbs of this type form a large group.

Wir *müssen* uns darüber *unterhalten,* wie wir die Ausstellung *organisieren werden.*	We *have to talk about* how we *are going to organize* the exhibition.
Ist das Videogerät schon *repariert worden?*	*Has* the videorecorder *been repaired* yet?
Ja, ich *habe* es *ausprobiert.*	Yes, I *'ve tried* it *out.*
Ich *hätte* früher mit dem Techniker *telefoniert,* wenn ich gewusst hätte, dass es nicht *funktioniert.*	I *would have called* the technician sooner if I had known that it *wasn't working.*
Firma XY *hat* ihren Auftrag *storniert.*	Company XY *has canceled* its contract.

IMPERATIVE
probier(e)! (du)   probieren Sie!   probiert! (ihr)

PRESENT PERFECT
ich habe ... probiert

PAST PERFECT (PLUPERFECT)
ich hatte ... probiert

FUTURE
ich werde ... probieren

FUTURE PERFECT
ich werde ... probiert haben

COMPOUND CONDITIONAL
ich würde ... probieren

PAST CONDITIONAL
ich hätte ... probiert

Ich habe gehört, dass Sie *sich*
für ein neues Computersystem
interessieren.

I have heard that you *are*
interested in a new computer
system.

Wie *wollen* **Sie das** *finanzieren?*

How *do* you *want to finance* it?

Unsere Firma *wird* **im nächsten**
Jahr auch Laserdrucker
produzieren.

Our company *will* also *produce*
laser printers next year.

Wir *haben uns* **in München gut**
amüsiert.

We *enjoyed ourselves* in Munich.

Das Hotel *ist* **letztes Jahr**
modernisiert worden.

The hotel *was modernized* last
year.

Ich weiß nicht, wie man so
etwas *arrangiert.*
Ich *werde mich informieren*
müssen.

I don't know how you *arrange*
something like that.
I *will have to find out.*

Regular inseparable weak verb, stress on stem **-kauf-**

PRESENT PARTICIPLE	PAST PARTICIPLE
verkaufend	verkauft

PRESENT	SIMPLE PAST
ich verkaufe	ich verkaufte
du verkaufst	du verkauftest
er/sie/es verkauft	er/sie/es verkaufte
wir verkaufen	wir verkauften
ihr verkauft	ihr verkauftet
sie/Sie verkaufen	sie/Sie verkauften

KONJUNKTIV I	KONJUNKTIV II
ich verkaufe	ich verkaufte

Note   Regular inseparable weak verbs of this type form a large group. **Interviewen** is included in this group as it takes no **ge-** in the past participle.

Ich *besuchte* meinen alten Freund, als ich in Leipzig war. Ich *erzählte* ihm von meinem Leben in den USA.	I *visited* my old friend when I was in Leipzig. I *told* him about my life in the U.S.A.
Ich habe ihn mehrmals gefragt, aber er hat meine Frage nicht *beantwortet*.	I asked him several times, but he didn't *answer* my question.
Ich *bin* zufällig meinem früheren Chef *begegnet*. Er *hat* mich sehr freundlich *begrüßt* und *hat* mich zu meiner neuen Stellung *beglückwünscht*.	I *ran into* my former boss by chance. He *greeted* me very warmly and *congratulated* me on my new job.
Ich dachte, ich *würde* den Zug *verpassen*. Aber er *hatte* Verspätung.	I thought I *would miss* the train. But it *had been delayed*.

IMPERATIVE
verkauf(e)! (du)   verkaufen Sie!   verkauft! (ihr)

PRESENT PERFECT
ich habe ... verkauft

PAST PERFECT (PLUPERFECT)
ich hatte ... verkauft

FUTURE
ich werde ... verkaufen

FUTURE PERFECT
ich werde ... verkauft haben

COMPOUND CONDITIONAL
ich würde ... verkaufen

PAST CONDITIONAL
ich hätte ... verkauft

Ich *habe mich erkältet.*
Ich würde dich aber gern nächste Woche nach Stuttgart *begleiten.*

I *have caught cold.*
But I would be happy to *accompany* you to Stuttgart next week.

Erinnern Sie *sich* an das Hotel in Stuttgart, in dem die Pressekonferenz stattfand?
Wir *hatten uns* dort *versammelt,* um den Minister zu *interviewen.*
Im letzten Augenblick *hat* er *sich entschuldigen lassen.*
Der Bericht *wurde* ohne das Interview *veröffentlicht.*

Do you *remember* the hotel in Stuttgart where the press conference took place?
We *had assembled* there to *interview* the minister.
At the last moment he *sent* his *apologies.*
The report *was published* without the interview.

Regular separable weak verb, stress on particle, e.g., **ab, auf, heraus-**

PRESENT PARTICIPLE	*PAST PARTICIPLE*
abstellend	abgestellt

PRESENT	*SIMPLE PAST*
ich stelle ab	ich stellte ab
du stellst ab	du stelltest ab
er/sie/es stellt ab	er/sie/es stellte ab
wir stellen ab	wir stellten ab
ihr stellt ab	ihr stelltet ab
sie/Sie stellen ab	sie/Sie stellten ab

KONJUNKTIV I	*KONJUNKTIV II*
ich stelle ab	ich stellte ab

Note   Regular separable weak verbs of this type form a large group.

Ich *höre* mit der Arbeit um 16.00 Uhr *auf*.	I *will stop* work at four o'clock p.m.
Dann *kann* ich *mich* noch etwas ausruhen bevor ich nach Hause aufbreche.	Then I *can* still *rest* a little before I *head* home.
Ich *kann* heute auf die Kinder aufpassen, während Sie einkaufen gehen.	I *can watch* the children today while you're *going shopping*.
Können wir uns morgen abwechseln?	*Can* we *trade places* tomorrow?
Als ich vom Schreibtisch aufblickte, sah ich, dass es geschneit hatte.	When I *looked up* from the desk, I saw that it had snowed.

IMPERATIVE

stell(e) ab! (du)   stellen Sie ab!   stellt ab! (ihr)

PRESENT PERFECT
ich habe ... abgestellt

PAST PERFECT (PLUPERFECT)
ich hatte ... abgestellt

FUTURE
ich werde ... abstellen

FUTURE PERFECT
ich werde ... abgestellt haben

COMPOUND CONDITIONAL
ich würde ... abstellen

PAST CONDITIONAL
ich hätte ... abgestellt

Ich *habe* die Theaterkarten für heute Abend *abbestellt*.
Das Stück, das ich mir eigentlich hatte ansehen wollen, *stellt* das Leben Galileos *dar*.
Ich *kann mir vorstellen*, dass es sehr interessant ist, aber es *hat sich herausgestellt*, dass ich keine Zeit habe.
Ich *kann* mir morgen ein anderes Stück *ansehen*.

Mein Freund Jean-Claude *hat* mir *mitgeteilt*, dass er nächstes Jahr nach Frankreich *zurückkehren wird*.

I *have cancelled* the theater tickets for this evening.
The play that I had actually wanted to see *depicts* the life of Galileo.

I *can imagine* that it is very interesting, but it *turns out* I have no time.

I *can see* another play tomorrow.

My friend Jean-Claude *told* me that he *will return* to France next year.

16 kennen

Irregular weak verb, stress on stem **kenn-**

PRESENT PARTICIPLE	PAST PARTICIPLE
kennend	gekannt

PRESENT	SIMPLE PAST
ich kenne	ich kannte
du kennst	du kanntest
er/sie/es kennt	er/sie/es kannte
wir kennen	wir kannten
ihr kennt	ihr kanntet
sie/Sie kennen	sie/Sie kannten

KONJUNKTIV I
ich kenne

Similar verbs

brennen	burn
nennen	name, call
rennen	run

Es *brennt!*	There's a fire!
Das Buchenholz *brennt* im Kamin.	The beechwood *is burning* in the fireplace.
Es *brennt* besser als Kiefer.	It *burns* better than pine.
Die Sonne *brannte* am Himmel.	The sun *burned* in the sky.
Wir *haben* das Licht die ganze Nacht *brennen lassen*.	We *left* the light *burning* all night.
Das Haus *hat* die ganze Nacht *gebrannt*.	The house *burned* all night.

IMPERATIVE
kenn(e)! (du)   kennen Sie!   kennt! (ihr)

PRESENT PERFECT   **PAST PERFECT (PLUPERFECT)**
ich habe ... gekannt   ich hatte ... gekannt

FUTURE   **FUTURE PERFECT**
ich werde ... kennen   ich werde ... gekannt haben

COMPOUND CONDITIONAL   **PAST CONDITIONAL**
ich würde ... kennen   ich hätte ... gekannt

Kennen Sie Frau Freising? **Ja, wir kennen uns schon seit langem.**	*Do* you *know* Mrs. Freising? Yes, we *have known each other* for a long time.
Der Preis, den mir jemand genannt hatte, war zu hoch.	The price that I *was quoted* was too high.
Wir rennen heute um die Wette.	We *have a race* today.
Er ist mit dem Kopf gegen die Mauer gerannt.	He *ran* head first against the wall.

Irregular inseparable weak verb, stress on stem **kenn-**

PRESENT PARTICIPLE	PAST PARTICIPLE
erkennend	erkannt

PRESENT	SIMPLE PAST
ich erkenne	ich erkannte
du erkennst	du erkanntest
er/sie/es erkennt	er/sie/es erkannte
wir erkennen	wir erkannten
ihr erkennt	ihr erkanntet
sie/Sie erkennen	sie/Sie erkannten

KONJUNKTIV I
ich erkenne

Similar verbs

bekennen	confess
ernennen (zu)	appoint (to)
verbrennen (+sein/haben)	burn up
verkennen	misjudge

IMPERATIVE
erkenn(e)! (du)   erkennen Sie!   erkennt! (ihr)

PRESENT PERFECT	**PAST PERFECT (PLUPERFECT)**
ich habe ... erkannt	ich hatte ... erkannt

FUTURE	**FUTURE PERFECT**
ich werde ... erkennen	ich werde ... erkannt haben

COMPOUND CONDITIONAL	**PAST CONDITIONAL**
ich würde ... erkennen	ich hätte ... erkannt

Er *wurde* zum Minister *ernannt.*	He *was appointed* minister.
Ich *hätte* meinen alten Freund fast nicht *erkannt.*	I almost *didn't recognize* my old friend.
Er *hat sich* so stark *verändert,* er ist kaum *wiederzuerkennen.*	He *has change*d so much that he is barely *recognizable.*
Sie *verkannte* den Ernst der Sache – unser Haus *ist* völlig *ausgebrannt.*	She *misjudged* the seriousness of the situation — our house *has been burned* to the ground.
Wir *werden* die Briefe sofort *verbrennen.*	We *will burn* the letters at once.
Er *gab* seine Absichten deutlich *zu erkennen.*	He *made* his intentions *clear.*
Sein Gesicht *war von der Sonne verbrannt.*	His face *was sunburned.*
Ich *habe* mir den Mund an der heißen Kartoffel *verbrannt.*	I *burned* my mouth on the hot potato.

18 niederbrennen   burn down

Irregular separable weak verb, stress on particle, e.g., **nieder-, aus-, durch-**

PRESENT PARTICIPLE	PAST PARTICIPLE
niederbrennend	niedergebrannt

PRESENT	SIMPLE PAST
ich brenne nieder	ich brannte nieder
du brennst nieder	du branntest nieder
er/sie/es brennt nieder	er/sie/es brannte nieder
wir brennen nieder	wir brannten nieder
ihr brennt nieder	ihr branntet nieder
sie/Sie brennen nieder	sie/Sie brannten nieder

KONJUNKTIV I
ich brenne nieder

Similar verbs

anerkennen	acknowledge, respect
sich auskennen *(auf/in+dat.)*	know a lot about
durchbrennen *(+sein)*	blow (fuse)
hinterherrennen *(+sein)*	chase

IMPERATIVE
brenn(e) nieder! (du)   brennen Sie nieder!   brennt nieder! (ihr)

PRESENT PERFECT
ich habe ... niedergebrannt

PAST PERFECT (PLUPERFECT)
ich hatte ... niedergebrannt

FUTURE
ich werde ... niederbrennen

FUTURE PERFECT
ich werde ... niedergebrannt haben

COMPOUND CONDITIONAL
ich würde ... niederbrennen

PAST CONDITIONAL
ich hätte ... niedergebrannt

Er *erkannte* das Kind als sein eigenes *an*.	He *acknowledged* the child as his own.
In dieser Sache *kenne* ich *mich* gut *aus*.	I *know a lot* about this matter.
Ich *kannte mich* in der Stadt nicht gut *aus*.	I *did* not *know* the town very well/*did* not *know my way around* the town very well.
Wenn die Sicherung nur nicht *durchgebrannt wäre!*	If only the fuse *had* not *burned through!*
Er *ist* hinter mir *hergerannt*.	He *ran along* behind me.

Irregular weak verb, stress on stem **wend-/send-**

PRESENT PARTICIPLE	PAST PARTICIPLE
wendend	gewendet (gewandt)

PRESENT	SIMPLE PAST
ich wende	ich wendete (wandte)
du wendest	du wendetest (wandtest)
er/sie/es wendet	er/sie/es wendete (wandte)
wir wenden	wir wendeten (wandten)
ihr wendet	ihr wendetet (wandtet)
sie/Sie wenden	sie/Sie wendeten (wandten)

KONJUNKTIV I	KONJUNKTIV II
ich wende	ich wendete
	wandte

Similar verbs

senden *(nach)*   send (for)

Notes   **wenden** (regular weak) [➤**arbeiten 12**] has the literal meaning "to turn" or "change direction." The irregular strong form (refl.), **sich wenden an**, has the figurative meaning of turning to someone for support.

        senden (regular weak) [➤**arbeiten 12**] has the literal meaning "to broadcast." It is sometimes used to mean "to send." The irregular form always means "to send."

Wir sind in einer Einbahn-straße. Sie müssen *wenden*.	We're in a one-way street. You have to *turn around*.
Er *wandte sich um*.	He *turned around*.

IMPERATIVE
wend(e)! (du)   wenden Sie!   wendet! (ihr)

PRESENT PERFECT
ich habe ... gewandt
　　　　gewendet

ich habe mich an (+Akk.) gewandt

PAST PERFECT (PLUPERFECT)
ich hatte ... gewandt
　　　　gewendet

FUTURE
ich werde ... wenden

FUTURE PERFECT
ich werde ... gewandt haben
　　　　gewendet

COMPOUND CONDITIONAL
ich würde ... wenden

PAST CONDITIONAL
ich hätte ... gewandt
　　　　gewendet

Das Schicksal *hat sich gewendet*.

Fate *has changed.*

Ich *werde* den Fisch in der Pfanne *wenden*.

I *will turn* the fish in the pan.

Ich *wandte mich* an meinen Bruder um Rat.

I *turned* to my brother for advice.

Der Rundfunk *sendete* Nachrichten.

The radio *broadcast* the news.

Sie *wandte sich* an mich mit einer Bitte.

She *turned* to me with a request.

Alles *hat sich* zum Guten *gewendet*.

Everything *has changed* for the good.

20 verwenden   use

Irregular inseparable weak verb, stress on stem **-wend- / -send-**

PRESENT PARTICIPLE	*PAST PARTICIPLE*
verwendend	verwendet (verwandt)

PRESENT	*SIMPLE PAST*
ich verwende	ich verwendete (verwandte)
du verwendest	du verwendetest (verwandtest)
er/sie/es verwendet	er/sie/es verwendete (verwandte)
wir verwenden	wir verwendeten (verwandten)
ihr verwendet	ihr verwendetet (verwandtet)
sie/Sie verwenden	sie/Sie verwendeten (verwandten)

KONJUNKTIV I	*KONJUNKTIV II*
ich verwende	ich verwendete

Similar verbs

entsenden	dispatch
entwenden	purloin, steal
versenden	send out

Note   The past simple and past participle forms in **-andt** are rarely found.

Ich *werde* diesen Stoff für ein Kleid *verwenden*.	I *will use* this material for a dress.
In dem Film *wurde* viel Mühe auf die Kostüme *verwendet*.	In the film, a lot of effort *was put* into the costumes.
Er *verwendete* die besten Zutaten für die Torte.	He *used* the best ingredients for the cake.

IMPERATIVE
verwend(e)! (du)   verwenden Sie!   verwendet! (ihr)

PRESENT PERFECT
ich habe ... verwendet (verwandt)

PAST PERFECT (PLUPERFECT)
ich hatte ... verwendet (verwandt)

FUTURE
ich werde ... verwenden

FUTURE PERFECT
ich werde ... verwendet (verwandt)
haben

COMPOUND CONDITIONAL
ich würde ... verwenden

PAST CONDITIONAL
ich hätte ... verwendet (verwandt)

Ich *würde* dieses Holz nie *verwenden* — wir *haben* immer nur das beste Material *verwendet.*

I *would* never *use* this wood – we *have* always *used* only the best materials.

Ich *bin* mit ihm *verwandt.*

I *am related* to him.

Die Dokumente *sind* der Firma *entwendet worden.*

The documents *have been stolen* from the firm.

Die Jacke hat einen Fleck. Ich *werde* dieses Reinigungsmittel *verwenden.*

The jacket has a spot.
I *will use* this cleaning product.

Irregular weak verb, stress on particle, e.g., **an-, ab-, ein-**

PRESENT PARTICIPLE	*PAST PARTICIPLE*
anwendend	angewandt (angewendet)

PRESENT	*SIMPLE PAST*
ich wende an	ich wandte (wendete) an
du wendest an	du wandtest (wendetest) an
er/sie/es wendet an	er/sie/es wandte (wendete) an
sir wenden an	wir wandten (wendeten) an
ihr wendet an	ihr wandtet (wendetet) an
sie/Sie wenden an	sie/Sie wandten (wendeten) an

KONJUNKTIV I	*KONJUNKTIV II*
ich wende	ich wendete

Similar verbs

abwenden	turn away
absenden	send away
einwenden	object

Note   The weak form is common in compounds of **wenden.**

Ich *werde* meine Englischkenntnisse im Urlaub in den USA gut *anwenden* *können.*	I *will be able to make good use of* my knowledge of English during my vacation in the U.S.A.
Wir *werden* für die neue Produktkampagne eine verbesserte Strategie *anwenden.*	We *will employ* an improved strategy for the new product campaign.

IMPERATIVE

wend(e) an! (du)   wenden Sie an!   wendet an! (ihr)

PRESENT PERFECT	***PAST PERFECT (PLUPERFECT)***
ich habe ... angewandt	ich hatte ... angewandt
(angewendet)	(angewendet)

FUTURE	***FUTURE PERFECT***
ich werde ... anwenden	ich werde ... angewandt (angewendet)
	haben

COMPOUND CONDITIONAL	***PAST CONDITIONAL***
ich würde ... anwenden	ich hätte ... angewandt (angewendet)

Als er sah wie ich reagierte, *wandte* der den Blick von mir *ab*.

When he saw how I reacted, he *turned* his gaze *away* from me.

Der Chef *hatte* nichts gegen meine Vorschläge *einzuwenden*.

The boss *had no objections* to my recommendations.

Das Unheil *ließ sich* gerade noch *abwenden*.

The disaster *could* just *be averted*.

Irregular weak verb, stress on stem **denk-**

PRESENT PARTICIPLE	PAST PARTICIPLE
denkend	gedacht

PRESENT	SIMPLE PAST
ich denke	ich dachte
du denkst	du dachtest
er/sie/es denkt	er/sie/es dachte
wir denken	wir dachten
ihr denkt	ihr dachtet
sie/Sie denken	sie/Sie dachten

KONJUNKTIV I	KONJUNKTIV II
ich denke	ich dächte

Similar verbs

bringen	bring, take, (publish)

Er *dachte* lange *nach,* bevor er antwortete.	He *thought* for a long time before answering.
Ich *denke*, er wird sein Studium in einem Jahr abschließen.	I *think* he will finish his studies in a year.
Er *wird* es sicher bis zum Facharzt *bringen*.	He *will* certainly *make it* to medical specialist.
Sie *denkt* nicht daran, hier in Bonn zu bleiben.	She *is* not *thinking* of staying here in Bonn.
Ich *bringe* Sie zum Bahnhof. *Denken* Sie daran, dass Sie noch eine Fahrkarte lösen müssen.	I *will take* you to the station. *Remember* that you still have to buy a ticket.
Ich *muss* die Kinder ins Bett *bringen*.	I *must put* the children to bed.
Ich *hätte* nie *gedacht,* dass ich so lange bei dieser Firma bleiben würde.	I never *would have thought* that I would stay this long at this company.

IMPERATIVE
denk(e)! (du)　　　　　denken Sie!　　　　　denkt! (ihr)

PRESENT PERFECT	**PAST PERFECT (PLUPERFECT)**
ich habe ... gedacht	ich hatte ... gedacht

FUTURE	**FUTURE PERFECT**
ich werde ... denken	ich werde ... gedacht haben

COMPOUND CONDITIONAL	**PAST CONDITIONAL**
ich würde ... denken	ich hätte ... gedacht

Die Zeitung *brachte* einen langen Artikel über den Streik in der Firma.	The paper *printed* a long article about the strike in the company.
Das *wird* uns viel Ärger *bringen*.	That *will give* us a lot of trouble.
Das *hätte* ich nicht von dem Redakteur *gedacht*.	I *would* never *have expected* that from the editor.
Der Briefträger *hat* ein Paket *gebracht*.	The mailman *has brought* a parcel.
Wir *haben* den Reiseführer *auf den neuesten Stand gebracht*.	We *have brought* the travel guide *up to date*.
Das *hätte* ich *mir denken können*.	I *might have guessed* that.
Ich *wurde* durch sein Benehmen *in* die größte *Verlegenheit gebracht*.	I *was greatly embarrassed* by his behavior.
Mein Kollege *bringt* mich mit seiner Telefoniererei noch *um den Verstand*.	My colleague *will cause* me *to lose my mind* with his frequent telephoning.

Irregular inseparable weak verb, stress on stem **-bring-**

PRESENT PARTICIPLE	*PAST PARTICIPLE*
verbringend	verbracht

PRESENT	*SIMPLE PAST*
ich verbringe	ich verbrachte
du verbringst	du verbrachtest
er/sie/es verbringt	er/sie/es verbrachte
wir verbringen	wir verbrachten
ihr verbringt	ihr verbrachtet
sie/Sie verbringen	sie/Sie verbrachten

KONJUNKTIV I	*KONJUNKTIV II*
ich verbringe	ich verbrächte

Similar verbs

bedenken	consider, think (about)
gedenken *(gen.)*	commemorate
vollbringen	accomplish

Bei der Planung des Skitrips **müssen** wir *bedenken*, dass am Wochenende viel Verkehr ist.	When planning the ski trip, we *have to take into consideration* that there is a lot of traffic on the weekend.
Die Heimatstadt des Dichters *gedachte* ihm anlässlich seines 200. Geburtstags mit einer Münze.	The poet's hometown *commemorated* his 200th birthday with a coin.

IMPERATIVE
verbring(e)! (du)   verbringen Sie!   verbringt! (ihr)

PRESENT PERFECT
ich habe ... verbracht

PAST PERFECT (PLUPERFECT)
ich hatte ... verbracht

FUTURE
ich werde ... verbringen

FUTURE PERFECT
ich werde ... verbracht haben

COMPOUND CONDITIONAL
ich würde ... verbringen

PAST CONDITIONAL
ich hätte ... verbracht

**Ich *verbringe* die Sommer-
monate immer in den USA.
Letztes Jahr *verbrachte* ich drei
Monate in Montana.**

I always *spend* the summer
months in the U.S.A.
Last year I *spent* three months in
Montana.

**Ich *sollte* mehr Zeit damit
verbringen, mit unseren Kindern
zu spielen.**

I *should spend* more time playing
with our children.

Er *hat* viele Wunder *vollbracht*.

He *performed* many miracles.

Irregular separable weak verb, stress on particle **nach-**

PRESENT PARTICIPLE	PAST PARTICIPLE
nachdenkend	nachgedacht

PRESENT	SIMPLE PAST
ich denke nach	ich dachte nach
du denkst nach	du dachtest nach
er/sie/es denkt nach	er/sie/es dachte nach
wir denken nach	wir dachten nach
ihr denkt nach	ihr dachtet nach
sie/Sie denken nach	sie/Sie dachten nach

KONJUNKTIV I	KONJUNKTIV II
ich denke nach	ich dächte nach

Similar verbs

abbringen (*von*)	dissuade (from)	**hervorbringen**	produce
ausdenken	think out/up	**mitbringen**	bring along
beibringen	tell, teach	**nahe bringen**	familiarize
durcheinander bringen	confuse, disorganize	**umbringen**	kill
herausbringen	bring out, publish, release	**unterbringen**	house, accommodate
		zurückbringen	bring back

Die Gäste *haben* **uns Blumen** *mitgebracht.*	The guests *brought* us some flowers.
Hans *brachte* **vor Schreck kein Wort** *heraus.*	In his horror, Hans *could* not *utter* a word.
Ich *war* **in dem Hotel gut** *untergebracht.*	*The accommodation* in the hotel *was* good.

IMPERATIVE
denk(e) nach! (du)   denken Sie nach!   denkt nach! (ihr)

PRESENT PERFECT
ich habe ... nachgedacht

PAST PERFECT (PLUPERFECT)
ich hatte ... nachgedacht

FUTURE
ich werde ... nachdenken

FUTURE PERFECT
ich werde ... nachgedacht haben

COMPOUND CONDITIONAL
ich würde ... nachdenken

PAST CONDITIONAL
ich hätte ... nachgedacht

Er *dachte* lange *nach,* bevor er antwortete.

He *thought* for a long time before answering.

Die Kinder *bringen* das ganze Haus *durcheinander.*
Sie *müssen* ihnen besseres Benehmen *beibringen.*

The children *make a mess* of the whole house.
You *must teach* them better behavior.

Ich *habe* mir einen besseren Plan *ausgedacht.*

I *have thought of* a better plan.

Leider *sind* die Folgen nicht ganz *abzusehen.*

Unfortunately, the consequences *are* not entirely *predictable.*

Das Buch *wurde* letztes Jahr *herausgebracht.*

The book *was published* last year.

Irregular weak verb, stress on stem **wiss-**

PRESENT PARTICIPLE	PAST PARTICIPLE
wissend	gewusst

PRESENT	SIMPLE PAST
ich weiß	ich wusste
du weißt	du wusstest
er/sie/es weiß	er/sie/es wusste
wir wissen	wir wussten
ihr wisst	ihr wusstet
sie/Sie wissen	sie/Sie wussten

KONJUNKTIV I	KONJUNKTIV II
ich wisse	ich wüsste

Note **wissen** is the only verb of this type.

IMPERATIVE
(du) wisse!   wissen Sie!   wisst! (ihr)

PRESENT PERFECT
ich habe ... gewusst

PAST PERFECT (PLUPERFECT)
ich hatte ... gewusst

FUTURE
ich werde ... wissen

FUTURE PERFECT
ich werde ... gewusst haben

COMPOUND CONDITIONAL
ich würde ... wissen

PAST CONDITIONAL
ich hätte ... gewusst

Wissen Sie vielleicht, wann der nächste Bus kommt?
Ich *würde es gerne wissen*.

Do you by chance *know* when the next bus is coming?
I *would like to know*.

Ich *weiß* nichts davon.
Wenn ich es *wüsste*, würde ich es Ihnen sofort sagen.

I *have* no *idea*.
If I *knew*, I would tell you at once.

Wissen Sie etwas über die Geschichte Jugoslawiens?

Do you *know* anything about the history of Yugoslavia?

Da *weiß* ich gar nicht Bescheid.

I *do* not *know* anything about that.

26 schreiben   write

Class I strong verb, stress on stem **schreib-**

PRESENT PARTICIPLE	PAST PARTICIPLE
schreibend	geschrieben

PRESENT	SIMPLE PAST
ich schreibe	ich schrieb
du schreibst	du schriebst
er/sie/es schreibt	er/sie/es schrieb
wir schreiben	wir schrieben
ihr schreibt	ihr schriebt
sie/Sie schreiben	sie/Sie schrieben

KONJUNKTIV I	KONJUNKTIV II
ich schreibe	ich schriebe

Similar verbs

bleiben (+*sein*)	remain
leihen	lend, borrow
meiden	avoid
preisen	praise
reiben	rub, grate
scheinen	shine
schreien	scream, call out
schweigen (+*sein*)	be silent
steigen(+*sein*)	climb, go up
treiben	drive
weisen (*auf+acc.*)	point (to)

Er *hat* mir *geschrieben*, dass er nächste Woche nach Tokio fliegt.	He *wrote* me that he's'flying to Tokyo next week.

IMPERATIVE
schreib(e)! (du)   schreiben Sie!   schreibt! (ihr)

PRESENT PERFECT
ich habe ... geschrieben

PAST PERFECT (PLUPERFECT)
ich hatte ... geschrieben

FUTURE
ich werde ... schreiben

FUTURE PERFECT
ich werde ... geschrieben haben

COMPOUND CONDITIONAL
ich würde ... schreiben

PAST CONDITIONAL
ich hätte ... geschrieben

Bleiben Sie ruhig!	Please *stay* calm!
Die Sonne *hat* den ganzen Tag lang *geschienen*.	The sun *shone* all day.
Die Temperatur *ist* bis auf 24 Grad *gestiegen*.	The temperature *rose* to 24 degrees.
Wir *sind* auf den Berg *gestiegen* und zwei Stunden dort oben *geblieben*.	We *climbed* the mountain and *stayed* at the top for two hours.
Ich *habe* meinem Bruder mein Fahrrad *geliehen*.	I *lent* my brother my bicycle.
Sabine *hat sich* 200 Euro von mir *geliehen*.	Sabine *borrowed* 200 euros from me.

27 erscheinen   appear

Class I inseparable verb, stress on stem **-schein-**

PRESENT PARTICIPLE	**PAST PARTICIPLE**
erscheinend	erschienen

PRESENT	**SIMPLE PAST**
ich erscheine	ich erschien
du erscheinst	du erschienst
er/sie/es erscheint	er/sie/es erschien
wir erscheinen	wir erschienen
ihr erscheint	ihr erschient
sie/Sie erscheinen	sie/Sie erschienen

KONJUNKTIV I	**KONJUNKTIV II**
ich erscheine	ich erschiene

Similar verbs

beschreiben	describe, characterize	**verbleiben** (+*sein*)	remain
besteigen	climb, mount	**verleihen**	lend
beweisen	prove, show	**vermeiden**	avoid
entscheiden	decide	**verschreiben**	prescribe
gedeihen (+*sein*)	flourish	**verschweigen**	keep quiet about
übersteigen	exceed	**vertreiben**	drive away
übertreiben	exaggerate	**verweisen**	expel, refer
unterscheiden	distinguish	**verzeihen** (*dat.*)	forgive (someone)
unterschreiben	sign		

Der Chef *erschien* pünktlich um 8 Uhr.	The boss *appeared* punctually at 8 o'clock.
Er *wird* seine Stelle so lange *behalten,* bis die Nachfolge *entschieden ist.*	He *will keep* his job until the successor *has been selected.*
Das Verbrechen *muss* zuerst *bewiesen werden.*	The crime *must* first *be proven.*

IMPERATIVE
erschein(e)! (du)   erscheinen Sie!   erscheint! (ihr)

PRESENT PERFECT
ich bin ... erschienen

PAST PERFECT (PLUPERFECT)
ich war ... erschienen

FUTURE
ich werde ... erscheinen

FUTURE PERFECT
ich werde ... erschienen sein

COMPOUND CONDITIONAL
ich würde ... erscheinen

PAST CONDITIONAL
ich wäre ... erschienen

Der Arzt *verschrieb* mir ein neues Mittel; er *hat* mir aber die möglichen Folgen der Behandlung *verschwiegen.*

The doctor *prescribed* a new medicine for me; however, he *kept quiet* about the possible consequences of the treatment.

Es *ist* heute *entschieden worden*, dass die Firma nach Berlin ziehen wird.

It *has been decided* today that the firm will move to Berlin.

Ich *werde mich* erst morgen *entscheiden*, ob ich mitgehe oder nicht.

I *will* not *decide* until tomorrow if I will go too or not.

Tut mir leid, aus dieser Entfernung *kann* ich die Farben nicht *unterscheiden.*

I'm sorry, from this distance I *can* not *distinguish* the colors.

Ich *sollte* jede Aufregung *vermeiden.*

I *should avoid* any upset.

Ich *werde* ihm nie *verzeihen*, dass er mein Auto *verliehen hat.*

I *will* never *forgive* him for *lending* my car.

Class I separable verb, stress on particle, e.g., **aus-, an-, auf-**

PRESENT PARTICIPLE	PAST PARTICIPLE
PRESENT PARTICIPLE	*PAST PARTICIPLE*
aussteigend	ausgestiegen

PRESENT	*SIMPLE PAST*
ich steige aus	ich stieg aus
du steigst aus	du stiegst aus
er/sie/es steigt aus	er/sie/es stieg aus
wir steigen aus	wir stiegen aus
ihr steigt aus	ihr stiegt aus
sie/Sie steigen aus	sie/Sie stiegen aus

KONJUNKTIV I	*KONJUNKTIV II*
ich steige aus	ich stiege aus

Similar verbs

abschreiben	copy	**hinweisen**	point (out)
absteigen (*+sein*)	get off, go down	(*auf+acc.*)	
ansteigen (*+sein*)	rise, increase	**nachweisen**	prove
aufschreiben	list, write down	**niederschreiben**	write down
aufschreien	yell	**stecken bleiben**	get stuck
ausleihen	lend, borrow	(*+sein*)	
ausscheiden	eliminate	**stehen bleiben**	stop, pause
ausschreiben	write out	(*+sein*)	
aussteigen (*+sein*)	get out/off	**umsteigen** (*+sein*)	change (trains)
einschreiben	enter, enroll	**vorschreiben**	specify
einsteigen (*+sein*)	get in/on, board	**zurückweisen**	turn down,
gleich bleiben	remain		refuse
(*+sein*)	unchanged	**zuschreiben** (*dat.*)	credit,
gutschreiben (*dat.*)	credit (to)		ascribe (to)
sich herumtreiben	hang around	**zuweisen**	assign
hinscheiden (*+sein*)	pass away		

IMPERATIVE
steig aus! (du)   steigen Sie aus!   steigt aus! (ihr)

PRESENT PERFECT   *PAST PERFECT (PLUPERFECT)*
ich bin ... ausgestiegen   ich war ... ausgestiegen

FUTURE   *FUTURE PERFECT*
ich werde ... aussteigen   ich werde ... ausgestiegen sein

COMPOUND CONDITIONAL   *PAST CONDITIONAL*
ich würde ... aussteigen   ich wäre ... ausgestiegen

Wir *schreiben uns* die Abfahrtzeiten *auf*.	We *are writing down* the departure times.
Wir *steigen* in Köln *um* und dann in Bremen *aus*.	We *are changing trains* in Cologne, and then *getting out* in Bremen.
Ich *habe mir* ein gutes Buch für die Reise *ausgeliehen*.	I *have borrowed* a good book for the trip.
Alles einsteigen!	*All aboard!*
Du *musst* hier vom Fahrrad *absteigen*.	You *must get off* your bicycle here.
Hier beginnt die Fußgängerzone.	The pedestrian zone starts here.
Der Wasserspiegel im Fluss *ist* sehr *angestiegen*.	The watertable of the river *rose* very high.
Seine Schuld *ist* nie *nachgewiesen worden*.	His guilt *was* never *proven*.
Die Teilnehmer der Exkursion *sind* auf die Gefahren des Dschungels *hingewiesen worden*.	The participants of the excursion *have been made aware* of the dangers of the jungle.

Class I verb, stress on stem **leid-**

PRESENT PARTICIPLE	PAST PARTICIPLE
leidend	gelitten

PRESENT	SIMPLE PAST
ich leide	ich litt
du leidest	du littest
er/sie/es leidet	er/sie/es litt
wir leiden	wir litten
ihr leidet	ihr littet
sie/Sie leiden	sie/Sie litten

KONJUNKTIV I	KONJUNKTIV II
ich leide	ich litte

Similar verbs

beißen	bite	**schleifen**	sharpen, drag
gleiten (+sein)	glide, slide	**schmeißen**	throw, chuck
greifen (nach)	grasp, reach (for)	**schneiden**	cut, slice
		schreiten	stride
kneifen	pinch	**streiten**	argue, quarrel
pfeifen	whistle		
reißen	tear		
reiten (+sein/haben)	ride		

Anne *hat* die vertrockneten Blumen in den Abfalleimer *geschmissen.*	Anne *threw* the dried-out flowers into the garbage bin.
Unser Hund *beißt!* Letzte Woche *hat* er den Briefträger ins Bein *gebissen* und ihm die Hose *zerrissen.*	Our dog *bites!* Last week he *bit* the mailman in the leg and *tore* his pants.

IMPERATIVE

leide! (du)   leiden Sie!   leidet! (ihr)

PRESENT PERFECT	**PAST PERFECT (PLUPERFECT)**
ich habe ... gelitten	ich hatte ... gelitten

FUTURE	**FUTURE PERFECT**
ich werde ... leiden	ich werde ... gelitten haben

COMPOUND CONDITIONAL	**PAST CONDITIONAL**
ich würde ... leiden	ich hätte ... gelitten

Jochen *ist* früher oft *geritten*.	In the past Jochen often *rode* a horse.
Die frisch *gestrichenen* Wände sehen gut aus.	The freshly *painted* walls look good.
Ich *bin* auf der vereisten Straße *ausgeglitten* und hingefallen.	I *slipped* on the icy road and fell down.
Sie *griff* nach dem Messer und *schnitt* das Fleisch in kleine Stücke.	She *reached* for the knife and *cut* the meat into small pieces.

30 zerreißen   tear up

Class I inseparable verb, stress on stem **-reiß-**

PRESENT PARTICIPLE	PAST PARTICIPLE
zerreißend	zerrissen

PRESENT	SIMPLE PAST
ich zerreiße	ich zerriss
du zerreißt	du zerrissest
er/sie/es zerreißt	er/sie/es zerriss
wir zerreißen	wir zerrissen
ihr zerreißt	ihr zerrisst
sie/Sie zerreißen	sie/Sie zerrissen

KONJUNKTIV I	KONJUNKTIV II
ich zerreiße	ich zerrisse

Similar verbs

begreifen	realize
bestreichen	spread
bestreiten	dispute
ergreifen	grasp, seize, reach for
umreißen	outline
unterstreichen	underline
verbleichen (*+sein*)	fade
vergleichen	compare

IMPERATIVE
zerreiße! (du)   zerreißen Sie!   zerreißt! (ihr)

PRESENT PERFECT	**PAST PERFECT (PLUPERFECT)**
ich habe ... zerrissen	ich hatte ... zerrissen

FUTURE	**FUTURE PERFECT**
ich werde ... zerreißen	ich werde ... zerrissen haben

COMPOUND CONDITIONAL	**PAST CONDITIONAL**
ich würde ... zerreißen	ich hätte ... zerrissen

Ich *habe* nie *begriffen*, warum Sie die Gelegenheit nie *ergriffen haben.*	I *have* never *understood* why you *didn't take advantage* of the opportunity.
Ich *bestreite*, dass sich die Angelegenheit so zugetragen hat.	I *dispute* that the matter occurred like that.
Er sagte mir, er *begreife* nicht, wie er den Scheck *habe zerreißen können.*	He told me that he can't *understand* how he *could have ripped up* the check.
Die Firma *kann* die Kosten nicht mehr *bestreiten.*	The company *cannot bear* the costs any longer.
Wir *haben* die beiden Bilder *verglichen* – sie sind kaum *zu unterscheiden.*	We *have compared* the two pictures – they *can* barely *be told apart.*
Die Farben *sind verblichen.* Aber die Konturen *sind* immer noch scharf *umrissen.*	The colors *have faded.* But the contours *are* still sharply *outlined.*
Das Brot *ist* mit Butter und Käse *bestrichen.*	The bread *is spread* with butter and cheese.

95

Class I separable verb, stress on particle **an-**

PRESENT PARTICIPLE	PAST PARTICIPLE
angreifend	angegriffen

PRESENT	SIMPLE PAST
ich greife an	ich griff an
du greifst an	du griffst an
er/sie/es greift an	er/sie/es griff an
wir greifen an	wir griffen an
ihr greift an	ihr grifft an
sie/Sie greifen an	sie/Sie griffen an

KONJUNKTIV I	KONJUNKTIV II
ich greife an	ich griffe an

Similar verbs

abreißen	tear off, demolish	**ausweichen** (+sein) (dat.)	avoid
abschneiden	cut off	**einschneiden** (in+acc.)	cut, carve into
abweichen (+sein) (von)	deviate, diverge (from)	**einschreiten**	intervene
anstreichen	decorate, paint	**glatt streichen**	smooth
ausgleichen	even out, equalize	**rausschmeißen**	throw out
ausschneiden	cut out	**zugreifen**	help oneself

Bitte *greifen* Sie *zu!*

Please *help yourself!*

Die Torte sieht gut aus – Oma *hat* den Guss *glatt gestrichen.*

The cake looks good – Grandma *smoothed out* the icing.

Wir wohnen jetzt auf dem Lande und fühlen uns von unserem alten Leben in der Stadt ziemlich *abgeschnitten.*

We are now living in the country and feel fairly *cut off* from our old life in the town.

IMPERATIVE

greif(e) an! (du)   greifen Sie an!   greift an! (ihr)

PRESENT PERFECT
ich habe ... angegriffen

PAST PERFECT (PLUPERFECT)
ich hatte ... angegriffen

FUTURE
ich werde ... angreifen

FUTURE PERFECT
ich werde ... angegriffen haben

COMPOUND CONDITIONAL
ich würde ... angreifen

PAST CONDITIONAL
ich hätte ... angegriffen

Unser Haus *wurde* letzte Woche frisch *angestrichen.*

Our house *was* freshly *painted* last week.

Die alte Garage *war* letztes Jahr *abgerissen worden.*

The old garage *was torn down* last year.

Der Fahrradfahrer *ist* vom Radweg *abgewichen,* und ich *konnte* ihm gerade noch *ausweichen.*

The bicycle rider *went off* the bike path and I *was* barely *able to avoid* him.

Wir *sind* bei der Sitzung immer wieder vom Thema *abgewichen, und* der Vorsitzende *hat einschreiten müssen.*

We continually *got off* the subject at the meeting, and the chairman *had to intervene.*

32 biegen   bend, turn

Class II verb, stress on stem **bieg-**

PRESENT PARTICIPLE	PAST PARTICIPLE
biegend	gebogen

PRESENT	SIMPLE PAST
ich biege	ich bog
du biegst	du bogst
er/sie/es biegt	er/sie/es bog
wir biegen	wir bogen
ihr biegt	ihr bogt
sie/Sie biegen	sie/Sie bogen

KONJUNKTIV I	KONJUNKTIV II
ich biege	ich böge

Similar verbs

biegen	bend, curve
bieten	offer, bid
fliegen *(+sein/haben)*	fly
fliehen *(+sein)*	flee
frieren	freeze
schieben	push, shove
wiegen	weigh

Notes wiegen meaning "*rock*" is weak [➤**machen**].

Die Flüchtlinge *wurden* nach Frankfurt *geflogen.*	The refugees *were flown* to Frankfurt.
Wir *fliegen* morgen nach Südamerika.	We *are flying* to South America tomorrow.
Sind Sie schon einmal mit dem neuen Airbus *geflogen?*	*Have* you *flown* with the new Airbus already?

IMPERATIVE
bieg(e)! (du)   biegen Sie!   biegt! (ihr)

PRESENT PERFECT
ich habe ... gebogen

PAST PERFECT (PLUPERFECT)
ich hatte ... gebogen

FUTURE
ich werde ... biegen

FUTURE PERFECT
ich werde ... gebogen haben

COMPOUND CONDITIONAL
ich würde ... biegen

PAST CONDITIONAL
ich hätte ... gebogen

Das ganze Haus *ist* in die Luft *geflogen*. — The whole house *blew up*.

Die Frauen und Kinder *haben gefroren*. — The women and children *were very cold*.

Es *hat* in der Nacht *gefroren*. Als wir aufwachten, *war* der Fluss *zugefroren*. — It *froze* during the night. When we woke up the river *was frozen over*.

Für das Gemälde *wurde* auf der Auktion 1 Million Euro *geboten*. — One million euros *were offered* for the painting at the auction.

Ich wäre schon früher in Urlaub gefahren, aber leider *hat sich* bisher keine Gelegenheit dazu *geboten*. — I would have gone on vacation sooner, but unfortunately there *has been* no opportunity until now.

33 ziehen · pull, move

Class II irregular verb with **-g-** in stem of past tenses, stress on stem **zieh-**

PRESENT PARTICIPLE	PAST PARTICIPLE
ziehend	gezogen

PRESENT	SIMPLE PAST
ich ziehe	ich zog
du ziehst	du zogst
er/sie/es zieht	er/sie/es zog
wir ziehen	wir zogen
ihr zieht	ihr zogt
sie/Sie ziehen	sie/Sie zogen

KONJUNKTIV I	KONJUNKTIV II
ich ziehe	ich zöge

Similar verbs

[For inseparable verbs ➤**verlieren** 34]
beziehen   cover

[For separable verbs ➤**anbieten** 35]

abziehen	take off,	**hinausziehen**	draw out
(+sein/haben)	make a copy	*(+sein/haben)*	
anziehen	attract, put on	**umziehen** *(+sein)*	move house
aufziehen	bring up	**vollziehen**	carry out
ausziehen	take off	**vorziehen** *(dat.)*	prefer (to)
(+sein/haben)		**zurückziehen**	draw back,
einziehen	draft, enlist	*(+sein/haben)*	move back
(+sein/haben)		**zusammenziehen**	move together
erziehen	bring up	*(+sein/haben)*	
großziehen	bring up, rear	**zuziehen**	close
herausziehen	pull out, extract		

IMPERATIVE
zieh(e)! (du)   ziehen Sie!   zieht! (ihr)

PRESENT PERFECT
ich habe/bin ... gezogen

PAST PERFECT (PLUPERFECT)
ich hatte/war ... gezogen

FUTURE
ich werde ... ziehen

FUTURE PERFECT
ich werde ... gezogen haben/sein

COMPOUND CONDITIONAL
ich würde ... ziehen

PAST CONDITIONAL
ich hätte/wäre ... gezogen

Wir *sind* von Bremen nach Hamburg *gezogen.*	We *have moved* from Bremen to Hamburg.
Welche Stadt *ziehen* Sie *vor?*	Which city *do* you *prefer?*
Als wir in das neue Haus *eingezogen waren,* fühlte ich mich zunächst von der Kultur der Großstadt *angezogen.*	When we *had* first *moved* into the new house, I felt *attracted* by the city culture.
Aber es fällt doch schwer *umzuziehen.*	But it is still difficult *to move.*
Es zieht hier im Haus.	*There is a draft* in the house.
Ich *habe* die finanzielle Lage auch in *Betracht gezogen.*	I *have* also *taken* the financial situation *into consideration.*
Ihre Kinder *sind* sehr gut *erzogen.*	Your children *have been raised* very well.
Die Unterlagen *beziehen sich* auf die Expansionspläne der Firma.	The files *pertain to* the expansion plans of the company.
Die finanzielle Lage *ist* auch *in Betracht gezogen worden.*	The financial situation *has* also *been taken into account.*

34 verlieren   lose

Class II inseparable verb, stress on stem **-lier-**

PRESENT PARTICIPLE	PAST PARTICIPLE
PRESENT PARTICIPLE	*PAST PARTICIPLE*
verlierend	verloren

PRESENT	*SIMPLE PAST*
ich verliere	ich verlor
du verlierst	du verlorst
er/sie/es verliert	er/sie/es verlor
wir verlieren	wir verloren
ihr verliert	ihr verlort
sie/Sie verlieren	sie/Sie verloren

KONJUNKTIV I	*KONJUNKTIV II*
ich verliere	ich verlöre

Similar verbs

entfliehen *(+sein) (dat.)*	escape (from)
überwiegen	outweigh, predominate
verbieten	forbid
verschieben	postpone

Du *solltest* die Abreise nicht *verschieben*.	You *should* not *postpone* the departure.
Wir *wollen* dem Lärm der Stadt *entfliehen*.	We *want* to *escape from* the noise of the city.
Ich *habe* meinen Schirm *verloren*.	I *have lost* my umbrella.
Das Projekt hat seine Nachteile, aber die Vorteile *überwiegen*.	The project has its disadvantages, but the advantages *outweigh* them.

IMPERATIVE
verlier(e)! (du)   verlieren Sie!   verliert! (ihr)

PRESENT PERFECT
ich habe ... verloren

PAST PERFECT (PLUPERFECT)
ich hatte ... verloren

FUTURE
ich werde ... verlieren

FUTURE PERFECT
ich werde ... verloren haben

COMPOUND CONDITIONAL
ich würde ... verlieren

PAST CONDITIONAL
ich hätte ... verloren

Der Verbrecher *ist* aus dem Gefängnis *entflohen*.
The criminal *has escaped* from prison.

Wir *hätten* viel Zeit *verloren*, wenn wir mit dem Auto gefahren wären.
We *would have lost* a lot of time if we had gone by car.

Wir *haben* den Termin auf einen späteren Zeitpunkt *verschoben*.
We *moved* the appointment to a later time.

Parken *verboten*.
No parking.

Class II separable verb, stress on particle **an-**

PRESENT PARTICIPLE	PAST PARTICIPLE
anbietend	angeboten

PRESENT	SIMPLE PAST
ich biete an	ich bot an
du bietest an	du botst an
er/sie/es bietet an	er/sie/es bot an
wir bieten an	wir boten an
ihr bietet an	ihr botet an
sie/Sie bieten an	sie/Sie boten an

KONJUNKTIV I	KONJUNKTIV II
ich biete an	ich böte an

Similar verbs

abbiegen	turn off (a road)
einbiegen *(+sein/haben) (in+acc.)*	turn in
einfrieren *(+sein/haben)*	freeze (food), to freeze up

Wir *haben* unseren Gästen Kaffee *angeboten.*	We *offered* our guests coffee.
Biegen* Sie an der Ampel rechts *ab!* Nach zwei Querstraßen *müssen* Sie dann links *einbiegen.	*Turn* right at the traffic light. Then *turn* left after the next two side streets.
Wenn wir links *abgebogen* wären, wären wir schneller zum Bahnhof gekommen.	If we *had turned* left, we would have gotten to the station quicker.
Er *bot* mir *an,* mich im Wagen mitzunehmen.	He *offered* me a lift in the car.

IMPERATIVE
biet(e) an! (du)   bieten Sie an!   bietet an! (ihr)

PRESENT PERFECT
ich habe ... angeboten

PAST PERFECT (PLUPERFECT)
ich hatte ... angeboten

FUTURE
ich werde ... anbieten

FUTURE PERFECT
ich werde ... angeboten haben

COMPOUND CONDITIONAL
ich würde ... anbieten

PAST CONDITIONAL
ich hätte ... angeboten

Ich *würde* ihm gern ein Glas Wein *anbieten,* aber er muss noch fahren.	I *would like* to *offer* him a glass of wine, but he has to drive.
Wir *werden* das Gemüse *einfrieren.*	We *will freeze* the vegetables.
Das Dach *hat sich* unter der Last des Schnees *gebogen,* und die *eingefrorenen* Wasserrohre sind geplatzt.	The roof *bent* under the weight of the snow, and the *frozen* water pipes burst.

Class II verb, stress on stem **heb-**

PRESENT PARTICIPLE	PAST PARTICIPLE
hebend	gehoben

PRESENT	SIMPLE PAST
ich hebe	ich hob
du hebst	du hobst
er/sie/es hebt	er/sie/es hob
wir heben	wir hoben
ihr hebet	ihr hobt
sie/Sie heben	sie/Sie hoben

KONJUNKTIV I	KONJUNKTIV II
ich hebe	ich höbe

Similar verbs

gären *(+sein/haben)*	ferment	**scheren**	shear, clip
lügen	lie	**schwören**	swear
saugen	suck	**trügen**	deceive
	vacuum	**weben**	weave

Notes There are vowel changes in the past tense in this sub-group; **saugen** and **weben** generally are used in a weak form (saugte, webte); **gären** is used figuratively in a weak form when it means to seethe or fester; **scheren** is used in a weak form when it means "to concern" or "clear off"; [➤**machen** 11].

Das Vorstandsmitglied *hob* **die Hand, um sich zu Wort zu melden.**	The board member *raised* his hand for an opportunity to speak.
Der Angeklagte *schwor*, **dass er die Wahrheit gesagt habe.**	The accused *swore* that he had told the truth.

IMPERATIVE
heb(e)! (du)   heben Sie!   hebt! (ihr)

PRESENT PERFECT
ich habe ... gehoben

PAST PERFECT (PLUPERFECT)
ich hatte ... gehoben

FUTURE
ich werde ... heben

FUTURE PERFECT
ich werde ... gehoben haben

COMPOUND CONDITIONAL
ich würde ... heben

PAST CONDITIONAL
ich hätte ... gehoben

Ich *könnte schwören,* dass ich ihn gestern gesehen habe.	I *could swear* I saw him yesterday.
Was *schert* mich das!	What *do I care* about that!
Hast du schon Staub *gesaugt?*	*Have* you *vacuumed* already?
Die Teppiche *wurden* von Hand *gewoben.*	The carpets *were woven* by hand.
Wenn mich meine Erinnerung *nicht trügt, hatte* er mir *geschworen,* dass er bis Montag fertig wird.	If my memory *serves me right,* he *had sworn* to me that he would be finished by Monday.
Der Wein *gärt* in großen Fässern.	The wine *ferments* in large casks.

37 erwägen

weigh up

Class II inseparable verb, stress on stem **-wäg-**

PRESENT PARTICIPLE	PAST PARTICIPLE
erwägend	erwogen

PRESENT	SIMPLE PAST
ich erwäge	ich erwog
du erwägst	du erwogst
er/sie/es erwägt	er/sie/es erwog
wir erwägen	wir erwogen
ihr erwägt	ihr erwogt
sie/Sie erwägen	sie/Sie erwogen

KONJUNKTIV I	KONJUNKTIV II
ich erwäge	ich erwöge

Similar verbs

beschwören	conjure up
betrügen	deceive
bewegen	persuade
erheben	raise, revolt
sich verschwören	conspire

Notes   **erwägen** is sometimes used in a weak form [➤**verkaufen** 14].
bewegen is always weak when it means to move[➤**verkaufen** 14].

Das Wetter *hat sich* **gegen uns** *verschworen.*	The weather *has conspired* against us.
Ich *habe* **den Plan gründlich** *erwogen.*	I *have weighed* the plan thoroughly.
Die Schüler *haben sich* **gegen die Schulleitung** *erhoben.*	The students *revolted* against the school administration.

IMPERATIVE

erwäg(e)! (du)   erwägen Sie!   erwägt! (ihr)

PRESENT PERFECT

ich habe ... erwogen

PAST PERFECT (PLUPERFECT)

ich hatte ... erwogen

FUTURE

ich werde ... erwägen

FUTURE PERFECT

ich werde ... erwogen haben

COMPOUND CONDITIONAL

ich würde ... erwägen

PAST CONDITIONAL

ich hätte ... erwogen

Ich weiß nicht, was ihn dazu *bewogen hat* **das Auto zu kaufen.**	I don't know what *persuaded* him to buy that car.
Ich *konnte* **ihn dazu** *bewegen,* **mir das Geld zu leihen.**	I *was able to persuade* him to lend me the money.
Wir *erhoben* **unser Glas und tranken auf das Wohl des Geburtstagskindes.**	We *raised* our glasses and drank to the heath of the birthday child.
Es *erhebt sich* **die Frage, ob wir uns einer anderen Partei anschließen sollten.**	The question *arises* whether we should join another party.
An Ihrer Stelle *würde* **ich jede Möglichkeit** *erwägen.*	In your place I *would weigh* every possibility.

38 aufheben

Class II separable verb, stress on particle **auf-**

PRESENT PARTICIPLE	PAST PARTICIPLE
aufhebend	aufgehoben

PRESENT	SIMPLE PAST
ich hebe auf	ich hob auf
du hebst auf	du hobst auf
er/sie/es hebt auf	er/sie/es hob auf
wir heben auf	wir hoben auf
ihr hebt auf	ihr hobt auf
sie/Sie heben auf	sie/Sie hoben auf

KONJUNKTIV I	KONJUNKTIV II
ich hebe auf	ich höbe auf

Similar verbs

abheben	pick up (phone), take off (plane) withdraw (money)
aufheben	abolish
abwägen	weigh
hervorheben	highlight
hochheben	hoist

Er *wägt* seine Worte immer vorsichtig *ab*.	He always *weighs* his words carefully.
Das Geld *ist* bei der Bank *gut aufgehoben*.	The money *is safe* at the bank.
Er ging zur Bank und *hob* das Geld *ab*.	He went to the bank and *withdrew* the money.

IMPERATIVE
heb(e) auf! (du)   heben Sie auf!   hebt auf! (ihr)

PRESENT PERFECT
ich habe ... aufgehoben

PAST PERFECT (PLUPERFECT)
ich hatte ... aufgehoben

FUTURE
ich werde ... aufheben

FUTURE PERFECT
ich werde ... aufgehoben haben

COMPOUND CONDITIONAL
ich würde ... aufheben

PAST CONDITIONAL
ich hätte ... aufgehoben

Man *muss* die Vorteile gegen die Nachteile gut *abwägen.*

You must *weigh* the advantages well against the disadvantages.

Die Werbebroschüre ist gut gelungen.

The advertising brochure turned out well.

Die Farben *heben sich* gut voneinander *ab.*

The colors *contrast* well.

Das Gesetz *ist aufgehoben worden.*

The law *was abolished.*

Kurz nachdem das Flugzeug *abgehoben hatte*, ist es in Turbulenzen geraten.

Shortly after the plane *took off*, it experienced turbulence.

39 schießen   shoot

Class II verb, stress on stem **schieß-**

PRESENT PARTICIPLE	PAST PARTICIPLE
schießend	geschossen

PRESENT	SIMPLE PAST
ich schieße	ich schoss
du schießt	du schossest
er/sie/es schießt	er/sie/es schoss
wir schießen	wir schossen
ihr schießt	ihr schosst
sie/Sie schießen	sie/Sie schossen

KONJUNKTIV I	KONJUNKTIV II
ich schieße	ich schösse

Similar verbs

dreschen	thresh	riechen *(nach)*	smell (of)
fechten	fence	saufen	drink (of
flechten	twine		animals),
	braid		drink (alcohol)
fließen *(+sein)*	flow	schießen *(+sein/haben)*	shoot, fire
gießen	cast, pour	schließen	close,
glimmen	glow		conclude
kriechen *(+sein)*	crawl	schmelzen *(+sein/haben)*	melt
melken	milk	schwellen *(+sein/haben)*	swell
quellen *(+sein)*	well up		

Note   Vowel changes in the second and third person singular present tense are as follows: **-e-** to **-i-** and **-au-** to **-äu-**, with the exception of **melken**. **Saufen** and **triefen** double the **f** in the simple past and past participle **soff**.

IMPERATIVE
schieß(e)! (du)   schießen Sie!   schießt! (ihr)

PRESENT PERFECT ich habe ... geschossen	*PAST PERFECT (PLUPERFECT)* ich hatte ... geschossen
FUTURE ich werde ... schießen	*FUTURE PERFECT* ich werde ... geschossen haben
COMPOUND CONDITIONAL ich würde ... schießen	*PAST CONDITIONAL* ich hätte ... geschossen

---

Aus den Untersuchungen *haben* wir *geschlossen*, dass das Eis vor Millionen von Jahren *geschmolzen war*.	We *have concluded* from our research that the ice *melted* millions of years ago.
An den Vortrag *schloss sich* eine lebhafte Diskussion an.	A lively discussion *followed* the lecture.
Das Boot *ist* durch das Wasser *geschossen*.	The boat *shot* through the water.
Der Bach *fließt* mitten durch die Stadt.	The brook *flows* through the middle of the town.
Die Tür *schließt* von selbst.	The door *shuts* automatically.
Mein Hund *hat* die Schüssel Wasser leer *gesoffen*.	My dog *drank* the entire bowl of water.
Das ganze Haus *riecht* nach frischer Farbe.	The whole house *smells* of fresh paint.

40 genießen   enjoy

Class II inseparable verb, stress on stem **-nieß-**

PRESENT PARTICIPLE	PAST PARTICIPLE
genießend	genossen

PRESENT	SIMPLE PAST
ich genieße	ich genoss
du genießt	du genossest
er/sie/es genießt	er/sie/es genoss
wir genießen	wir genossen
ihr genießt	ihr genosst
sie/Sie genießen	sie/Sie genossen

KONJUNKTIV I	KONJUNKTIV II
ich genieße	ich genösse

Similar verbs

begießen	water, celebrate	**erschießen**	shoot dead
beschießen	shoot at, shell	**erschließen**	open up, infer
beschließen	decide	**umschließen**	border
sich entschließen	make up one's mind	**verdrießen**	annoy
		vergießen	spill
erlöschen (+sein)	go out (fire)	**verschließen**	lock, seal

Note **erlöschen** changes the vowel in the second and third person singular present tense to **-i-**.

Haben Sie *sich entschlossen* zu verreisen?	*Have* you *made up your mind* to go away?
Ja, wir *haben beschlossen,* nach Frankreich zu fahren.	Yes, we *have decided* to go to France.
Unser Erfolg wurde mit einer Flasche Sekt *begossen.*	Our success was *celebrated* with a bottle of champagne.

IMPERATIVE
genieß(e)! (du)   genießen Sie!   genießt! (ihr)

PRESENT PERFECT
ich habe ... genossen

PAST PERFECT (PLUPERFECT)
ich hatte ... genossen

FUTURE
ich werde ... genießen

FUTURE PERFECT
ich werde ... genossen haben

COMPOUND CONDITIONAL
ich würde ... genießen

PAST CONDITIONAL
ich hätte ... genossen

Was mich *verdrießt*, ist die Tatsache, dass er sich nie schnell *entschließen kann*.

What *annoys* me is the fact that he *can* never *make up his mind* quickly.

Die Verhandlungen wurden hinter *verschlossenen* Türen geführt.

The negotiations were carried out behind *locked* doors.

Das Essen *war nicht zu genießen;* wir *beschlossen,* in ein anderes Restaurant zu gehen.

The meal *was inedible;* we *decided* to go to another restaurant.

Wir *werden* nächstes Jahr neue Märkte *erschließen*.

We *will open up* new markets next year.

Es *wurde beschlossen*, die Gegend als Reisegebiet *zu erschließen*.

It *was decided to open up* the region as a tourist area.

Man *kann* dort in Ruhe die Berglandschaft *genießen*.

You *can enjoy* the mountain landscape at leisure there.

Class II separable verb, stress on particle **ab-**

PRESENT PARTICIPLE	PAST PARTICIPLE
abschließend	abgeschlossen

PRESENT	SIMPLE PAST
ich schließe ab	ich schloss ab
du schließt ab	du schlossest ab
er/sie/es schließt ab	er/sie/es schloss ab
wir schließen ab	wir schlossen ab
ihr schließt ab	ihr schlosst ab
sie/Sie schließen ab	sie/Sie schlossen ab

KONJUNKTIV I	KONJUNKTIV II
ich schließe ab	ich schlösse ab

Similar verbs

anschließen	connect
aufschließen	unlock
ausschließen	bar, exclude
einschließen	enclose, include
kurzschließen	short-circuit
sich zusammenschließen	join together

Ich *habe mich* **schon wieder** *ausgeschlossen.*	I *have locked* myself *out* again.
Ist **der neue Computer schon** *angeschlossen?*	*Has* the new computer *been connected* yet?
Das Naturschutzgebiet *ist ganz* **vom Wasser** *eingeschlossen.*	The nature preserve *is surrounded* by water.
Der Garten *schließt* **direkt an den Wald** *an.*	The garden *adjoins* the woods.

IMPERATIVE
schließ(e) ab! (du)   schließen Sie ab!   schließt ab! (ihr)

PRESENT PERFECT	**PAST PERFECT (PLUPERFECT)**
ich habe ... abgeschlossen	ich hatte ... abgeschlossen

FUTURE	**FUTURE PERFECT**
ich werde ... abschließen	ich werde ... abgeschlossen haben

COMPOUND CONDITIONAL	**PAST CONDITIONAL**
ich würde ... abschließen	ich hätte ... abgeschlossen

Wir *haben* uns zu einer Bürgerrechtsbewegung *zusammengeschlossen.*	We *have joined together* in a civil rights action.
Alle, ich *eingeschlossen, haben sich* dem Sportverein *angeschlossen.*	All of us, *including me, have joined* the sports club.
Man *kann* diese Möglichkeit nicht *ausschließen.*	One *can* not *rule out* this possibility.

42 trinken   drink

Class III verb, stress on stem **trink-**

PRESENT PARTICIPLE	PAST PARTICIPLE
trinkend	getrunken

PRESENT	SIMPLE PAST
ich trinke	ich trank
du trinkst	du trankst
er/sie/es trinkt	er/sie/es trank
wir trinken	wir tranken
ihr trinkt	ihr trankt
sie/Sie trinken	sie/Sie tranken

KONJUNKTIV I	KONJUNKTIV II
ich trinke	ich tränke

Similar verbs

dringen *(+sein)*	penetrate
klingen	sound
ringen	wrestle, wring, wrench
schwingen	swing, oscillate
singen	sing
sinken *(+sein)*	sink, fall
springen *(+sein)*	jump
stinken	stink
wringen	wring
zwingen	force, compel

Trinken Sie ein Glas Wein!	*Have* a glass of wine!
Der Dollar *ist* wieder *gesunken*.	The dollar *has gone down* again.
Wir *waren gezwungen*, unser Haus zu verkaufen.	We *were forced* to sell our house.
Das Motorboot *ist* im Sturm *gesunken*.	The motorboat *sank* in the storm.

IMPERATIVE
trink(e)! (du)   trinken Sie!   trinkt! (ihr)

PRESENT PERFECT   *PAST PERFECT (PLUPERFECT)*
ich habe ... getrunken   ich hatte ... getrunken

FUTURE   *FUTURE PERFECT*
ich werde ... trinken   ich werde ... getrunken haben

COMPOUND CONDITIONAL   *PAST CONDITIONAL*
ich würde ... trinken   ich hätte ... getrunken

Der Lärm von der Party *ist* durch die dünnen Wände bis zu uns *gedrungen*.	The noise from the party *went* right *through* the thin walls all the way to our place.
Der Hund *ist* in den Teich *gesprungen*.	The dog *jumped* into the lake.
Es *klang* so, als ob Peter nächstes Wochenende nicht zu Hause wäre.	It *sounded* as if Peter wouldn't be home next weekend.
Sie *hat* lange mit *sich gerunge*n, bevor sie die teure Uhr kaufte.	She *wrestled* long *with herself* before she bought the expensive watch.

43 durchdringen   penetrate

Class III inseparable verb, stress on stem **-dring-**

PRESENT PARTICIPLE	PAST PARTICIPLE
durchdringend	durchdrungen

PRESENT	SIMPLE PAST
ich durchdringe	ich durchdrang
du durchdringst	du durchdrangst
er/sie/es durchdringt	er/sie/es durchdrang
wir durchdringen	wir durchdrangen
ihr durchdringt	ihr durchdrangt
sie/Sie durchdringen	sie/Sie durchdrangen

KONJUNKTIV I	KONJUNKTIV II
ich durchdringe	ich durchdränge

Similar verbs

sich betrinken	get drunk
entspringen *(+sein) (dat.)*	rise (from)
ertrinken *(+sein)*	drown
gelingen *(+sein) (dat.)*	succeed
misslingen *(+sein) (dat.)*	fail
überspringen	jump over
verklingen *(+sein)*	fade
verschlingen	devour, gobble

Note   **durchdringen** can also be used intransitively as a separable verb with the auxiliary **sein**.

Als die Musik *verklungen war*, applaudierte das Publikum.	When the music *had faded away*, the audience applauded.
Der Fluss *entspringt* in den Alpen.	The river *rises* in the Alps.

IMPERATIVE
durchdringe! (du)   durchdringen Sie!   durchdringet! (ihr)

PRESENT PERFECT	*PAST PERFECT (PLUPERFECT)*
ich habe ... durchdrungen	ich hatte ... durchdrungen

FUTURE	*FUTURE PERFECT*
ich werde ... durchdringen	ich werde ... durchdrungen haben

COMPOUND CONDITIONAL	*PAST CONDITIONAL*
ich würde ... durchdringen	ich hätte ... durchdrungen

Es *ist* mir *misslungen,* ihn von seinen Umzugsplänen *abzubringen.*	I *was unsuccessful* in *dissuading* him from his plans to move.
Er *verschlingt* jedes Buch in ein paar Tagen.	He *consumes* each book in a few days.
Die Inszenierung *ist* gut *gelungen.*	The production *was* very *successful.*
Das Licht der Taschenlampe *durchdringt* die Dunkelheit.	The beam of the flashlight *penetrates* the darkness.
Die Kinder *haben* das Popcorn *verschlungen.*	The children *have devoured* the popcorn.
Die Restaurierung des Opernhauses *wird* Millionen *verschlingen.*	The restoration of the opera house *will cost* millions.
Es *ist* mir bisher nicht *gelungen,* ihn telefonisch zu erreichen.	I *have been unable* so far to reach him by telephone.

44 aufspringen   jump up

Class III separable verb, stress on particle **auf-**

PRESENT PARTICIPLE	***PAST PARTICIPLE***
aufspringend	aufgesprungen

PRESENT	***SIMPLE PAST***
ich springe auf	ich sprang auf
du springst auf	du sprangst auf
er/sie/es springt auf	er/sie/es sprang auf
wir springen auf	wir sprangen auf
ihr springt auf	ihr sprangt auf
sie/Sie springen auf	sie/Sie sprangen auf

KONJUNKTIV I	***KONJUNKTIV II***
ich springe auf	ich spränge auf

Similar verbs

absinken *(+sein)*	sink, subside
abspringen *(+sein)*	jump down, come off
anspringen *(+sein)*	jump, start
austrinken	drink up
einspringen *(+sein) (für)*	stand in (for)

Er *hat* den Wein *ausgetrunken*.	He *drank all of* the wine.
Wenn du nicht so schnell *aufgesprungen wärst*, wäre das nicht passiert.	If you *had* not *jumped up* so fast, that would not have happened.

IMPERATIVE

spring(e) auf! (du)   springen Sie auf!   springt auf! (ihr)

PRESENT PERFECT	*PAST PERFECT (PLUPERFECT)*
ich bin ... aufgesprungen	ich war ... aufgesprungen

FUTURE	*FUTURE PERFECT*
ich werde ... aufspringen	ich werde ... aufgesprungen sein

COMPOUND CONDITIONAL	*PAST CONDITIONAL*
ich würde ... aufspringen	ich wäre ... aufgesprungen

Er *springt* immer *ein*, wenn jemand fehlt.	He always *steps in* when someone is absent.
***Könnten* Sie heute mal für mich *einspringen*?**	*Could* you *work for me* today?
Er *sprang auf*.	He *jumped up*.
Der Motor *ist* nicht *angesprungen*.	The engine *would* not *start*.
Wir hätten das Haus fast verkauft, aber dann *ist* der Käufer *abgesprungen*.	We almost sold our house, but then the buyer *backed out*.

45 binden

bind, tie

Class III verb, stress on stem **bind-**

PRESENT PARTICIPLE	PAST PARTICIPLE
bindend	gebunden

PRESENT	SIMPLE PAST
ich binde	ich band
du bindest	du bandst
er/sie/es bindet	er/sie/es band
wir binden	wir banden
ihr bindet	ihr bandet
sie/Sie binden	sie/Sie banden

KONJUNKTIV I	KONJUNKTIV II
ich binde	ich bände

Similar verbs

finden	find
schwinden *(+sein)*	dwindle, fade
winden	curl, wind, squirm

Mir *schwindet* **allmählich die Hoffnung, dass wir noch einen günstigen Flug bekommen.**	I'm gradually *losing* hope that we'll still get a reasonable flight.
Ich *kann* **meine Brille nicht** *finden.* **Sie** *wird sich* **schon wieder** *finden.*	I *can't find* my glasses. They *will turn up* again.

IMPERATIVE
binde! (du)   binden Sie!   bindet! (ihr)

PRESENT PERFECT   **PAST PERFECT (PLUPERFECT)**
ich habe ... gebunden   ich hatte ... gebunden

FUTURE   **FUTURE PERFECT**
ich werde ... binden   ich werde ... gebunden haben

COMPOUND CONDITIONAL   **PAST CONDITIONAL**
ich würde ... binden   ich hätte ... gebunden

Binde dir die Schuhe zu!	Tie your shoes!
Er band sich einen Schal um den Hals.	He tied a scarf around his neck.
Fandst du den Film auch langweilig?	Did you find the movie boring too?
Ich finde, dass wir uns am Wochenende ausruhen sollten.	I think that we should relax on the weekend.
Er findet sich immer bereit, ihr bei der Arbeit zu helfen.	He is always ready to help her with the work.
Wir dachten, wir hätten die Lösung gefunden.	We thought we had found the solution.
Sie hat sich das Bein gebrochen und windet sich vor Schmerzen.	She has broken her leg and is squirming in pain.

46 verschwinden

disappear

Class III inseparable verb, stress on stem -**schwind**-

PRESENT PARTICIPLE	PAST PARTICIPLE
verschwindend	verschwunden

PRESENT	SIMPLE PAST
ich verschwinde	ich verschwand
du verschwindest	du verschwandst
er/sie/es verschwindet	er/sie/es verschwand
wir verschwinden	wir verschwanden
ihr verschwindet	ihr verschwandet
sie/Sie verschwinden	sie/Sie verschwanden

KONJUNKTIV I	KONJUNKTIV II
ich verschwinde	ich verschwände

Similar verbs

sich befinden	be located
erfinden	invent, make up
überwinden	overcome
verbinden *(mit)*	bind, connect (with)

Können Sie mich mit dem Personalchef verbinden?	*Can* you *connect* me with the head of personnel?
Das Hotel befindet sich in einer schönen Gegend.	The hotel *is located* in a beautiful area.
Die Bahn verbindet das Dorf mit der Stadt.	The railroad *links* the village with the town.
Verschwinde!	*Get lost!*

IMPERATIVE
verschwinde! (du)   verschwinden Sie!   verschwindet! (ihr)

PRESENT PERFECT
ich bin ... verschwunden

PAST PERFECT (PLUPERFECT)
ich war ... verschwunden

FUTURE
ich werde ... verschwinden

FUTURE PERFECT
ich werde ... verschwunden sein

COMPOUND CONDITIONAL
ich würde ... verschwinden

PAST CONDITIONAL
ich wäre ... verschwunden

Sie *sind* falsch *verbunden.*

You *have the wrong number.*

Wer *hat* die Nähmaschine *erfunden?*

Who *invented* the sewing machine?

Die ganze Geschichte *ist* frei *erfunden.*

The whole story *is a* complete *invention.*

Wir *befanden uns* in einer schwierigen Lage.

We *found ourselves* in a difficult situation.

Die Krise *konnte überwunden werden.*

The crisis *could be overcome.*

Meine Unterlagen *sind verschwunden.*

My files *have disappeared.*

Class III separable verb, stress on particle **heraus-**

PRESENT PARTICIPLE	*PAST PARTICIPLE*
herausfindend	herausgefunden

PRESENT	*SIMPLE PAST*
ich finde heraus	ich fand heraus
du findest heraus	du fandst heraus
er/sie/es findet heraus	er/sie/es fand heraus
wir finden heraus	wir fanden heraus
ihr findet heraus	ihr fandet heraus
sie/Sie finden heraus	sie/Sie fanden heraus

KONJUNKTIV I	*KONJUNKTIV II*
ich finde heraus	ich fände heraus

Similar verbs

sich abfinden *(mit)*	put up (with)
festbinden	tie up
losbinden	untie, loosen
stattfinden	take place
wiederfinden	find again
sich zurechtfinden	find one's way

Die Festspiele *finden* **jedes Jahr in Salzburg** *statt*.	The festivals *take place* in Salzburg every year.
Bitte *finden* **Sie** *heraus*, **um wie viel Uhr das Konzert anfängt.**	Please *find out* at what time the concert starts.

IMPERATIVE
finde heraus! (du)   finden Sie heraus!   findet heraus! (ihr)

PRESENT PERFECT
ich habe ... herausgefunden

PAST PERFECT (PLUPERFECT)
ich hatte ... herausgefunden

FUTURE
ich werde ... herausfinden

FUTURE PERFECT
ich werde ... herausgefunden haben

COMPOUND CONDITIONAL
ich würde ... herausfinden

PAST CONDITIONAL
ich hätte ... herausgefunden

Ich *habe mich* in Berlin nicht *zurechtfinden können*.	I *could* not *find my way* around Berlin.
Endlich *fand* ich meine Schlüssel *wieder*.	Finally I *found* my keys *again*.
Konnten Sie *herausfinden*, wo der Zug abfährt?	*Could* you *find out* where the train leaves?
Du *wirst dich* mit dem Preisanstieg *abfinden müssen*.	You *will have to accept* the price increase.

48 sprechen speak

Class IV verb, stress on stem **sprech-**

PRESENT PARTICIPLE	PAST PARTICIPLE
sprechend	gesprochen

PRESENT	SIMPLE PAST
ich spreche	ich sprach
du sprichst	du sprachst
er/sie/es spricht	er/sie/es sprach
wir sprechen	wir sprachen
ihr sprecht	ihr spracht
sie/Sie sprechen	sie/Sie sprachen

KONJUNKTIV I	KONJUNKTIV II
ich spreche	ich spräche

Similar verbs

bergen	rescue, salvage	**sinnen**	ponder
bersten *(+sein)*	burst	**spinnen**	spin
brechen	break, beat	**stechen**	sting, stab, bite
gelten	be worth, valid	**sterben** *(+sein)*	die
helfen *(dat.) (bei)*	help, aid (with)	**werben (für)**	recruit, advertise
rinnen *(+sein)*	run, trickle	**werfen**	throw, cast
schwimmen	swim, float		
(+sein/haben)			

Note **werden** also belongs to this group.

Die Kinder *haben* **mit Steinen** *geworfen.* **Du** *musst* **mit ihnen** *sprechen.*	The children *have been throwing* stones. You *must speak* to them.
Unser jüngster Sohn *kann* **noch nicht** *schwimmen.*	Our youngest son *can*not *swim* yet.
Gerhard *half* **seiner Frau beim Abwaschen.**	Gerhard *helped* his wife to wash the dishes.
Frau Hort *wurde* **Abteilungsleiterin.**	Mrs. Hort *became* head of the department.

IMPERATIVE
sprich! (du)   sprechen Sie!   sprecht! (ihr)

PRESENT PERFECT
ich habe ... gesprochen

PAST PERFECT (PLUPERFECT)
ich hatte ... gesprochen

FUTURE
ich werde ... sprechen

FUTURE PERFECT
ich werde ... gesprochen haben

COMPOUND CONDITIONAL
ich würde ... sprechen

PAST CONDITIONAL
ich hätte ... gesprochen

Hättest du lieber mit Karin *gesprochen?*

Would you have preferred to *speak* with Karin?

Das Kind *konnte* mit einem Jahr schon *sprechen.*

The child *could talk* when only one year old.

Herr Smith *spricht* fließend Deutsch, und *das gilt* auch für seinen Kollegen George.
Wir *haben* viel über Europa *gesprochen.*

Mr. Smith *speaks* German fluently and *that is* also *true of* his colleague George.
We *have talked* a lot about Europe.

Er *spricht* nie von sich selbst.

He never *talks* of himself.

Sabines Vater *ist* vor einem Jahr an Krebs *gestorben.*

Sabine's father *died* a year ago of cancer.

Vor der Wahl haben die Parteien um neue Mitglieder *geworben.*

Before the election the parties *were recruiting* new members.

Diese Vorschrift *gilt* schon seit langem nicht mehr.

This regulation *has been void* for quite some time.

49 stehlen steal

Class IV verb, stress on stem **stehl-**

PRESENT PARTICIPLE	PAST PARTICIPLE
stehlend	gestohlen

PRESENT	SIMPLE PAST
ich stehle	ich stahl
du stiehlst	du stahlst
er/sie/es stiehlt	er/sie/es stahl
wir stehlen	wir stahlen
ihr stehlt	ihr stahlt
sie/Sie stehlen	sie/Sie stahlen

KONJUNKTIV I	KONJUNKTIV II
ich stehle	ich stähle

Similar verbs

With inseparable prefix

befehlen *(dat.)*	order, tell (someone)
bestehlen	rob
empfehlen	recommend
gebären	give birth (to)

With separable particle

sich hinausstehlen	sneak out

Mir *ist* das Portemonnaie *gestohlen worden*.	My wallet *was stolen*.
Der Kellner *empfiehlt* uns Steak mit Kartoffeln.	The waiter *recommends* steak with potatoes to us.
Jemand *hat* zwei meiner Kollegen *bestohlen*.	Someone *stole from* two of my colleagues.
Hier habe ich *zu befehlen*!	I *am in charge* here!

IMPERATIVE
stiehl! (du)   stehlen Sie!   stehlt! (ihr)

PRESENT PERFECT   *PAST PERFECT (PLUPERFECT)*
ich habe ... gestohlen   ich hatte ... gestohlen

FUTURE   *FUTURE PERFECT*
ich werde ... stehlen   ich werde ... gestohlen haben

COMPOUND CONDITIONAL   *PAST CONDITIONAL*
ich würde ... stehlen   ich hätte ... gestohlen

Er *stahl sich* aus dem Haus *hinaus*, als er seinen Vermieter kommen sah.	He *sneaked out* of the house when he saw his landlord coming.
Der Chef *befahl* und alle gehorchten.	The boss *commanded* and everybody obeyed.
Uns *wurde befohlen*, sofort auszusteigen.	We *were ordered* to get off at once.
Was *würdest* du mir *empfehlen*?	What *would* you *recommend* to me?
Ich *hätte* diesen Fotoapparat *empfohlen*, aber ich weiß nicht, wie viel Geld Sie ausgeben wollen.	I *would have recommended* this camera, but I do not know how much money you want to spend.
Der Arzt *hat* mir *befohlen*, das Bein nicht zu bewegen.	The doctor *ordered me* not to move my leg.

Class IV inseparable verb, stress on stem **-winn-**

PRESENT PARTICIPLE	PAST PARTICIPLE
gewinnend	gewonnen

PRESENT	SIMPLE PAST
ich gewinne	ich gewann
du gewinnst	du gewannst
er/sie/es gewinnt	er/sie/es gewann
wir gewinnen	wir gewannen
ihr gewinnt	ihr gewannt
sie/Sie gewinnen	sie/Sie gewannen

KONJUNKTIV I	KONJUNKTIV II
ich gewinne	ich gewönne (gewänne)

Similar verbs

beginnen *(mit)*	begin (on)	**erwerben**	acquire
sich behelfen	manage, cope	**gewinnen**	win, obtain
		übertreffen	surpass
sich besinnen	reflect	**unterbrechen**	break off,
besprechen	discuss		interrupt
bestechen	corrupt, bribe	**unterwerfen**	subject
sich bewerben *(um)*	apply (for)	**verbergen** *(vor+dat.)*	conceal
durchstechen	pierce		(from)
sich entsinnen *(gen.)*	recall	**verderben**	spoil
entsprechen *(dat.)*	correspond (to)	**verschwimmen** *(+sein)*	become blurred
entwerfen	sketch, design	**versprechen**	promise
		widersprechen *(dat.)*	contradict
sich erbrechen	throw up	**zerbrechen**	break,
sich erschrecken	be frightened	*(+sein/haben)*	smash

Note   **erschrecken** has simple past **erschrak**. Used tr. (frighten) it is weak [➤**verkaufen** 14].

Wenn du kein Werkzeug hast, *wirst* du *dich* anders *behelfen müssen*.	If you don't have any tools, you *will have to manage* otherwise.

IMPERATIVE
gewinne! (du)   gewinnen Sie!   gewinnt! (ihr)

PRESENT PERFECT
ich habe ... gewonnen

PAST PERFECT (PLUPERFECT)
ich hatte ... gewonnen

FUTURE
ich werde ... gewinnen

FUTURE PERFECT
ich werde ... gewonnen haben

COMPOUND CONDITIONAL
ich würde ... gewinnen

PAST CONDITIONAL
ich hätte ... gewonnen

Ich *habe* im Lotto *gewonnen.*
Der Gewinn *entspricht* meinem Jahresgehalt.

I *won* the lottery.
The winnings *equal* my yearly salary.

Sollte man die Lage nicht erst einmal *besprechen?*

Shouldn't we *discuss* the situation first?

Sie *müssen sich* um eine neue Stellung *bewerben.*

You *must apply* for a new job.

Ich *verspreche* Ihnen, dass ich sofort mit der Arbeit *beginnen werde.*

I *promise* you that I *will start* with the work at once.

Die Feier *hat* all unsere Erwartungen *übertroffen.*

The party *exceeded* all of our expectations.

Der Regen *hatte* uns den Spaß am Tennis *verdorben.*

The rain *had spoiled* the fun of playing tennis.

Jemand *hat* eine Flasche *zerbrochen.*

Someone *broke* a bottle.

Widersprich (mir) nicht!

Don't *answer back!*

51 zusammenbrechen collapse

Class IV separable verb, stress on particle **zusammen-**

PRESENT PARTICIPLE	PAST PARTICIPLE
zusammenbrechend	zusammengebrochen

PRESENT	SIMPLE PAST
ich breche zusammen	ich brach zusammen
du brichst zusammen	du brachst zusammen
er/sie/es bricht zusammen	er/sie/es brach zusammen
wir brechen zusammen	wir brachen zusammen
ihr brecht zusammen	ihr bracht zusammen
sie/Sie brechen zusammen	sie/Sie brachen zusammen

KONJUNKTIV I	KONJUNKTIV II
ich breche zusammen	ich bräche zusammen

Similar verbs

abbrechen	break off	**einbrechen** *(+sein)*	burglarize/
absterben *(+sein)*	die out		burgle,
anbrechen	open		break in
(+sein/haben)		**einwerfen**	drop off mail
ansprechen	address	**freisprechen**	acquit
aufbrechen	break	**hervorbrechen** *(+sein)*	burst out
(+sein/haben)	open/up/out	**umwerfen**	knock over,
ausbrechen *(+sein)*	burst/break		down
	out, erupt	**vorwerfen** *(dat.)*	reproach
aussprechen	speak out,	**wegwerfen**	throw away
	pronounce	**zurückwerfen**	reflect,
aussterben *(+sein)*	become		throw back
	extinct	**zusprechen**	award

Wirf diese Papiere nicht **weg**!	Don't *throw* these papers *away*!
Ich *werde* die Briefe *einwerfen*.	I *will mail* the letters.
Alle *sind* vor einer Stunde *aufgebrochen*.	They all *set off* an hour ago.
Einige Tierarten *sind* bereits *ausgestorben*.	Some animal species *have* already *become extinct*.

IMPERATIVE
brich zusammen! (du)   brechen Sie zusammen!   brecht zusammen! (ihr)

PRESENT PERFECT
ich bin ... zusammengebrochen

PAST PERFECT (PLUPERFECT)
ich war ... zusammengebrochen

FUTURE
ich werde ... zusammenbrechen

FUTURE PERFECT
ich werde ... zusammengebrochen sein

COMPOUND CONDITIONAL
ich würde ... zusammenbrechen

PAST CONDITIONAL
ich wäre ... zusammengebrochen

Bei uns *ist eingebrochen worden.*	We *have been burglarized.*
Das Türschloss *wurde aufgebrochen.*	The doorlock *was broken open.*
Die Verbrecher *sind* aus dem Gefängnis *ausgebrochen.*	The criminals *have broken out* of prison.
Der Angeklagte *ist freigesprochen worden.*	The accused *was acquitted.*
Als die Eltern sich scheiden ließen, *wurde* der Mutter das Kind *zugesprochen.*	When the parents divorced, the mother *was given custody* of the child.
Man *hat* ihm *vorgeworfen,* dass er sich zu wenig um seine Familie kümmert.	He *was accused* of paying too little attention to his family.
Wir *werden* die Verhandlungen *abbrechen müssen.*	We *will have to break off* the negotiations.

Class IV irregular verb, stress on stem **nehm-**

PRESENT PARTICIPLE	PAST PARTICIPLE
nehmend	genommen

PRESENT	SIMPLE PAST
ich nehme	ich nahm
du nimmst	du nahmst
er/sie/es nimmt	er/sie/es nahm
wir nehmen	wir nahmen
ihr nehmt	ihr nahmt
sie/Sie nehmen	sie/Sie nahmen

KONJUNKTIV I	KONJUNKTIV II
ich nehme	ich nähme

Note   **nehmen** is the only verb of this type. However, note the compound verbs ➤**sich benehmen** 53; **annehmen** 54.

Bitte, *nimm* die Butter aus dem Kühlschrank!	Please, *take* the butter out of the refrigerator!
***Nehmen* wir ein Taxi oder fahren wir mit dem Bus?**	*Shall* we *take* a taxi or go by bus?
Ich *nehme* mir jeden Tag die Zeit zum Zeitunglesen.	Everyday I *take* the time to read the newspaper.
Woher *soll* ich das Geld für ein neues Auto *nehmen*?	Where *am* I *supposed to get* the money for a new car?
Bitte *nehmen Sie Platz*!	Please, *take a seat!*

IMPERATIVE
nimm! (du)   nehmen Sie!   nehmt! (ihr)

PRESENT PERFECT
ich habe ... genommen

PAST PERFECT (PLUPERFECT)
ich hatte ... genommen

FUTURE
ich werde ... nehmen

FUTURE PERFECT
ich werde ... genommen haben

COMPOUND CONDITIONAL
ich würde ... nehmen

PAST CONDITIONAL
ich hätte ... genommen

Sie *haben Abschied* voneinander *genommen.*

They *said good-bye* to each other.

Unser Sohn *wird* bei unserer Nachbarin Musikunterricht *nehmen.*

Our son *will take* music lessons from our neighbor.

Der Unfall *hat* ihm jede Hoffnung auf eine Sportlerkarriere *genommen.*

The accident *took away* all his hopes for a career in sports.

Nehmen Sie die Tabletten dreimal täglich.

Take these tablets three times a day.

53　sich benehmen　　　　　　　　behave

Class IV inseparable irregular verb, stress on stem **-nehm-**

PRESENT PARTICIPLE	PAST PARTICIPLE
sich benehmend	sich benommen

PRESENT	SIMPLE PAST
ich benehme mich	ich benahm mich
du benimmst dich	du benahmst dich
er/sie/es benimmt sich	er/sie/es benahm sich
wir benehmen uns	wir benahmen uns
ihr benehmt euch	ihr benahmt euch
sie/Sie benehmen sich	sie/Sie benahmen sich

KONJUNKTIV I	KONJUNKTIV II
ich benehme mich	ich benähme mich

Similar verbs

entnehmen *(dat.)*	withdraw (from)
(sich) übernehmen	take over, overextend
vernehmen	hear, perceive
sich vornehmen	intend

Unser Sohn *benimmt sich* in der Schule besser als zu Hause.	Our son *behaves* better in school than at home.
Ich *habe* im Keller ein leises Geräusch *vernommen*.	I *heard* some noise in the basement.
Herbert *hat sich* gestern beim Fußballspiel *übernommen*.	Herbert *overextended himself* yesterday while playing soccer.
Kinder, *benehmt euch*!	Children, *behave yourselves*!

IMPERATIVE

benimm dich (du)!   benehmen Sie sich!   benehmt euch (ihr)!

PRESENT PERFECT

ich habe mich ... benommen

PAST PERFECT (PLUPERFECT)

ich hatte mich ... benommen

FUTURE

ich werde mich ... benehmen

FUTURE PERFECT

ich werde mich ... benommen haben

COMPOUND CONDITIONAL

ich würde mich ... benehmen

PAST CONDITIONAL

ich hätte mich ... benommen

Die Polizei *vernahm* den Unfallzeugen.	The police *interrogated* the accident witness.
Ich *entnahm* deinem Brief, dass der Chef die Firma verlassen hatte.	I *gathered* from your letter, that the boss had left the firm.
Wer *hat* seine Stelle *übernommen*?	Who *has taken over* his position?
Ich *habe* der Kasse 200 Euro *entnommen*.	I *have taken* 200 euros from the petty-cash box.
Würden Sie es *übernehmen*, die Blumen zu besorgen?	*Would* you *take charge* of getting the flowers?

Class IV separable irregular verb, stress on particle **an-**

PRESENT PARTICIPLE	PAST PARTICIPLE
annehmend	angenommen

PRESENT	SIMPLE PAST
ich nehme an	ich nahm an
du nimmst an	du nahmst an
er/sie/es nimmt an	er/sie/es nahm an
wir nehmen an	wir nahmen an
ihr nehmt an	ihr nahmt an
sie/Sie nehmen an	sie/Sie nahmen an

KONJUNKTIV I	KONJUNKTIV II
ich nehme an	ich nähme an

Similar verbs

abnehmen	take off, lose weight	**teilnehmen** *(an+dat.)*	take part (in)
aufnehmen	receive	**übel nehmen**	take amiss
auseinander nehmen	dismantle	**sich** *(dat.)*	absorb
einnehmen	earn, take in	**vornehmen**	intend
festnehmen	arrest	**wahrnehmen**	perceive
gefangen nehmen	take prisoner	**wegnehmen** *(dat.)*	take away (from)
malnehmen *(mit)*	multiply (by)	**zunehmen**	increase, grow
mitnehmen	take along	**sich zusammennehmen**	pull oneself together

Ich *nehme an*, Sie wollen den ganzen Tag hier bleiben.	I *assume* you want to stay here all day.
Wir werden die Kinder *mit* ins Kino *nehmen*.	We *will take* the children with us to the movies.
Ich *hatte* mir *vorgenommen*, am Sportfest *teilzunehmen*.	I *had intended to take part* in the sports festival.
Hat Erika die Einladung *angenommen*?	*Has* Erika *accepted* the invitation?

IMPERATIVE
nimm an! (du)   nehmen Sie an!   nehmt an! (ihr)

PRESENT PERFECT	**PAST PERFECT (PLUPERFECT)**
ich habe ... angenommen	ich hatte ... angenommen

FUTURE	**FUTURE PERFECT**
ich werde ... annehmen	ich werde ... angenommen haben

COMPOUND CONDITIONAL	**PAST CONDITIONAL**
ich würde ... annehmen	ich hätte ... angenommen

Er *hat* ihr *übel genommen*, dass sie ihm das Buch *weggenommen hat*.	He *was cross* with her for *taking* the book *away* from him.
Der Verbrecher *wurde* gestern *festgenommen*.	The criminal *was arrested* yesterday.
Nehmen Sie den Motor *auseinander*, dann sehen wir, was damit los ist.	*Take* the engine *apart*, then we will see what's the matter with it.
Diese Fernsehsendung *werden* wir auf Video *aufnehmen*!	This TV show we *will videotape*!
Nimm dich *zusammen!*	*Pull* yourself *together*.
Man *hat* uns sehr freundlich *aufgenommen*.	We *were* very warmly *received*.
Im Oktober *wird* er sein Studium an der Uni *aufnehmen*.	In October, he *will start* his studies at the university.

55 kommen

come

Class IV irregular verb, stress on stem **komm-**

PRESENT PARTICIPLE	PAST PARTICIPLE
kommend	gekommen

PRESENT	SIMPLE PAST
ich komme	ich kam
du kommst	du kamst
er/sie/es kommt	er/sie/es kam
wir kommen	wir kamen
ihr kommt	ihr kamt
sie/Sie kommen	sie/Sie kamen

KONJUNKTIV I	KONJUNKTIV II
ich komme	ich käme

Note   **kommen** is the only verb of this type. However, note the compound verbs ►**bekommen** 57; **ankommen** 58.

Kommen Sie doch zum Abendessen zu uns!	*Come* and have dinner with us!
Er *kommt* erst um acht Uhr.	He *is* not *coming* until eight o'clock.
Ich freue mich sehr, dass Sie *gekommen sind.*	I am very glad you *have come.*
Sind Sie mit dem Wagen *gekommen?*	*Did* you *come* by car?
Wir *wollten* mit dem Auto *kommen*, aber es ist nicht angesprungen.	We *wanted to come* by car but it didn't start.
Seid ihr aus England?	*Are* you guys from England?

IMPERATIVE
komme! (du)   kommen Sie!   kommt! (ihr)

PRESENT PERFECT	*PAST PERFECT (PLUPERFECT)*
ich bin ... gekommen	ich war ... gekommen

FUTURE	*FUTURE PERFECT*
ich werde ... kommen	ich werde ... gekommen sein

COMPOUND CONDITIONAL	*PAST CONDITIONAL*
ich würde ... kommen	ich wäre ... gekommen

Unsere Tochter *kommt* im *kommenden* Monat in *die* Schule.	Our daughter *starts school next* month.
Ich *habe* es *kommen sehen*.	I *saw* it *coming*.
Das *kommt* davon, wenn man nicht aufpasst.	That *comes* from not paying attention.
Er *wäre* bei dem Unfall fast *ums Leben gekommen*.	He nearly *died* in the accident.
***Ist* Post für mich *gekommen*?**	*Has* any mail *arrived* for me?
Wenn ich könnte, *würde* ich früher *kommen*.	I *would come* sooner if I could.

Class IV irregular verb, stress on stem **treff-**

PRESENT PARTICIPLE	PAST PARTICIPLE
treffend	getroffen

PRESENT	SIMPLE PAST
ich treffe	ich traf
du triffst	du trafst
er/sie/es trifft	er/sie/es traf
wir treffen	wir trafen
ihr trefft	ihr traft
sie/Sie treffen	sie/Sie trafen

KONJUNKTIV I	KONJUNKTIV II
ich treffe	ich träfe

Similar verbs

[With an inseparable prefix ➤**bekommen** 57]
betreffen	concern, affect
übertreffen	surpass

[With a separable particle ➤**ankommen** 58]
eintreffen *(+sein)*	arrive
zutreffen	apply

Was mich betrifft, ist es egal, ob wir **uns** heute oder morgen **treffen**.	*As for me*, it's all the same whether we *meet* today or tomorrow.
Wir *treffen uns* seit Jahren im selben Restaurant.	We *have been meeting* for years in the same restaurant.
Ich *traf* ihn öfters im Turnverein.	I *used to meet* him frequently at the gym.

STRONG VERBS

IMPERATIVE
triff! (du)   treffen Sie!   trefft! (ihr)

PRESENT PERFECT
ich habe ... getroffen

PAST PERFECT (PLUPERFECT)
ich hatte ... getroffen

FUTURE
ich werde ... treffen

FUTURE PERFECT
ich werde ... getroffen haben

COMPOUND CONDITIONAL
ich würde ... treffen

PAST CONDITIONAL
ich hätte ... getroffen

Er *ist* pünktlich bei uns *eingetroffen*.

He *arrived* punctually at our house.

Es *ist* genau das *eingetroffen*, was ich befürchtet habe!

Exactly what I had feared *did happen*!

***Trifft es zu*, dass Frau Schweiss unsere Abteilung übernehmen wird?**

It is correct that Mrs. Schweiss will take over our department?

Gestern *traf* ich einen alten Freund.

Yesterday I *met* an old friend.

Class IV inseparable irregular verb, stress on stem **-komm-**

PRESENT PARTICIPLE	PAST PARTICIPLE
bekommend	bekommen

PRESENT	SIMPLE PAST
ich bekomme	ich bekam
du bekommst	du bekamst
er/sie/es bekommt	er/sie/es bekam
wir bekommen	wir bekamen
ihr bekommt	ihr bekamt
sie/Sie bekommen	sie/Sie bekamen

KONJUNKTIV I	KONJUNKTIV II
ich bekomme	ich bekäme

Similar verbs

entkommen *(+sein) (dat.)*	escape (from)
verkommen *(+sein)*	go to pieces

Note   **bekommen,** meaning "to agree with" (of food), is intransitive and takes **sein**.

Sonja *bekommt* ihr Kind im Herbst.	Sonja *is having* her baby in the fall.
Er *wird* dieses Jahr mehr Geld *bekommen*.	He *will get* more money this year.
Was *bekommen* Sie bitte?	What *can* I *get* you?
Sie *bekommen* noch drei Euro von mir.	I still *owe you three euros*.

bekommen 57

IMPERATIVE
bekomme! (du)   bekommen Sie!   bekommt! (ihr)

PRESENT PERFECT
ich habe ... bekommen

PAST PERFECT (PLUPERFECT)
ich hatte ... bekommen

FUTURE
ich werde ... bekommen

FUTURE PERFECT
ich werde ... bekommen haben

COMPOUND CONDITIONAL
ich würde ... bekommen

PAST CONDITIONAL
ich hätte ... bekommen

Wir *bekamen* keine Antworten auf unsere Fragen.

We *got* no answers to our questions.

Er sagt uns, er *bekomme* eine neue Jacke zum Geburtstag. Er sagt, er *werde* auch neue Schuhe *bekommen*.

He told us he *was getting* a new jacket for his birthday. He said he *would* also *get* new shoes.

Er *ist* der Gefahr *entkommen*.

He *escaped* the danger.

Habt ihr auch gutes Essen *bekommen*?

Did you also *get* good food?

Class IV separable irregular verb, stress on particle **an-**

PRESENT PARTICIPLE	PAST PARTICIPLE
ankommend	angekommen

PRESENT	SIMPLE PAST
ich komme an	ich kam an
du kommst an	du kamst an
er/sie/es kommt an	er/sie/es kam an
wir kommen an	wir kamen an
ihr kommt an	ihr kamt an
sie/Sie kommen an	sie/Sie kamen an

KONJUNKTIV I	KONJUNKTIV II
ich komme an	ich käme an

Similar verbs

abkommen *(+sein) (von)*	deviate (from)
ankommen *(+sein) (in+dat.)*	arrive
auskommen *(+sein)*	get by, manage
davonkommen *(+sein)*	escape, get away
gleichkommen *(+sein) (dat.)*	equal, match
herausbekommen	find out, work out
hereinkommen *(+sein)*	enter, come in
herkommen *(+sein)*	come here, come from
herüberkommen *(+sein)*	come across, come over
herunterkommen *(+sein)*	come down
nachkommen *(+sein)*	come later
reinkommen *(+sein)*	come in
umkommen *(+sein)*	perish
vorbeikommen *(+sein)*	come by, drop by
vorkommen *(+sein)*	occur
zugute kommen *(+sein) (dat.)*	benefit
zurechtkommen *(+sein) (mit)*	cope (with)
zurückkommen *(+sein)*	come back, get back
zusammenkommen *(+sein)*	come together
zuvorkommen *(+sein) (dat.)*	anticipate

IMPERATIVE
komme an! (du)   kommen Sie an!   kommt an! (ihr)

PRESENT PERFECT	**PAST PERFECT (PLUPERFECT)**
ich bin ... angekommen	ich war ... angekommen

FUTURE	**FUTURE PERFECT**
ich werde ... ankommen	ich werde ... angekommen sein

COMPOUND CONDITIONAL	**PAST CONDITIONAL**
ich würde ... ankommen	ich wäre ... angekommen

Wann ist Paul *zurückgekommen?*	When *did* Paul *come back*?
Komm doch mal am Wochenende *vorbei!*	*Drop by* on the weekend!
Er erzählte uns, er *sei* vor ein paar Tagen aus England *zurückgekommen.*	He told us he *had come back* from England a few days ago.
Sie *werden* ohne uns *auskommen müssen.*	You *will have to do* without us.
Er *ist* öfters vom Thema *abgekommen,* aber wir *haben* dann doch *herausbekommen,* was vorgefallen war.	He frequently *got off the subject,* but we eventually *found out* what had happened.
Viele Menschen *sind* bei dem Schiffsunglück *umgekommen.*	Many people *died* in the ship accident.
Wir *sind* endlich dahinter *gekommen,* wo er *herkommt.* Er *kommt* aus New York.	We *have* finally *found out* where he *comes from.* He *comes* from New York.
Kommen Sie bitte *herein!*	Please *come in!*

59 geben

give

Class V verb, stress on stem **geb-**

PRESENT PARTICIPLE	PAST PARTICIPLE
gebend	gegeben

PRESENT	SIMPLE PAST
ich gebe	ich gab
du gibst	du gabst
er/sie/es gibt	er/sie/es gab
wir geben	wir gaben
ihr gebt	ihr gabt
sie/Sie geben	sie/Sie gaben

KONJUNKTIV I	KONJUNKTIV II
ich gebe	ich gäbe

Similar verbs

liegen   lie, be located

Wer *gibt* Englisch in eurer Klasse?	Who *teaches* English in your class?
***Gibst* du mir bitte noch etwas Brot?**	Would you please *give* me some more bread?
Ich *habe* mir viel Mühe mit dem Essen *gegeben*.	I *have put* a lot of effort into this meal.
Gestern *wurde* "Othello" im Theater *gegeben*.	Yesterday "Othello" *was performed* at the theater.
Die Ministerin *gab* gestern Abend einen großen Empfang.	The minister *gave* a big reception last night.
Das *gibt's* doch nicht!	That *can't be true*!

IMPERATIVE
gib! (du)   geben Sie!   gebt! (ihr)

PRESENT PERFECT   *PAST PERFECT (PLUPERFECT)*
ich habe ... gegeben   ich hatte ... gegeben

FUTURE   *FUTURE PERFECT*
ich werde ... geben   ich werde ... gegeben haben

COMPOUND CONDITIONAL   *PAST CONDITIONAL*
ich würde ... geben   ich hätte ... gegeben

Was *gibt's* zu Mittag? | *What's* for lunch?

Es gab keinen Zweifel daran, wer der Täter war. | *There was* no doubt who was the perpetrator.

Ich *gäbe* viel *darum* zu wissen, was er für das Auto bezahlt hat. | I *would give* a lot to know what he had paid for the car.

Hamburg *liegt* an der Elbe. | Hamburg *lies* on the Elbe.

Unsere Mutter *liegt* seit zwei Wochen *krank* im Bett. | Our mother *has been sick* in bed for two weeks.

Es *läge* eigentlich *an* meiner Schwester am Samstag sauber zu machen. | It *would* really *be up to* my sister to clean on Saturday.

Bis kurz vor Spielende *lag* unsere Mannschaft ganz *vorn*. | Our team *was in the lead* until shortly before the end of the game.

Es liegt nicht an mir, dass der Kühlschrank leer ist. | *It's not my fault* that the refrigerator is empty.

60 vergeben   forgive, give away

Class V inseparable verb, stress on stem **-geb-**

PRESENT PARTICIPLE	PAST PARTICIPLE
vergebend	vergeben

PRESENT	SIMPLE PAST
ich vergebe	ich vergab
du vergibst	du vergabst
er/sie/es vergibt	er/sie/es vergab
wir vergeben	wir vergaben
ihr vergebt	ihr vergabt
sie/Sie vergeben	sie/Sie vergaben

KONJUNKTIV I	KONJUNKTIV II
ich vergebe	ich vergäbe

Similar verbs

sich begeben	happen
(sich) ergeben	produce, result in, surrender
(sich) übergeben	hand over, throw up
umgeben	surround

Unsere Stadt ist von Hügeln *umgeben.*	Our town *is surrounded* by hills.
Wir haben die Dokumente unserem Anwalt *übergeben.*	We *have handed over* the documents to our attorney.
Wegen dem schlechten Essen musste ich mich zweimal *übergeben.*	Because of the bad food I *had to throw up* twice.

IMPERATIVE
vergib! (du)   vergeben Sie!   vergebt! (ihr)

PRESENT PERFECT
ich habe ... vergeben

PAST PERFECT (PLUPERFECT)
ich hatte ... vergeben

FUTURE
ich werde ... vergeben

FUTURE PERFECT
ich werde ... vergeben haben

COMPOUND CONDITIONAL
ich würde ... vergeben

PAST CONDITIONAL
ich hätte ... vergeben

Du *hast* die Freikarten fürs Theater *weggegeben*! Das *vergebe* ich dir nie!

You *gave away* the free tickets for the theater! I *will* never *forgive* you for that!

Eine Umfrage *hatte ergeben*, dass viele Leute gegen eine Parteienkoalition waren.

A poll *had shown* that many people were against a party coalition.

Wir *werden uns* nie *ergeben*!

We *will* never *surrender*!

Dem Schauspieler *wurde* ein Preis *übergeben*.

The actor *was given* an award.

Das *ergibt* keinen Sinn!

That *makes* no sense!

61 zurückgeben   give back

Class V separable verb, stress on particle **zurück-**

PRESENT PARTICIPLE	PAST PARTICIPLE
zurückgebend	zurückgegeben

PRESENT	SIMPLE PAST
ich gebe zurück	ich gab zurück
du gibst zurück	du gabst zurück
er/sie/es gibt zurück	er/sie/es gab zurück
wir geben zurück	wir gaben zurück
ihr gebt zurück	ihr gabt zurück
sie/Sie geben zurück	sie/Sie gaben zurück

KONJUNKTIV I	KONJUNKTIV II
ich gebe zurück	ich gäbe zurück

Similar verbs

abgeben	hand in	**brachliegen**	lie fallow
abliegen	be at a distance	**durchgeben**	radio
Acht geben (auf+acc.)	pay attention (to)	**herausgeben**	issue, publish
angeben	state, show off	**hergeben**	hand over
		nachgeben	give way
anliegen	fit closely	**nahe liegen**	suggest itself
aufgeben	give up, renounce	**vorliegen**	be available
ausgeben	spend, pay out	**weggeben**	give away
		wiedergeben	give back
ausliegen	be displayed	**zugeben**	admit, concede
bekannt geben	disclose		

Gib Acht!	*Watch out!*
Peter *hat* das Rauchen *aufgegeben.*	Peter *has given up* smoking.
Gib nicht so *an!*	*Don't brag like that!*

IMPERATIVE
gib zurück! (du)   geben Sie zurück!   gebt zurück! (ihr)

PRESENT PERFECT
ich habe ... zurückgegeben

PAST PERFECT (PLUPERFECT)
ich hatte ... zurückgegeben

FUTURE
ich werde ... zurückgeben

FUTURE PERFECT
ich werde ... zurückgegeben haben

COMPOUND CONDITIONAL
ich würde ... zurückgeben

PAST CONDITIONAL
ich hätte ... zurückgegeben

Achten Sie darauf, dass Sie das Gepäck am richtigen Schalter *abgeben*.

Make sure that you *check in* the luggage at the right counter.

Die Nachricht *wurde* im Radio *durchgegeben*.
Näheres *wird* morgen in der Zeitung *bekannt gegeben*.

The news *was announced* on the radio.
Further details *will be disclosed* in the paper tomorrow.

Der Verlag *gab* eine neue Zeitschrift *heraus*.

The publisher *published* a new magazine.

Ich *gebe zu*, wir *würden* nicht so viel Geld *ausgeben*, wenn wir weniger verdienen würden.

I *admit* we *would* not *spend* so much money if we didn't earn that much.

Ich *werde* Ihnen das Geld, das Sie mir gestern *gegeben haben*, morgen *zurückgeben*.

Tomorrow I *will give* you *back* the money you *gave* me yesterday.

Der neue Buchkatalog *liegt* jetzt *vor*.

The new book catalog *is* now *available*.

Class V verb, stress on stem **tret-**

PRESENT PARTICIPLE	PAST PARTICIPLE
tretend	getreten

PRESENT	SIMPLE PAST
ich trete	ich trat
du trittst	du tratst
er/sie/es tritt	er/sie/es trat
wir treten	wir traten
ihr tretet	ihr tratet
sie/Sie treten	sie/Sie traten

KONJUNKTIV I	KONJUNKTIV II
ich trete	ich träte

Notes **treten** (to kick, pedal, step) takes **haben**.
treten is the only verb of this type. However, note the compound
verbs ►**betreten** 64; **hinaustreten** 65.

Treten Sie näher!	*Step* closer!
Er *trat* ans Fenster.	He *went* to the window.
Warum *trittst* du mich gegen das Schienbein?	Why do you *kick* me on the shin?
Beim Zwiebelschälen *traten* mir Tränen in die Augen.	While peeling onions, tears *came* to my eyes.

IMPERATIVE
tritt! (du)   treten Sie!   tretet! (ihr)

PRESENT PERFECT
ich bin ... getreten

PAST PERFECT (PLUPERFECT)
ich war ... getreten

FUTURE
ich werde ... treten

FUTURE PERFECT
ich werde ... getreten sein

COMPOUND CONDITIONAL
ich würde ... treten

PAST CONDITIONAL
ich wäre ... getreten

Ich *wäre* zur Seite *getreten*, wenn ich Sie hätte kommen sehen.

I *would have stepped* aside if I had seen you coming.

Er *hat* gegen die Tür *getreten*.

He *kicked* against the door.

Man berichtet, der Fluss *sei* über die Ufer *getreten*.

It is reported that the river *has gone over* its banks.

Er *hat* stark in die Pedale *getreten*.

He has *pedalled* hard.

63 bitten

ask, request

Class V irregular verb, stress on stem **bitt-**

PRESENT PARTICIPLE	PAST PARTICIPLE
bittend	gebeten

PRESENT	SIMPLE PAST
ich bitte	ich bat
du bittest	du batst
er/sie/es bittet	er/sie/es bat
wir bitten	wir baten
ihr bittet	ihr batet
sie/Sie bitten	sie/Sie baten

KONJUNKTIV I	KONJUNKTIV II
ich bitte	ich bäte

Similar verbs

sich *(dat.)* **verbitten**   refuse to tolerate

Darf ich *bitten?*	*May* I *have* this dance?
Er *bat* mich um einen großen Gefallen.	He *asked* me for a big favor.
Dieses Benehmen *verbitte* ich *mir!*	I *won't tolerate* this behavior.
Er *hat* tausendmal um Entschuldigung *gebeten.*	He *begged* my pardon a thousand times.

IMPERATIVE
bitte! (du)   bitten Sie!   bittet! (ihr)

PRESENT PERFECT	*PAST PERFECT (PLUPERFECT)*
ich habe ... gebeten	ich hatte ... gebeten
FUTURE	*FUTURE PERFECT*
ich werde ... bitten	ich werde ... gebeten haben
COMPOUND CONDITIONAL	*PAST CONDITIONAL*
ich würde ... bitten	ich hätte ... gebeten

Ich *werde* ihn nächste Woche um Hilfe *bitten*.	I *will ask* him for help next week.
Wir *haben* Manfred *gebeten*, im Café auf uns zu warten.	We *have asked* Manfred to wait for us in the Café.
Darf ich um ein Glas Wasser *bitten*?	*May* I *ask* for a glass of water?
Maria *bat* mich, ihre Blumen zu gießen.	Maria *asked* me to water her plants.

64 betreten   enter

Class V inseparable verb, stress on stem **-tret-**

PRESENT PARTICIPLE	PAST PARTICIPLE
betretend	betreten

PRESENT	SIMPLE PAST
ich betrete	ich betrat
du betrittst	du betratst
er/sie/es betritt	er/sie/es betrat
wir betreten	wir betraten
ihr betretet	ihr betratet
sie/Sie betreten	sie/Sie betraten

KONJUNKTIV I	KONJUNKTIV II
ich betrete	ich beträte

Similar verbs

vertreten	replace, represent
zertreten	trample

Das Betreten der Baustelle ist verboten.	It is forbidden *to enter* the construction site.
Kaum *hatte* ich das Haus *betreten*, als es anfing zu regnen.	I *had* hardly *entered* the house, when it started to rain.
Die Kinder *dürfen* den Rasen nicht *betreten*.	The children *may* not *walk* on the lawn.
Sie *zertreten* alle meine Blumen.	They *trample* all my flowers.

IMPERATIVE
betritt! (du)   betreten Sie!   betretet! (ihr)

PRESENT PERFECT
ich habe ... betreten

PAST PERFECT (PLUPERFECT)
ich hatte ... betreten

FUTURE
ich werde ... betreten

FUTURE PERFECT
ich werde ... betreten haben

COMPOUND CONDITIONAL
ich würde ... betreten

PAST CONDITIONAL
ich hätte ... betreten

Ich *habe mir die Füße vertreten.*
I *have gone for a short walk.*

Wer *vertritt* Ihre Firma?
Who *represents* your company?

Die Gewerkschaft *sollte* die Interessen ihrer Mitglieder *vertreten!*
The labor union *should represent* the interests of its members!

Ich *werde* morgen den Geschäftsleiter *vertreten.*
I *will be standing in* for the manager tomorrow.

Betreten verboten!
Off limits!

Class V separable verb, stress on particle **hinaus-**

PRESENT PARTICIPLE	*PAST PARTICIPLE*
hinaustretend	hinausgetreten

PRESENT	*SIMPLE PAST*
ich trete hinaus	ich trat hinaus
du trittst hinaus	du tratst hinaus
er/sie/es tritt hinaus	er/sie/es trat hinaus
wir treten hinaus	wir traten hinaus
ihr tretet hinaus	ihr tratet hinaus
sie/Sie treten hinaus	sie/Sie traten hinaus

KONJUNKTIV I	*KONJUNKTIV II*
ich trete hinaus	ich träte hinaus

Similar verbs

abtreten *(+sein/haben)*	resign
auftreten *(+sein)*	appear, come on
austreten *(+sein/haben)*	step out, resign, wear out
beitreten *(+sein) (dat.)*	join
eintreten *(+sein)*	enter
herantreten *(+sein)*	approach
hervortreten *(+sein)*	step forward
zurücktreten *(+sein)*	resign, step back

Er *hatte* seine Schuhe ganz *ausgetreten.*	He had completely *worn out* his shoes.
Meine Mutter sagte, ich *solle* die Schuhe *abtreten.*	My mother said I *should wipe* my feet.
Wir *sind* aus dem Sportverein *ausgetreten.*	We *have terminated* our membership at the sports club.
Wir *sind* vor Jahren dem Autoklub *beigetreten.*	We *joined* the auto club years ago.

IMPERATIVE

tritt hinaus! (du)   treten Sie hinaus!   tretet hinaus! (ihr)

PRESENT PERFECT

ich bin ... hinausgetreten

PAST PERFECT (PLUPERFECT)

ich war ... hinausgetreten

FUTURE

ich werde ... hinaustreten

FUTURE PERFECT

ich werde ... hinausgetreten sein

COMPOUND CONDITIONAL

ich würde ... hinaustreten

PAST CONDITIONAL

ich wäre ... hinausgetreten

Treten Sie von der Bahnsteigkante *zurück!*

Step back from the edge of the platform!

Der Minister *ist* letzte Woche *zurückgetreten.*

The minister *resigned* last week.

Der Schauspieler *trat* im "Faust" *auf.*

The actor appeared in "Faust."

Die Sonne *trat* aus den Wolken *hervor.*

The sun *came out* of the clouds.

Class V irregular verb, stress on stem **ess-**

PRESENT PARTICIPLE	PAST PARTICIPLE
essend	gegessen

PRESENT	SIMPLE PAST
ich esse	ich aß
du isst	du aßest
er/sie/es isst	er/sie/es aß
wir essen	wir aßen
ihr esst	ihr aßt
sie/Sie essen	sie/Sie aßen

KONJUNKTIV I	KONJUNKTIV II
ich esse	ich äße

Similar verbs

| **fressen** | eat (of animals), devour |
| **messen** | measure |

Was *wollen* wir zum Frühstück *essen?*	What *shall* we *have* for breakfast?
Ich *möchte* gern ein gekochtes Ei *essen.*	I *would like* to eat a boiled egg.
Wir *gehen* heute Mittag *essen.*	We *are going out for lunch.*
Was *möchten* Sie *essen?* Ich *würde* gern Gulasch *essen.*	What *would* you *like to eat?* I *would like* some goulash.
Wir *werden* abends *kalt essen.*	We *will have a cold meal* in the evening.

IMPERATIVE
iss! (du)   essen Sie!   esst! (ihr)

PRESENT PERFECT
ich habe ... gegessen

PAST PERFECT (PLUPERFECT)
ich hatte ... gegessen

FUTURE
ich werde ... essen

FUTURE PERFECT
ich werde ... gegessen haben

COMPOUND CONDITIONAL
ich würde ... essen

PAST CONDITIONAL
ich hätte ... gegessen

Was gibt's *zu essen?*	What is there *to eat?*
Gib* dem Hund was *zu fressen.	*Give* the dog something *to eat.*
Der Wagen *hat* immer zu viel Benzin *gefressen.*	The car *always consumed* too much gasoline.
Iss* nicht so schnell.** **Er *isst* nicht, er *frisst.	*Don't eat* so fast. He *doesn't eat,* he *devours.*
Er *hat* immer gut und gern *gegessen.*	He *has* always *been fond of* his food.
In manchen Ländern *wird* die Temperatur in Fahrenheit *gemessen.*	In some countries temperature *is measured* in Fahrenheit.

67 sitzen   sit

Class V irregular verb, stress on stem **sitz-**

PRESENT PARTICIPLE	PAST PARTICIPLE
sitzend	gesessen

PRESENT	SIMPLE PAST
ich sitze	ich saß
du sitzt	du saßest
er/sie/es sitzt	er/sie/es saß
wir sitzen	wir saßen
ihr sitzt	ihr saßt
sie/Sie sitzen	sie/Sie saßen

KONJUNKTIV I	KONJUNKTIV II
ich sitze	ich säße

Similar verbs

[Inseparable verb ➤**vergessen** 68]
besitzen — possess

[Separable verb ➤**aufessen** 69]
aus/absitzen — sit out
nachsitzen — stay after (at school)

Bitte *bleiben Sie sitzen!* — Please *stay seated!*

Der Schüler hatte seine Hausaufgaben nicht gemacht und *musste nachsitzen*. — The student had not done his homework and *had to stay after* school.

Ich *habe* zu lange am Computer *gesessen*. — I *sat* too long at the computer.

IMPERATIVE
sitz(e)! (du)   sitzen Sie!   sitzt! (ihr)

PRESENT PERFECT
ich habe ... gesessen

PAST PERFECT (PLUPERFECT)
ich hatte ... gesessen

FUTURE
ich werde ... sitzen

FUTURE PERFECT
ich werde ... gesessen haben

COMPOUND CONDITIONAL
ich würde ... sitzen

PAST CONDITIONAL
ich hätte ... gesessen

Das Kleid *sitzt* gut!	The dress *fits* well.
Als Studenten *saßen* wir manchmal lange über den Büchern.	As students, we sometimes *sat* long hours over our books.
Wir *saßen* gerade beim Frühstück, als unsere Freunde vorbeikamen.	We *were sitting* at breakfast when our friends dropped by.
Wir *besitzen* ein großes Grundstück.	We *own* a large piece of land.
Wenn wir nur ein größeres Haus *besäßen*!	If only we *owned* a bigger house!
Mein Bruder *besaß* viel Phantasie.	My brother *had* a lot of imagination.

68 vergessen

forget

Class V inseparable verb, stress on stem **-gess-**

PRESENT PARTICIPLE	PAST PARTICIPLE
vergessend	vergessen

PRESENT	SIMPLE PAST
ich vergesse	ich vergaß
du vergisst	du vergaßest
er/sie/es vergisst	er/sie/es vergaß
wir vergessen	wir vergaßen
ihr vergesst	ihr vergaßt
sie/Sie vergessen	sie/Sie vergaßen

KONJUNKTIV I	KONJUNKTIV II
ich vergesse	ich vergäße

Similar verbs

vermessen	survey, measure
zerfressen	corrode

Vergiss nicht, die Schlüssel mitzunehmen!	*Don't forget* to take your keys!
Als Kind *vergaß* er immer seine Brille.	As a child, he always *forgot* his glasses.
Sie *haben* Ihren Schirm bei uns *vergessen*.	You *forgot* your umbrella at our house.

IMPERATIVE
vergiss! (du)   vergessen Sie!   vergesst! (ihr)

PRESENT PERFECT
ich habe ... vergessen

PAST PERFECT (PLUPERFECT)
ich hatte ... vergessen

FUTURE
ich werde ... vergessen

FUTURE PERFECT
ich werde ... vergessen haben

COMPOUND CONDITIONAL
ich würde ... vergessen

PAST CONDITIONAL
ich hätte ... vergessen

Das Grundstück *wird vermessen*.	The property *is being surveyed*.
Der Rost *hat* die Türen meines Autos *zerfressen*.	Rust *has corroded* the doors of my car.
Ich *hätte beinahe vergessen*, ihn anzurufen.	I *almost forgot* to call him.
Ich *werde* dieses Konzert nie *vergessen*.	I *will* never *forget* this concert.
Das kannst du vergessen!	*Forget about it!*

Class V separable irregular verb, stress on particle -**auf**-

PRESENT PARTICIPLE	PAST PARTICIPLE
aufessend	aufgegessen

PRESENT	SIMPLE PAST
ich esse auf	ich aß auf
du isst auf	du aßest auf
er/sie/es isst auf	er/sie/es aß auf
wir essen auf	wir aßen auf
ihr esst auf	ihr aßt auf
sie/Sie essen auf	sie/Sie aßen auf

KONJUNKTIV I	KONJUNKTIV II
ich esse auf	ich äße auf

Similar verbs

abmessen	measure (off)
aufessen	eat up, finish eating
beimessen	attach value to
nachmessen	measure again, check
zumessen	measure out, apportion

Iss dein Essen auf!	*Finish* your meal!
Die Kinder *haben* **den ganzen Kuchen** *aufgegessen*.	The children *have finished* the whole cake.

IMPERATIVE
iss auf! (du)   essen Sie auf!   esst auf! (ihr)

PRESENT PERFECT
ich habe ... aufgegessen

PAST PERFECT (PLUPERFECT)
ich hatte ... aufgegessen

FUTURE
ich werde ... aufessen

FUTURE PERFECT
ich werde ... aufgegessen haben

COMPOUND CONDITIONAL
ich würde ... aufessen

PAST CONDITIONAL
ich hätte ... aufgegessen

Bevor ich das Regal bestelle, **muss** ich **nachmessen**, wie viel Platz ich habe.	Before I order the shelf, I *have to measure* how much space I have.
Der Stoff **wurde** genau **abgemessen**.	The material *was measured off* exactly.
Man **sollte** den Statistiken keine zu große Bedeutung **beimessen**.	You *should* not *attach* too much *value* to statistics.
Ich **werde** seine Temperatur **nachmessen**.	I *will check* his temperature again.

Class V verb, stress on stem **les-**

PRESENT PARTICIPLE	PAST PARTICIPLE
lesend	gelesen

PRESENT	SIMPLE PAST
ich lese	ich las
du liest	du lasest
er/sie/es liest	er/sie/es las
wir lesen	wir lasen
ihr lest	ihr last
sie/Sie lesen	sie/Sie lasen

KONJUNKTIV I	KONJUNKTIV II
ich lese	ich läse

Similar verbs

sehen	see, glance

Note **sehen** has an alternative second person imperative form **siehe!** (du).

Michael *lernt lesen.* **Seine Mutter sagt, er** *lese* **sehr** *gern.*	Michael *is learning to read.* His mother says he *enjoys reading* very much.
"Faust" *wurde* **oft in der Schule** *gelesen.*	"Faust" *was read* at school often.
Ich *habe* **in der Zeitung** *gelesen*, **dass Kinder heutzutage weniger** *lesen.*	I *read* in the paper that children *read* less nowadays.

IMPERATIVE
lies! (du)   lesen Sie!   lest! (ihr)

PRESENT PERFECT
ich habe ... gelesen

PAST PERFECT (PLUPERFECT)
ich hatte ... gelesen

FUTURE
ich werde ... lesen

FUTURE PERFECT
ich werde ... gelesen haben

COMPOUND CONDITIONAL
ich würde ... lesen

PAST CONDITIONAL
ich hätte ... gelesen

Als Kind *habe* ich viel *gelesen*.
As a child I *read* a lot.

Die Trauben *werden* im Herbst *gelesen*.
The grapes *are gathered* in the fall.

Frank *sieht* sehr schlecht.
Frank's *eye sight is* very bad.

Mein Chef *sah* alle fünf Minuten auf die Uhr.
My boss *kept looking* at his watch every five minutes

Sieh mal *nach*, ob die Maschine läuft.
See if the machine is running.

Er lud Dichter ein, aus ihren Werken *zu lesen*.
He invited poets *to read* from their works.

Class V inseparable verb, stress on stem **-seh-**

PRESENT PARTICIPLE	*PAST PARTICIPLE*
versehend	versehen

PRESENT	*SIMPLE PAST*
ich versehe	ich versah
du versiehst	du versahst
er/sie/es versieht	er/sie/es versah
wir versehen	wir versahen
ihr verseht	ihr versaht
sie/Sie versehen	sie/Sie versahen

KONJUNKTIV I	*KONJUNKTIV II*
ich versehe	ich versähe

Similar verbs

geschehen *(+sein)*	happen
übersehen	overlook, ignore
verlesen	read out
sich verlesen	make a slip

Ich *kann* nicht *übersehen*, ob wir noch Arbeitskräfte werden einstellen müssen.	I *cannot judge* whether we will have to hire more employees.
Der Nachrichtensprecher *hat sich verlesen*.	The anchorman *misread* something.
Sie *haben* einen Fehler *übersehen*.	You *have overlooked* a mistake.

IMPERATIVE

versieh(e)! (du) versehen Sie! verseht! (ihr)

PRESENT PERFECT	**PAST PERFECT (PLUPERFECT)**
ich habe ... versehen	ich hatte ... versehen
FUTURE	**FUTURE PERFECT**
ich werde ... versehen	ich werde ... versehen haben
COMPOUND CONDITIONAL	**PAST CONDITIONAL**
ich würde ... versehen	ich hätte ... versehen

Was *geschieht*, wenn man hier auf den Knopf drückt?	What *happens* when you press this knob?
Was *wäre geschehen*, wenn ich zu spät gekommen wäre?	What *would have happened* if I had been late?
Der Moderator hat die Namen der Gewinner *verlesen*.	The moderator *read* the names of the winners.
Er *hat* mich absichtlich *übersehen*.	He *ignored* me on purpose.

72 ansehen   look at

Class V separable verb, stress on particle **an-**

PRESENT PARTICIPLE	PAST PARTICIPLE
ansehend	angesehen

PRESENT	SIMPLE PAST
ich sehe an	ich sah an
du siehst an	du sahst an
er/sie/es sieht an	er/sie/es sah an
wir sehen an	wir sahen an
ihr seht an	ihr saht an
sie/Sie sehen an	sie/Sie sahen an

KONJUNKTIV I	KONJUNKTIV II
ich sehe an	ich sähe an

Similar verbs

absehen *(von)*	foresee, disregard	**nachsehen**	look up s.th.
aussehen	look like	**sich umsehen** *(nach)*	look around (at)
durchlesen	read through	**vorhersehen**	foresee
durchsehen	check over	**vorlesen**	read aloud
einsehen	see, realize	**zusehen** *(dat.)*	watch, look on
fernsehen	watch TV		
hinwegsehen *(über + acc.)*	ignore		

Lies mir bitte etwas *vor.*	Please *read aloud* to me.
Ich *sah* ihm bei der Arbeit *zu.*	I *watched* him at work.
Es *sieht* so *aus*, als ob es bald regnet.	It *looks* as if it will rain soon.
Sie *hat sich* nach einer neuen Stelle *umgesehen.*	She *was looking around* for a new job.

IMPERATIVE
sieh(e) an! (du)   sehen Sie an!   seht an! (ihr)

PRESENT PERFECT
ich habe ... angesehen

PAST PERFECT (PLUPERFECT)
ich hatte ... angesehen

FUTURE
ich werde ... ansehen

FUTURE PERFECT
ich werde ... angesehen haben

COMPOUND CONDITIONAL
ich würde ... ansehen

PAST CONDITIONAL
ich hätte ... angesehen

Sie *sieht* jünger *aus*, als sie ist.

She *looks* younger than she is.

Sehen Sie im Wörterbuch *nach*, ob das Wort richtig geschrieben ist.

Check the dictionary to see whether the word is spelled correctly.

Ein Ende der Rezession *ist* nicht *abzusehen*.

An end to the recession *cannot* be *predicted*.

Ich *werde* diesmal darüber *hinwegsehen*, dass du deine Hausaufgaben nicht gemacht hast.

This time I *will ignore* the fact that you have not done your homework.

Wir *müssen zusehen*, dass wir möglichst schnell nach Hause kommen.

We *must see* that we get home as fast as possible.

Die Kinder *haben* den ganzen Abend *ferngesehen*.

The kids *watched television* all evening.

73 fahren

drive, go, travel

Class VI verb, stress on stem **fahr-**

PRESENT PARTICIPLE	PAST PARTICIPLE
fahrend	gefahren

PRESENT	SIMPLE PAST
ich fahre	ich fuhr
du fährst	du fuhrst
er/sie/es fährt	er/sie/es fuhr
wir fahren	wir fuhren
ihr fahrt	ihr fuhrt
sie/Sie fahren	sie/Sie fuhren

KONJUNKTIV I	KONJUNKTIV II
ich fahre	ich führe

Similar verbs

graben	dig, mine	tragen	carry, wear
laden	load, charge	wachsen (+sein)	grow
schlagen	hit, strike	waschen	wash
(+sein/haben) (auf+acc.)			

Note **laden** present tense: **du lädst**, **er/sie/es lädt**.

Dieser Zug _fährt_ nur noch werktags.	This train only _runs_ on weekdays.
Er _ist_ früher auch samstags _gefahren_.	Formerly it _ran_ on Saturdays as well.
Wir _werden_ erster Klasse _fahren_.	We _will travel_ first class.
Kannst du Auto _fahren_?	_Can_ you _drive_ a car?
Wir _sind_ sehr langsam _gefahren_, weil es schneite.	We _drove_ very slowly, because it was snowing.
Wer _wird_ die Kosten _tragen_?	Who _will cover_ the costs?

IMPERATIVE
fahr(e)! (du)   fahren Sie!   fahrt! (ihr)

PRESENT PERFECT
ich bin ... gefahren

PAST PERFECT (PLUPERFECT)
ich war ... gefahren

FUTURE
ich werde ... fahren

FUTURE PERFECT
ich werde ... gefahren sein

COMPOUND CONDITIONAL
ich würde ... fahren

PAST CONDITIONAL
ich wäre ... gefahren

Wollen wir das nächste Mal lieber zu Fuß *gehen*, anstatt zu *fahren?*

Should we *walk* the next time rather than *drive?*

Sie *trägt lieber* Jeans als ein Kleid.

She *prefers wearing* jeans to a dress.

Wasch dir die Hände!

Wash your hands!

Ulrichs Jeans *müssen gewaschen werden*.

Ulrich's jeans *have to be washed*.

Das Kind *ist* zwei Zentimeter *gewachsen*.

The child *has grown* two centimeters.

Die Orangen *sind* auf den Lastwagen *geladen worden*.

The oranges *have been loaded* onto the truck.

Bitte *tragen* Sie mir den Koffer zum Taxi.

Please *carry* my suitcase to the taxi!

Class VI verb, stress on stem **schaff-**

PRESENT PARTICIPLE	PAST PARTICIPLE
PRESENT PARTICIPLE	*PAST PARTICIPLE*
schaffend	geschaffen

PRESENT	SIMPLE PAST
PRESENT	*SIMPLE PAST*
ich schaffe	ich schuf
du schaffst	du schufst
er/sie/es schafft	er/sie/es schuf
wir schaffen	wir schufen
ihr schafft	ihr schuft
sie/Sie schaffen	sie/Sie schufen

KONJUNKTIV I	KONJUNKTIV II
KONJUNKTIV I	*KONJUNKTIV II*
ich schaffe	ich schüfe

Notes **schaffen** (do, achieve, get done) is always weak [➤**machen** 11].

beschaffen and **verschaffen** (procure) are always weak [➤**verkaufen** 14].

Der Künstler *hat* mit dieser Skulptur ein Meisterwerk *geschaffen*.	With this sculpture the artist *has created* a masterpiece.
Dieser Posten *ist* wie für ihn *geschaffen*.	This position *is made* for him.
Du hast es geschafft!	*You made it!*

IMPERATIVE
schaff(e)! (du)   schaffen Sie!   schafft! (ihr)

PRESENT PERFECT
ich habe ... geschaffen

PAST PERFECT (PLUPERFECT)
ich hatte ... geschaffen

FUTURE
ich werde ... schaffen

FUTURE PERFECT
ich werde ... geschaffen haben

COMPOUND CONDITIONAL
ich würde ... schaffen

PAST CONDITIONAL
ich hätte ... geschaffen

Ich *schaffe* es nicht, vor Ladenschluss einzukaufen.

I *am* not *able* to go shopping before closing hours.

Heute *haben* wir viel von unserem Arbeitspensum *geschafft*.

Today we *accomplished* a lot of our work load.

Können Sie mir einen billigen CD-Spieler *beschaffen*?

Can you get me a cheap CD player?

Wir *haben* es *geschafft*, in die zweite Liga aufzusteigen.

We *accomplished the move* up to the second division.

Das ist nicht zu schaffen!

It cannot be done!

75 ertragen   bear

Class VI inseparable verb, stress on stem **-trag-**

PRESENT PARTICIPLE	**PAST PARTICIPLE**
ertragend	ertragen

PRESENT	**SIMPLE PAST**
ich ertrage	ich ertrug
du erträgst	du ertrugst
er/sie/es erträgt	er/sie/es ertrug
wir ertragen	wir ertrugen
ihr ertragt	ihr ertrugt
sie/Sie ertragen	sie/Sie ertrugen

KONJUNKTIV I	**KONJUNKTIV II**
ich ertrage	ich ertrüge

Similar verbs

begraben	bury so.	**überschlagen**	pass over, skip
beladen	load	**übertragen**	transmit
beschlagen	shoe (a horse)	**unterschlagen**	embezzle
betragen	amount to	**sich verfahren**	get lost (car)
erfahren	find out, hear	**vergraben**	bury s.th.
erschlagen	kill, slay	**vertragen**	tolerate
überfahren	run over	**zerschlagen**	smash

Die Kinder *vertragen sich* gut.	The children *get on* well *together*.
Ich *kann* es nicht länger *ertragen*.	I *can*'t *stand* it any longer.
Wann *werden* wir das Ergebnis *erfahren*?	When *will* we *find out* the result?

IMPERATIVE
ertrag(e)! (du)   ertragen Sie!   ertragt! (ihr)

PRESENT PERFECT ich habe ... ertragen	**PAST PERFECT (PLUPERFECT)** ich hatte ... ertragen
FUTURE ich werde ... ertragen	**FUTURE PERFECT** ich werde ... ertragen haben
COMPOUND CONDITIONAL ich würde ... ertragen	**PAST CONDITIONAL** ich hätte ... ertragen

Die Miete *beträgt* 1000 Euro.	The rent *comes to* 1000 euros.
Er *hat* mehrere Seiten des Buchs *überschlagen*.	He *skipped* several pages of the book.
Ich *kann* nicht viel Sonne *vertragen*.	I *can* not *take* much sun.
Wir *erfuhren* gestern, dass dein Hund *überfahren worden ist*.	We *found out* yesterday that your dog *had been run over*.
In seinem Leben *ist* ihm nur wenig Gutes *widerfahren*.	He *has experienced* few good things in his life.
Das Theaterstück *wurde* aus dem Englischen *übertragen*.	The play *had been translated* from English.
Das Spiel *wird* nächste Woche im Radio *übertragen*.	The game *will be broadcast* next week on the radio.

Class VI separable verb, stress on particle **ein-**

PRESENT PARTICIPLE	PAST PARTICIPLE
einladend	eingeladen

PRESENT	SIMPLE PAST
ich lade ein	ich lud ein
du lädst ein	du ludst ein
er/sie/es lädt ein	er/sie/es lud ein
wir laden ein	wir luden ein
ihr ladet ein	ihr ludet ein
sie/Sie laden ein	sie/Sie luden ein

KONJUNKTIV I	KONJUNKTIV II
ich lade ein	ich lüde ein

Similar verbs

abfahren *(+sein)*	depart, leave	**niederschlagen**	knock down
abladen	unload, dump	**hinauffahren**	go up (car)
abtragen	wear out, remove	*(+sein)*	
abwaschen	wash up	**losfahren** *(+sein)*	set off (car),
anschlagen	post, chip		get started
auffahren	jump up	**schwarzfahren**	travel with
(+sein)		*(+sein)*	no ticket
aufladen	load	**umfahren**	run down (car)
aufschlagen	open	**vorbeifahren**	drive past
auftragen	apply	*(+sein) (an+dat.)*	
aufwachsen	grow up	**vorschlagen**	suggest,
(+sein)			propose
ausgraben	dig up, unearth	**vortragen**	deliver (speech)
auswaschen	wash out, erode	**wegtragen**	carry off
beitragen *(zu)*	contribute (to)	**zerschlagen**	smash
einfahren	drive in	**zurückfahren**	drive back
(+sein)		*(+sein)*	
eintragen	register	**zusammenfahren**	crash
fortfahren	go away (car)	*(+sein)*	
(+sein/haben)	continue	**zuschlagen**	slam, bang
nachschlagen	look up		

Note **fortfahren** (continue) takes either **haben** or **sein**.

IMPERATIVE
lad(e) ein! (du)   laden Sie ein!   ladet ein! (ihr)

PRESENT PERFECT
ich habe ... eingeladen

PAST PERFECT (PLUPERFECT)
ich hatte ... eingeladen

FUTURE
ich werde ... einladen

FUTURE PERFECT
ich werde ... eingeladen haben

COMPOUND CONDITIONAL
ich würde ... einladen

PAST CONDITIONAL
ich hätte ... eingeladen

Wir *fahren* jetzt *los!*

Off we *go* now!

Wir *sind* früh *abgefahren.*

We *had set off* early.

Wir *sind* schon an der Gaststätte *vorbeigefahren.*

We *already passed* the restaurant.

Morgen *sind* wir bei unseren Nachbarn *eingeladen.*

Tomorrow we *are invited* to our neighbors'.

Er *ist* heute *fortgefahren.*

He *went away* today.

Bitte, *schlagen Sie* im Wörterbuch *nach!*

Please *look* it *up* in the dictionary!

Schlag die Tür nicht *zu!*

*Do*n't *slam* the door!

Bitte *fahren* Sie mit Ihrem Vortrag *fort!*

Please *continue* with your lecture!

Jeder *hat* zum Erfolg des Projekts *beigetragen.*

Everyone *contributed* to the success of the project.

Class VII verb, stress on stem **schlaf-**

PRESENT PARTICIPLE	PAST PARTICIPLE
schlafend	schlafen

PRESENT	SIMPLE PAST
ich schlafe	ich schlief
du schläfst	du schliefst
er/sie/es schläft	er/sie/es schlief
wir schlafen	wir schliefen
ihr schlaft	ihr schlieft
sie/Sie schlafen	sie/Sie schliefen

KONJUNKTIV I	KONJUNKTIV II
ich schlafe	ich schliefe

Similar verbs

blasen	blow
braten	fry, roast
fallen *(+sein)*	fall
lassen	let
raten *(dat.)*	advise

Note   **lassen** belongs in this group, but is listed with its compounds under the modal auxiliaries [➤10].

Schlaf gut!	*Sleep* well!
Rate mal, wer uns gestern besucht hat.	*Guess* who visited us yesterday.
Was *würdest* du mir *raten*?	What *would* you *advise* me?
Der Wind *blies*, und es *fiel* die ganze Nacht Schnee.	The wind *blew* and snow *fell* all night.

IMPERATIVE
schlaf(e)! (du)　　　　　schlafen Sie!　　　　　schlaft! (ihr)

PRESENT PERFECT	*PAST PERFECT (PLUPERFECT)*
ich habe ... geschlafen	ich hatte ... geschlafen

FUTURE	*FUTURE PERFECT*
ich werde ... schlafen	ich werde ... geschlafen haben

COMPOUND CONDITIONAL	*PAST CONDITIONAL*
ich würde ... schlafen	ich hätte ... geschlafen

Er *ist* vor Schreck fast vom Stuhl *gefallen*.	He nearly *fell off* the chair with fright.
Ich *habe* meinem Kollegen *geraten*, dass er erstmal abwarten soll.	I *advised* my colleague to wait and see.
Ich *riet* ihm Geduld zu haben.	I *advised* him to have patience.
Der Fisch *sollte* in Butter *gebraten werden*.	The fish *should be fried* in butter.
Das Fleisch *brät* schon in der Pfanne, und die Hähnchen *werden* wir am Spieß *braten*.	The meat *is* already *frying* in the pan, and we *will roast* the chicken on a spit.

Class VII inseparable verb, stress on stem **-halt-**

PRESENT PARTICIPLE	PAST PARTICIPLE
behaltend	behalten

PRESENT	SIMPLE PAST
ich behalte	ich behielt
du behältst	du behieltst
er/sie/es behält	er/sie/es behielt
wir behalten	wir behielten
ihr behaltet	ihr behieltet
sie/Sie behalten	sie/Sie behielten

KONJUNKTIV I	KONJUNKTIV II
ich behalte	ich behielte

Similar verbs

beraten	advise	**überfallen**	attack
enthalten	include, hold	**unterhalten**	support
erhalten	receive,	**sich unterhalten**	talk, enjoy
	preserve	**verfallen** *(+sein)*	decay,
erraten	guess		deteriorate
gefallen *(dat.)*	please	**sich verhalten**	behave
geraten	get (into)	**verraten**	betray
(+sein) (in/an+acc.)		**verschlafen**	oversleep
missfallen *(dat.)*	displease	**zerfallen** *(+sein)*	disintegrate

Er *hat* **das Haus nicht renoviert, und jetzt** *verfällt* **es langsam.**	He *has* not *renovated* the house and now it is slowly *deteriorating*.
Hat **Ihnen der Abend gut** *gefallen?*	*Did* you *enjoy* the evening?
Ja, wir *haben uns* **gut** *unterhalten.*	Yes, we *enjoyed ourselves*.

IMPERATIVE
behalt(e)! (du)   behalten Sie!   behaltet! (ihr)

PRESENT PERFECT
ich habe ... behalten

PAST PERFECT (PLUPERFECT)
ich hatte ... behalten

FUTURE
ich werde ... behalten

FUTURE PERFECT
ich werde ... behalten haben

COMPOUND CONDITIONAL
ich würde ... behalten

PAST CONDITIONAL
ich hätte ... behalten

Er *hat* sich bei der Krisensitzung völlig falsch *verhalten*.

He *behaved* totally inappropriately at the crisis meeting.

Sie *ist* in der Firma in große Schwierigkeiten *geraten* und wird ihre Stellung nur bis Oktober *behalten*.

She *got into* great difficulties at her company and *will* only *keep* her position until October.

Der Film *hat* mir gut *gefallen*. Wir *haben uns* lange darüber *unterhalten*.

I *liked* the movie a lot. We *talked about* it for a long time.

Ich *wäre* nie *auf den Gedanken verfallen*, ihm Geld zu leihen.

It never *would have occurred* to me to lend him money.

Ich *hätte* heute Morgen *verschlafen*, wenn ich nicht den Wecker gestellt hätte.

I *would have overslept* this morning if I hadn't set the alarm.

Class VII separable verb, stress on particle **herunter-**

PRESENT PARTICIPLE	PAST PARTICIPLE
herunterfallend	heruntergefallen

PRESENT	SIMPLE PAST
ich falle herunter	ich fiel herunter
du fällst herunter	du fielst herunter
er/sie/es fällt herunter	er/sie/es fiel herunter
wir fallen herunter	wir fielen herunter
ihr fallt herunter	ihr fielt herunter
sie/Sie fallen herunter	sie/Sie fielen herunter

KONJUNKTIV I	KONJUNKTIV II
ich falle herunter	ich fiele herunter

Similar verbs

abhalten (von)	keep from	**einschlafen**	fall asleep
abraten *(dat.)*	advise against	*(+sein)*	
	(someone)	**fern halten**	keep away
anhalten	stop	**festhalten**	grasp, hold on
aufblasen	blow up,	**herunterfallen**	fall down
	inflate	*(+sein)*	
auffallen *(+sein)*	notice, stand out	**hinfallen** *(+sein)*	fall down
aufhalten	stop, delay	**hinunterfallen**	fall down
ausfallen *(+sein)*	turn out	*(+sein)*	
aushalten	endure	**innehalten**	pause
ausschlafen	have a good	**mithalten** *(mit)*	keep up (with)
(+sein/haben)	sleep	**stillhalten**	keep still
durchfallen	fail	**zurückfallen**	fall back
(+sein)		*(+sein)*	
durchhalten	hold out	**zurückhalten**	hold back
einfallen	occur (to)	**zusammenfallen**	collapse,
(+sein) (dat.)	to have an idea	*(+sein)*	coincide

IMPERATIVE

fall(e) herunter! (du)   fallen Sie herunter!   fallt herunter! (ihr)

PRESENT PERFECT
ich bin ... heruntergefallen

PAST PERFECT (PLUPERFECT)
ich war ... heruntergefallen

FUTURE
ich werde ... herunterfallen

FUTURE PERFECT
ich werde ... heruntergefallen sein

COMPOUND CONDITIONAL
ich würde ... herunterfallen

PAST CONDITIONAL
ich wäre ... heruntergefallen

Das Theaterstück war langweilig, aber wir *haben* bis zum Ende *durchgehalten*.	The play was boring, but we *stuck it out* to the end.
Wir *wurden* lange am Zoll *aufgehalten*.	We *were delayed* a long time at customs.
Unser Neffe *ist* beim Staatsexamen *durchgefallen*.	Our nephew *failed* his state exam.
Ich *habe* ihm von der Reise *abgeraten*.	I *advised* him *against* the trip.
Ist dir *eingefallen,* wo du den Schlüssel hingelegt hast?	*Did* you *remember* where you *put* the key?
Ich *bin* gestern vor dem Fernseher *eingeschlafen*.	Yesterday I *fell asleep* in front of the TV.
Ich *bin* über den Stuhl gestolpert und *hingefallen*.	I tripped over the chair and *fell down*.
Mir *ist aufgefallen*, dass die Termine für die beiden Sitzungen *zusammenfallen*.	I *noticed* that the dates of the two meetings *coincide*.
Wir *müssen* den Streik *durchhalten*.	We *must hold out* to the end of the strike.

Class VII verb, stress on stem **ruf-**

PRESENT PARTICIPLE	*PAST PARTICIPLE*
rufend	gerufen

PRESENT	*SIMPLE PAST*
ich rufe	ich rief
du rufst	du riefst
er/sie/es ruft	er/sie/es rief
wir rufen	wir riefen
ihr ruft	ihr rieft
sie/Sie rufen	sie/Sie riefen

KONJUNKTIV I	*KONJUNKTIV II*
ich rufe	ich riefe

Similar verbs

hauen	hew, bash, beat
heißen	be called
laufen *(+sein)*	run, go
stoßen *(+sein/haben)*	bump, push

Note   **hauen** has a past simple stem **hieb.** The verb is also used in a weak form [➤**machen** 11].

Wie *heißen* Sie?	What *are* you *called/what is your name?*
Sie *stießen* das Boot zusammen ins Wasser und *sind* dabei an einen Stein *gestoßen*.	*Together they pushed the boat into the water and hit a stone while doing so.*
Lauf nicht so schnell!	*Don't run so fast!*

IMPERATIVE

ruf(e)! (du)   rufen Sie!   ruft! (ihr)

PRESENT PERFECT
ich habe ... gerufen

PAST PERFECT (PLUPERFECT)
ich hatte ... gerufen

FUTURE
ich werde ... rufen

FUTURE PERFECT
ich werde ... gerufen haben

COMPOUND CONDITIONAL
ich würde ... rufen

PAST CONDITIONAL
ich hätte ... gerufen

Unser Garten *stößt* an eine Wiese.

Our garden *adjoins* a meadow.

Als sie die Kinder zum Essen *rief*, *liefen* sie ins Haus.

When she *called* the children to lunch, they *ran* into the house.

Was *soll* das *heißen?*

What *is the meaning* of this?

Ich *habe mich* am Fuß *gestoßen.*

I *bumped* my foot.

Wir *haben* lange nach dem Hund *gerufen.*

We *called* the dog for a long time.

Class VII inseparable verb, stress on stem **-stoß-**

PRESENT PARTICIPLE	PAST PARTICIPLE
verstoßend	verstoßen

PRESENT	SIMPLE PAST
ich verstoße	ich verstieß
du verstößt	du verstießst
er/sie/es verstößt	er/sie/es verstieß
wir verstoßen	wir verstießen
ihr verstoßt	ihr verstieß
sie/Sie verstoßen	sie/Sie verstießen

KONJUNKTIV I	KONJUNKTIV II
ich verstoße	ich verstieße

Similar verbs

sich belaufen (auf+acc.)	amount (to)
entlaufen (dat.) (+sein)	run away (pet)
verlaufen (+sein)	smudge
sich verlaufen	lose one's way
zerstoßen	crush

verstoß(e)! (du)   verstoßen Sie!   verstoßt! (ihr)

PRESENT PERFECT
ich habe ... verstoßen

PAST PERFECT (PLUPERFECT)
ich hatte ... verstoßen

FUTURE
ich werde ... verstoßen

FUTURE PERFECT
ich werde ... verstoßen haben

COMPOUND CONDITIONAL
ich würde ... verstoßen

PAST CONDITIONAL
ich hätte ... verstoßen

Der Firmenleiter *hat* gegen die Steuergesetze *verstoßen.*	The head of the company *committed an offense* against the tax laws.
Unsere Reise *ist gut verlaufen.*	Our trip *went well.*
Wir *haben* uns einmal im Wald *verlaufen.*	We *got lost* once in the woods.
Die Zahl der Touristen *beläuft sich* auf 100 000 in der Woche.	The number of tourists *amounts* to 100,000 a week.
Die Einnahmen *belaufen sich* auf mehrere Millionen Euro.	The earnings *come* to several million euros.
Peter *ist* sein Hund *entlaufen.*	Peter's dog *ran away from* him.
Die Landesgrenze *verläuft* entlang dem Fluss.	The border *runs* along the river.

Class VII separable verb, stress on particle **weg-**

PRESENT PARTICIPLE	PAST PARTICIPLE
weglaufend	weggelaufen

PRESENT	SIMPLE PAST
ich laufe weg	ich lief weg
du läufst weg	du liefst weg
er/sie/es läuft weg	er/sie/es lief weg
wir laufen weg	wir liefen weg
ihr lauft weg	ihr lieft weg
sie/Sie laufen weg	sie/Sie liefen weg

KONJUNKTIV I	KONJUNKTIV II
ich laufe weg	ich liefe weg

Similar verbs

ablaufen *(+sein)*	run out	**überlaufen** *(+sein)*	overflow
anlaufen *(+sein)*	start	**umstoßen**	upset, turn
anrufen	ring up,		upside down
	phone, call	**zurückrufen**	call back
anstoßen (auf)	drink to the	**zurufen**	shout at, hail
	health of	**zusammenlaufen**	merge, run
ausrufen	call out	*(+sein)*	together
davonlaufen *(+sein)*	run away	**zusammenrufen**	summon,
einlaufen *(+sein)*	come in		convene
hervorrufen	evoke	**zusammenstoßen**	crash
hinauslaufen	amount (to)	*(+sein)*	
(+sein) (auf+acc.)	run out		
	(person)		

Note   **abhauen** *(+sein)* (to clear off) has a weak simple past **haute ab** and a past participle **abgehauen**.

IMPERATIVE
lauf(e) weg! (du)   laufen Sie weg!   lauft weg! (ihr)

PRESENT PERFECT	**PAST PERFECT (PLUPERFECT)**
ich bin ... weggelaufen	ich war ... weggelaufen

FUTURE	**FUTURE PERFECT**
ich werde ... weglaufen	ich werde ... weggelaufen sein

COMPOUND CONDITIONAL	**PAST CONDITIONAL**
ich würde ... weglaufen	ich wäre ... weggelaufen

Sie *rief aus*: "Pass auf, du *hast* das Glas *umgestoßen!*"	She *called out:* "Look out, you *knocked over* the glass."
Die beiden Fahrzeuge *sind* auf der Autobahn *zusammengestoßen.*	The two vehicles *crashed into each other* on the Autobahn.
Wir hörten einen Knall und *liefen* auf die Straße *hinaus.*	We heard a bang and *ran out* into the street.
Ob wir alle Kollegen *zusammenrufen* oder sie nur *anrufen, läuft* auf dasselbe *hinaus.*	Whether we *convene* all our colleagues or simply *telephone* them *amounts* to the same thing.
Kannst du morgen *zurückrufen?*	*Can* you *call back* tomorrow?
Du *kannst* ab neun Uhr *anrufen.*	You *can call* from nine o'clock on.

Class VII verb, stress on stem **häng-**

PRESENT PARTICIPLE	*PAST PARTICIPLE*
hängend	gehangen

PRESENT	*SIMPLE PAST*
ich hänge	ich hing
du hängst	du hingst
er/sie/es hängt	er/sie/es hing
wir hängen	wir hingen
ihr hängt	ihr hingt
sie/Sie hängen	sie/Sie hingen

KONJUNKTIV I	*KONJUNKTIV II*
ich hänge	ich hinge

Similar verbs

fangen	capture, catch
hängen an jdm./etwas	attached to someone or something

Note   **hängen** (transitive) is weak [➤**machen** II].

IMPERATIVE
häng(e)! (du)   hängen Sie!   hängt! (ihr)

PRESENT PERFECT
ich habe ... gehangen

PAST PERFECT (PLUPERFECT)
ich hatte ... gehangen

FUTURE
ich werde ... hängen

FUTURE PERFECT
ich werde ... gehangen haben

COMPOUND CONDITIONAL
ich würde ... hängen

PAST CONDITIONAL
ich hätte ... gehangen

Unsere Tochter *hängt* stundenlang am Telefon.	Our daughter *talks* on the telephone for hours.
Bisher *hat* das Bild im Flur *gehangen*.	Until now the picture *has hung* in the hallway.
In der neuen Wohnung *soll* es im Wohnzimmer *hängen*.	In the new apartment it *is supposed to hang* in the living room.
Unsere Katze *fängt* viele Mäuse. Aber gestern *hat* sie einen Vogel *gefangen*.	Our cat *catches* a lot of mice. But yesterday she *caught* a bird.
Eva *hängt* sehr an ihrem Hund.	Eva *is* very *attached* to her dog.
Ich *habe* bei der Angeltour den größten Fisch *gefangen*.	I *caught* the biggest fish during the fishing trip.

Class VII inseparable verb, stress on stem **-fang-**

PRESENT PARTICIPLE	**PAST PARTICIPLE**
empfangend	empfangen

PRESENT	**SIMPLE PAST**
ich empfange	ich empfing
du empfängst	du empfingst
er/sie/es empfängt	er/sie/es empfing
wir empfangen	wir empfingen
ihr empfangt	ihr empfingt
sie/Sie empfangen	sie/Sie empfingen

KONJUNKTIV I	**KONJUNKTIV II**
ich empfange	ich empfinge

Note   **empfangen** is the only common inseparable compound of **fangen**.

IMPERATIVE
empfang(e)! (du)   empfangen Sie!   empfangt! (ihr)

PRESENT PERFECT
ich habe ... empfangen

PAST PERFECT (PLUPERFECT)
ich hatte ... empfangen

FUTURE
ich werde ... empfangen

FUTURE PERFECT
ich werde ... empfangen haben

COMPOUND CONDITIONAL
ich würde ... empfangen

PAST CONDITIONAL
ich hätte ... empfangen

Wir *empfangen* den Südwestfunk nur schlecht.

We *get* poor *reception* of radio station Southwest.

Wir *sind* vom Bürgermeister sehr freundlich *empfangen worden*.

We *were* very warmly *received* by the mayor.

Meine Hose *hat sich* in der Fahrradkette *verfangen*.

My pants *got caught* in the bicycle chain.

Der Angeklagte *hat sich* in einem Netz von Lügen *verfangen*.

The accused *has caught himself* in a net of lies.

Class VII separable verb, stress on particle **an-**

PRESENT PARTICIPLE	PAST PARTICIPLE
anfangend	angefangen

PRESENT	SIMPLE PAST
ich fange an	ich fing an
du fängst an	du fingst an
er/sie/es fängt an	er/sie/es fing an
wir fangen an	wir fingen an
ihr fangt an	ihr fingt an
sie/Sie fangen an	sie/Sie fingen an

KONJUNKTIV I	KONJUNKTIV II
ich fange an	ich finge an

Similar verbs

abhängen *(von)*	depend (on)
anfangen	begin, start
auffangen	catch
aushängen	display, post
zusammenhängen *(mit)*	link, relate (to)

Note   **anhängen** (append), **aufhängen** (hang up, suspend), and **aushängen** (display, post, unhinge) are weak [►**abstellen** 15].

Ich *hätte lieber* gestern mit den Vorbereitungen *angefangen.*	I *would rather have started* yesterday with the preparations.
Ob wir am Wochenende wandern gehen, *hängt davon ab,* wie das Wetter ist.	Whether we go hiking on the weekend *depends on* how the weather is.

IMPERATIVE
fang(e) an! (du)   fangen Sie an!   fangt an! (ihr)

PRESENT PERFECT	*PAST PERFECT (PLUPERFECT)*
ich habe ... angefangen	ich hatte ... angefangen

FUTURE	*FUTURE PERFECT*
ich werde ... anfangen	ich werde ... angefangen haben

COMPOUND CONDITIONAL	*PAST CONDITIONAL*
ich würde ... anfangen	ich hätte ... angefangen

Häng die Wäsche zum Trocknen *auf!*	*Hang* the wash up to dry.
Dass ich Kopfschmerzen habe, *hängt* mit dem Wetterumschwung *zusammen.*	The fact that I have a headache *is related to* the change in the weather.
Klaus hat mir den Schlüssel zugeworfen, und ich *habe* ihn *aufgefangen.*	Klaus threw the key to me and I *caught* it.

Strong irregular verb, stress on stem **geh-**

PRESENT PARTICIPLE	PAST PARTICIPLE
gehend	gegangen

PRESENT	SIMPLE PAST
ich gehe	ich ging
du gehst	du gingst
er/sie/es geht	er/sie/es ging
wir gehen	wir gingen
ihr geht	ihr gingt
sie/Sie gehen	sie/Sie gingen

KONJUNKTIV I	KONJUNKTIV II
ich gehe	ich ginge

Note **gehen** is the only verb of this type. However, note the compound verbs ➤**begehen** 87; **ausgehen** 88.

Wie *geht es Ihnen?*	How *are you?*
Mir *geht's gut*, danke.	I *am well*, thank you.
Und Ihnen?	And you?
Ich *bin* gestern zum Arzt *gegangen*.	I *went* to the doctor yesterday.
Wenn alles gut *geht*, können wir nächste Woche in Urlaub fahren.	If all *goes* well, we can go on vacation next week
***Wollen* wir *spazieren gehen*?**	*Shall* we *go for a walk?*
Ich *möchte* lieber *schwimmen gehen*.	I *would* rather *go swimming.*

STRONG VERBS gehen 86

IMPERATIVE
geh(e)! (du)　　　　　gehen Sie!　　　　　geht! (ihr)

PRESENT PERFECT
ich bin ... gegangen

PAST PERFECT (PLUPERFECT)
ich war ... gegangen

FUTURE
ich werde ... gehen

FUTURE PERFECT
ich werde ... gegangen sein

COMPOUND CONDITIONAL
ich würde ... gehen

PAST CONDITIONAL
ich wäre ... gegangen

Wenn es nach mir *ginge*, würden wir meine Oma besuchen.	If it *were* up to me, we would visit my Grandma.
Gehen wir oder fahren wir?	Should we *walk* or drive?
Thomas *muss schlafen gehen*. Er *geht* um 8 Uhr in die Schule.	Thomas *must go to bed*. He *goes* to school at 8 o'clock.
Die Firma *ist Pleite gegangen*.	The firm *went bankrupt*.
Es *geht* mir nicht nur *ums* Geld.	I'*m* not just *concerned* about the money.
Gehen wir nach Hause!	*Let's go* home!
Heute *geht's* nach München. Der Zug *geht* über Frankfurt.	*We are off* to Munich today. The train *goes* via Frankfurt.

207

Strong irregular inseparable verb, stress on stem **-geh-**

PRESENT PARTICIPLE	PAST PARTICIPLE
begehend	begangen

PRESENT	SIMPLE PAST
ich begehe	ich beging
du begehst	du begingst
er/sie/es begeht	er/sie/es beging
wir begehen	wir begingen
ihr begehet	ihr beging
sie/Sie begehen	sie/Sie begingen

KONJUNKTIV I	KONJUNKTIV II
ich begehe	ich beginge

Similar verbs

entgehen *(+sein) (dat.)*	avoid, overlook
umgehen	go around, avoid
vergehen *(+sein)*	pass, vanish

Note   **umgehen** can also be used as a separable verb [➤**ausgehen** 88].

IMPERATIVE
begeh(e)! (du) begehen Sie! begeht! (ihr)

PRESENT PERFECT	**PAST PERFECT (PLUPERFECT)**
ich habe ... begangen	ich hatte ... begangen

FUTURE	**FUTURE PERFECT**
ich werde ... begehen	ich werde ... begangen haben

COMPOUND CONDITIONAL	**PAST CONDITIONAL**
ich würde ... begehen	ich hätte ... begangen

Wir *begehen* (feiern) morgen den 80. Geburtstag meiner Mutter.	We *are celebrating* my mother's 80th birthday tomorrow.
Es *war* mir völlig *entgangen*, dass die Besprechung schon am Montag ist.	It completely *slipped my mind* that the meeting is on Monday already.
Er *hat* das Verbrechen *begangen* und *wird* der Strafe nicht *entgehen können*.	He *has committed* the crime, and he *will* not *be able to escape* the punishment.
Mir *ist* keines seiner Worte *entgangen*.	Not one of his words *escaped* me.
Das neue Gesetz *wird* öfters *umgangen*.	The new law *is* frequently *evaded*.
Die Zeit *vergeht*.	Time *passes*.
Der Appetit *ist* mir *vergangen*.	I *have lost* my appetite.

88 ausgehen

go out

Strong irregular separable verb, stress on particle **aus-**

PRESENT PARTICIPLE	*PAST PARTICIPLE*
ausgehend	ausgegangen

PRESENT	*SIMPLE PAST*
ich gehe aus	ich ging aus
du gehst aus	du gingst aus
er/sie/es geht aus	er/sie/es ging aus
wir gehen aus	wir gingen aus
ihr geht aus	ihr gingt aus
sie/Sie gehen aus	sie/Sie gingen aus

KONJUNKTIV I	*KONJUNKTIV II*
ich gehe aus	ich ginge aus

Similar verbs

angehen *(+sein)*	concern	**nahe gehen**	grieve, affect
aufgehen *(+sein)*	rise, dawn	*(+sein) (dat.)*	
durchgehen *(+sein)*	go through	**schief gehen** *(+sein)*	go wrong
eingehen *(+sein)*	die (plant)	**umgehen**	handle,
einlaufen *(+sein)*	shrink	*(mit) (+sein)*	evade
	(clothes)	**untergehen**	set, sink
entgegengehen	go (toward)	*(+sein)*	
(+sein) (dat.)		**vorangehen**	go ahead (of)
hinausgehen *(+sein)*	go out	*(+sein) (dat.)*	
hineingehen *(+sein)*	go in	**vorbeigehen**	go past
hinübergehen *(+sein)*	cross over	*(+sein) (an+dat.)*	
hinuntergehen	go down,	**vorgehen** *(+sein)*	proceed
(+sein)	descend	**weggehen** *(+sein)*	go away,
kaputtgehen *(+sein)*	break, bust		depart
losgehen *(+sein)*	go off, set off	**weitergehen** *(+sein)*	go on
mitgehen *(+sein)*	go along too	**zugehen**	approach
nachgehen	follow	*(+sein) (auf+acc.)*	
(+sein) (dat.)		**zurückgehen** *(+sein)*	go back

Meine schöne Begonie *ist* leider *eingegangen*.	Unfortunately my beautiful begonia *died*.

IMPERATIVE
geh(e) aus! (du)   gehen Sie aus!   geht aus! (ihr)

PRESENT PERFECT	*PAST PERFECT (PLUPERFECT)*
ich bin ... ausgegangen	ich war ... ausgegangen

FUTURE	*FUTURE PERFECT*
ich werde ... ausgehen	ich werde ... ausgegangen sein

COMPOUND CONDITIONAL	*PAST CONDITIONAL*
ich würde ... ausgehen	ich wäre ... ausgegangen

Wann *geht* die Messe *los?*	When *does* the trade show *start?*
Wir *müssen losgehen*, sonst kommen wir zu spät. *Gehen* Sie *mit?*	We *have to go* or we will be late. Are you *going with* us?
Er *ging* aus dem Zimmer *hinaus*, am Badezimmer *vorbei*, die Treppe *hinunter* und in die Küche.	He *went out* of the room, *past* the bathroom, *down* the stairs and *into* the kitchen.
Wir *würden* am Fluss *spazieren gehen*, wenn wir Zeit hätten. Wir *müssen* jetzt *zurückgehen*.	We *would walk* along the river if we had time. We *must go back* now.
Alles *ging schief.* Die Waschmaschine *war kaputtgegangen*, und alle Stricksachen *sind eingelaufen.*	Everything *went wrong.* The washing machine *had broken down* and all the sweaters *shrank.*
Das *geht* mich nichts *an.*	That's *none of my business.*
Die Sonne *geht* um sieben Uhr *auf* und um sechs *unter.*	The sun *rises* at seven o'clock and *sets* at six o'clock.
Ein Gespenst geht im Haus *um.*	A ghost is *walking around* the house.
Er *geht* sehr liebevoll mit den Kindern *um.*	He *handles* the children very caringly.

Strong irregular verb, stress on stem **steh-**

PRESENT PARTICIPLE	PAST PARTICIPLE
stehend	gestanden

PRESENT	SIMPLE PAST
ich stehe	ich stand
du stehst	du standst
er/sie/es steht	er/sie/es stand
wir stehen	wir standen
ihr steht	ihr standet
sie/Sie stehen	sie/Sie standen

KONJUNKTIV I	KONJUNKTIV II
ich stehe	ich stünde

Note stehen is the only verb of this type. However, note the compound verbs ➤**verstehen** 90; **aufstehen** 91.

IMPERATIVE

steh(e)! (du)   stehen Sie!   steht! (ihr)

PRESENT PERFECT	**PAST PERFECT (PLUPERFECT)**
ich habe/bin ... gestanden	ich hatte/war ... gestanden

FUTURE	**FUTURE PERFECT**
ich werde ... stehen	ich werde ... gestanden haben/sein

COMPOUND CONDITIONAL	**PAST CONDITIONAL**
ich würde ... stehen	ich hätte/wäre ... gestanden

Die Flasche *muss stehen*, nicht liegen.	The bottle *has to stand,* not lie down.
Die kleine Ute *kann* schon *stehen.*	Little Ute *can stand* already.
Das Kleid *steht* ihr gut.	The dress *looks* good on her.
Sie *stand* am Fenster und beobachtete die Leute auf der Straße.	She *stood* by the window and watched the people in the street.
Er sagte, der Garten *stehe* schon seit zwei Wochen *unter Wasser.*	He said that the garden *has been flooded* for two weeks already.
In der Zeitung *stand*, dass es morgen wieder regnen würde.	The newspaper *reported* that it would rain again tomorrow.
Wie *stehen Sie zu* der Sache?	What *is your position on* the matter?

Strong inseparable irregular verb, stress on stem **-steh-**

PRESENT PARTICIPLE	*PAST PARTICIPLE*
verstehend	verstanden

PRESENT	*SIMPLE PAST*
ich verstehe	ich verstand
du verstehst	du verstandst
er/sie/es versteht	er/sie/es verstand
wir verstehen	wir verstanden
ihr versteht	ihr verstandet
sie/Sie verstehen	sie/Sie verstanden

KONJUNKTIV I	*KONJUNKTIV II*
ich verstehe	ich verstünde

Similar verbs

bestehen	exist, pass (exam)
entstehen *(+sein) (dat.)*	arise, emerge (from)
gestehen	confess
missverstehen	misunderstand

Du *darfst* mich nicht *missverstehen*.	*Don't misunderstand* me.
Der Konflikt *besteht* seit Jahren.	The conflict *has existed* for years.
Verstehen Sie etwas Französisch?	*Do* you *understand* some French?
Ich *würde* Sie besser *verstehen*, wenn Sie langsam sprechen würden.	I *would understand* you better if you would speak slowly.
Aber es *ist* mir offen *gestanden* lieber, Deutsch zu sprechen.	But quite *frankly*, I would prefer to speak German.
Dieses Sportzentrum *ist* in den 80ern *entstanden*.	This sport center *was built* in the 80s.

IMPERATIVE
versteh(e)! (du)   verstehen Sie!   versteht! (ihr)

PRESENT PERFECT
ich habe ... verstanden

PAST PERFECT (PLUPERFECT)
ich hatte ... verstanden

FUTURE
ich werde ... verstehen

FUTURE PERFECT
ich werde ... verstanden haben

COMPOUND CONDITIONAL
ich würde ... verstehen

PAST CONDITIONAL
ich hätte ... verstanden

Die Gründe für sein Verhalten *habe* ich nie *verstanden*.

I *have* never *understood* the reasons for his behavior.

Es *versteht sich von selbst*, dass die beiden *sich* nicht gut *verstehen*.

It *goes without saying* that the two *do*n't *get along* well.

Ich *habe* meinen Freund am Telefon nur schwer *verstanden*.

I *understood* my friend on the phone only with great difficulty.

Er *hat* die Prüfung glänzend *bestanden*.

He *has passed* the examination with flying colors.

Er *verstand* etwas von Musik.

He *knew* something about music.

Er *versteht sich* auf das Kochen.

He *is* an expert cook.

Der Täter *hat* das Verbrechen *gestanden*.

The criminal *confessed* to his crime.

91 aufstehen

stand up

Strong separable irregular verb, stress on particle **auf-**

PRESENT PARTICIPLE	PAST PARTICIPLE
aufstehend	aufgestanden

PRESENT	SIMPLE PAST
ich stehe auf	ich stand auf
du stehst auf	du standst auf
er/sie/es steht auf	er/sie/es stand auf
wir stehen auf	wir standen auf
ihr steht auf	ihr standet auf
sie/Sie stehen auf	sie/Sie standen auf

KONJUNKTIV I	KONJUNKTIV II
ich stehe auf	ich stünde auf

Similar verbs

anstehen	line up, queue
ausstehen	endure, stand
beistehen *(dat.)*	help
feststehen	be certain
gegenüberstehen *(dat.)*	be opposite, face
hervorstehen	stick out

IMPERATIVE
steh(e) auf! (du)   stehen Sie auf!   steht auf! (ihr)

PRESENT PERFECT
ich bin ... aufgestanden

PAST PERFECT (PLUPERFECT)
ich war ... aufgestanden

FUTURE
ich werde ... aufstehen

FUTURE PERFECT
ich werde ... aufgestanden sein

COMPOUND CONDITIONAL
ich werde ... aufstehen

PAST CONDITIONAL
ich wäre ... aufgestanden

Wir *mussten* an der Kinokasse *anstehen*.

We *had to stand in line* at the movie theater box office.

Ich *muss* morgen früher *aufstehen*.

I *have to get up* earlier tomorrow.

Er *hat* mir immer *beigestanden*, wenn es mir schlecht ging. Trotzdem *stehe* ich seinem Vorhaben etwas skeptisch *gegenüber*.

He *has* always *stood by* me when things were bad for me. Nevertheless I *feel* somewhat doubtful *about* his plan.

Ich *kann* unseren neuen Abteilungsleiter nicht *ausstehen*.

I *can't stand* our new department head.

Eines *steht fest*, wir können die Konferenz nicht absagen.

One thing *is certain*, we cannot cancel the conference.

Das Programm für das Jazzfest *steht* jetzt *fest*.

The program for the jazz festival *is* now *fixed*.

92 tun   do

Strong irregular verb, stress on stem **tu-**

PRESENT PARTICIPLE	PAST PARTICIPLE
tuend	getan

PRESENT	SIMPLE PAST
ich tue	ich tat
du tust	du tatst
er/sie/es tut	er/sie/es tat
wir tun	wir taten
ihr tut	ihr tatet
sie/Sie tun	sie/Sie taten

KONJUNKTIV I	KONJUNKTIV II
ich tue	ich täte

Similar verbs

[Separable verbs ➤*aufstehen* 91]

gut tun *(dat.)*	benefit
leidtun *(dat.)*	be sorry
wehtun *(dat.)*	hurt
zusammentun	get/put together

Was *kann* man jetzt *tun*?	What *can* you *do* now?
***Tut* es *weh*?**	*Does* it *hurt*?
Ja, der Bauch *tut* mir *weh*.	Yes, my stomach *hurts*.
Das *tut* mir *leid*.	I *am sorry*.
Der Hund *tut* dir nichts.	The dog *will* not *hurt* you.

IMPERATIVE
tu(e)! (du)   tun Sie!   tut! (ihr)

PRESENT PERFECT	*PAST PERFECT (PLUPERFECT)*
ich habe ... getan	ich hatte ... getan

FUTURE	*FUTURE PERFECT*
ich werde ... tun	ich werde ... getan haben

COMPOUND CONDITIONAL	*PAST CONDITIONAL*
ich würde ... tun	ich hätte ... getan

Tu die Bücher ins Regal.	*Put* the books on the shelf.
Er *tat so*, als ob er nichts gesehen hätte.	He *acted* as if he had seen nothing.
Wir *haben* mit dem Finanzamt *zu tun*.	We *have to deal* with the Internal Revenue Service.
Wir *haben uns zusammengetan*, um Marita ein Geschenk zu kaufen.	We *have gotten together* to buy Marita a present.
Sie *tat* den ganzen Tag nichts anderes als arbeiten.	She *did* nothing else all day except work.
Ich *habe* mein Bestes *getan*, aber ich konnte die Situation nicht retten.	I *did* my best, but I couldn't salvage the situation.
Sie muss ihm etwas *zu tun* geben.	She has to give him something *to do*.

C

SUBJECT INDEX

Subject index

Note Where there is a major section devoted to any item, the reference is shown in bold type.

D

VERB INDEX

Verb index

Notes: for each verb only two or three of the most common meanings are given.

An asterisk * has been used to indicate that a verb is conjugated in the Model verbs section.

References are to entry numbers.

A

ab|bauen (tr. & intr.) — dismantle, break down 15
er baut das Zelt ab — *he takes down the tent*
ab|bestellen (tr.) — cancel 15
ab|bezahlen (tr.) — pay off 15
ab|biegen (tr. & intr.+s.) — turn off 35
ab|blenden (tr. & intr.) — dip, dim (lights) 12, 15
ab|brechen (tr. & intr.+s.) — break off 51
ab|bringen (von) (tr.) — dissuade (from) 24
ab|fahren (intr.+s.) — depart, leave 76
ab|färben (intr.) — run (of color) 15
ab|finden (mit) (refl.) — put up (with) 47
ab|geben (tr.) — hand in 61
sie gibt sich mit ... ab (refl.) — *she concerns herself with ...*
ab|gewöhnen (tr.) — break (of a habit) 15
ich gewöhne mir das Rauchen ab (dat. refl.) — *I am giving up smoking*
ab|haken (tr.) — check off 15
ab|halten (von) (tr. & refl.) — keep from 79
ab|hängen (von) (intr.) — depend (on) 85
ab|härten (tr. & refl.) — toughen up 12, 15
ab|hauen (tr.) — chop off 15
er haut ab (intr.+s.) — *he clears off*
ab|heben (tr.) — abolish 38
das Flugzeug hebt ab (intr.+s.) — *the plane takes off*
es hebt sich ab (refl.) — *it stands out*
ab|holen (tr.) — call for, fetch 15
ab|kommen (von) (intr.+s.) — deviate (from) 58
ab|kühlen (tr. & intr.+s.) — cool down 15
ab|kürzen (tr.) — abbreviate 15
ab|laden (tr.) — unload, dump 76
ab|lassen (tr.) — let out 10, 79

ab|laufen (intr.+s.)	run out 82
er läuft die Schuhe ab (tr.)	*he wears out his shoes*
ab|legen (tr. & intr.)	put down, file 15
er legt ab	*he takes his coat off*
sie legt Daten ab	*she stores data*
ab|lehnen (tr. & intr.)	refuse, reject 15
ab|lenken (tr. & intr.)	divert, distract 15
ab|liegen (intr.)	be at a disance 61
ab|lösen (tr.)	detach 15
es löst sich ab (refl.)	*it peels off*
ab|machen (tr.)	take off 15
wir machen den Termin ab	*we agree on the time (of the meeting)*
ab|melden (tr.)	cancel 12, 15
sie meldet sich ab (refl.)	*she checks out*
ab|messen (tr.)	measure (off) 69
ab|nehmen (tr.)	take off 54
sie nimmt ab	*she loses weight*
abonnieren (auf+acc.) (tr. & intr.)	subscribe (to) 13
ab|raten (dat.) (tr.)	advise against 79
ich rate ihm von ... ab	*I advise him against ...*
ab|räumen (tr. & intr.)	clear away 15
ab|rechnen (tr. & intr.)	cash up 12, 15
er rechnet mit mir ab	*he settles up with me*
ab|reisen (intr.+s.)	depart 15
ab|reißen (tr.)	tear off, demolish 31
ab|runden (tr.)	round down (numbers)12, 15
ab|rüsten (tr. & intr.)	disarm 12, 15
ab|sacken (intr.+s.)	subside 15
ab|sagen (tr. & intr.)	call off, cancel 15
ab|schaffen (tr.)	abolish, do away with 15
ab|schalten (tr. & intr.)	switch off 12, 15
ab|schicken (tr.)	send off 15
ab|schleppen (tr.)	tow away 15
*ab|schließen (tr. & intr.)	complete 41
er schließt die Tür ab	*he locks the door*
ab|schmecken (tr. & intr.)	taste, season 15
ab|schminken (refl.)	remove make-up 15
ab|schneiden (tr.)	cut off 29, 31
ab|schrauben (tr.)	unscrew 15
ab|schreiben (tr.)	copy 28
er schreibt es ab	*he writes it off*
ab|sehen (tr.)	foresee 72
sie sieht von ... ab	*she disregards ...*

*ab|senden (tr.)	send off 21
ab|setzen (tr.)	set down 15
er setzt den Hut ab	*he takes off his hat*
ab|sinken (intr.+s.)	sink, subside 44
ab|sitzen (tr.)	sit out 67
er sitzt ab	*he dismounts*
ab|sondern (tr.)	isolate 15
ab|speichern (tr.)	save, store 15
ab|springen (intr.+s.)	jump down, come off 44
ab|stauben (tr. & intr.)	dust 15
ab|steigen (intr.+s.)	get off, go down 28
*ab|stellen (tr. & intr.)	put down, turn off 15
ab|sterben (intr.+s.)	die out 51
ab|stimmen (über+acc.) (intr.)	vote (on) 15
er stimmt die Farben aufeinander ab (tr.)	*he coordinates the colors*
ab|streifen (tr.)	cast, shed 15
ab|stufen (tr.)	grade 15
ab|stürzen (intr.+s.)	crash 15
ab|teilen (tr.)	partition off 15
ab|tragen (tr.)	wear out 76
ab|trennen (tr.)	detach, cut off 15
ab|treten (intr.+s.)	resign 50
er tritt die Schuhe ab (tr.)	*he wipes his feet*
ab|trocknen (tr. & intr.)	wipe, dry up 15
ab|tropfen (intr.+s.)	drip, drain 15
ab|wägen (tr.)	weigh up 38
ab|warten (tr. & intr.)	wait (for) 12, 15
warten wir ab	*let's wait and see*
ab|waschen (tr. & intr.)	wash up 76
ab|wechseln (intr.)	alternate 15
sie wechseln sich ab (refl.)	*they take turns*
ab|wehren (tr. & intr.)	beat back, repulse 15
ab|weichen (von) (intr.+s.)	deviate, diverge (from) 31
ab|wenden (tr.)	turn away 21
ab|werten (tr. & intr.)	devalue 12, 15
ab|ziehen (tr.)	take off, print 33, 35
er zieht ab (intr.+s.)	*he moves off*
achten (tr.)	respect 12
er achtet auf sie	*he pays attention to her*
Acht geben (auf+acc.) (intr.)	pay attention (to) 61
addieren (tr. & intr.)	add 13
adoptieren (tr.)	adopt 13
ähneln (dat.) (intr.)	resemble, take after 11
ahnen (tr. & intr.)	suspect 11
akkumulieren (tr., intr. & refl.)	accumulate 13

akzeptieren (tr.)	accept 13
alarmieren (tr.)	alarm, alert 13
altern (intr.+s.)	age 11
amputieren (tr.)	amputate 13
amüsieren (tr.)	amuse 13
er amüsiert sich (refl.)	*he enjoys himself*
analysieren (tr.)	analyze 13
an|beten (tr.)	adore, worship 12, 15
*an|bieten (tr.)	offer 35
an|blicken (tr.)	look at 15
an|brechen (tr.)	open 51
der Tag bricht an (intr.+s.)	*the day dawns*
ändern (tr. & refl.)	change, alter 11
an|eignen (dat. refl.)	appropriate 12, 15
an|ekeln (tr.)	disgust 15
an|erkennen (tr.)	acknowledge, respect 17, 18
*an|fangen (tr. & intr.)	begin, start 85
ich fange mit ... an	*I make a start on ...*
an|fassen (tr.)	touch, seize 15
an|flehen (tr.)	beg, implore 15
an|geben (tr. & intr.)	state 61
sie gibt an	*she shows off/boasts*
an|gehen (tr.)	concern 88
es geht an (intr.+s.)	*it goes/switches on*
an|gehören (dat.) (intr.)	belong to 14, 15
angeln (tr. & intr.)	fish (for) 11
*an|greifen (tr. & intr.)	attack 31
an|haben (tr.)	have on, wear 2
an|halten (tr. & intr.)	stop, delay 79
an|hängen (tr.)	append 85
an|hören (tr.)	hear, listen to 15
ich höre es mir an (dat. refl.)	*I listen to it*
animieren (tr.)	encourage, animate 13
ankern (intr.)	anchor 11
an|ketten (tr.)	chain up 12, 15
an|klagen (tr. & intr.)	accuse, protest 15
an|knüpfen (tr.)	tie on 15
*an|kommen (in+dat.) (intr.+s.)	arrive 58
es kommt auf+acc ... an (impers.)	*it depends on ...*
an|kündigen (tr.)	announce, signal 15
an|lassen (tr.)	start 10, 79
an|laufen (intr.+s.)	start 82
an|legen (tr.)	lay out 15
das Boot legt an (intr.)	*the boat moors*

an|lehnen (an+acc.) (tr. & refl.) — lean (against) 15
an|liegen (intr.) — be on course for 61
es liegt an — *it fits closely*
an|machen (tr.) — attach 15
er macht das Radio an — *he switches on the radio*
an|melden (tr.) — announce 12, 15
er meldet sich an (refl.) — *he checks in*
*an|nehmen (tr.) — assume, accept 54
annektieren (tr.) — annex 13
an|passen (tr.) — fit, adapt 15
er passt sich (dat.) an (refl.) — *he conforms (to)*
an|probieren (tr.) — try on 13, 15
an|regen (tr.) — prompt, encourage 15
an|rufen (tr. & intr.) — ring up, phone, call 82
an|sagen (tr. & intr.) — announce, call out 15
an|sammeln (tr. & refl.) — accumulate, gather 15
an|schalten (tr.) — switch on 12, 15
an|schauen (tr.) — look at 15
an|schlagen (tr.) — nail on, chip 76
an|schließen (tr.) — connect 41
er schließt sich mir an (refl.) — *he joins me*
an|schnallen (tr.) — fasten, strap 15
er schnallt sich an (refl.) — *he fastens his seatbelt*
*an|sehen (tr.) — look at 72
an sein (intr.+s.) — be on 1
an|spannen (tr.) — tighten 15
er spannt sich an (refl.) — *he strains*
an|spielen (auf+acc.) (intr.) — allude (to) 15
an|sprechen (tr.) — address 51
an|springen (intr.+s.) — jump, start 44
an|starren (tr.) — stare at 15
an|stecken (tr.) — infect, ignite 15
an|stehen (intr.) — line up, queue 91
an|steigen (intr.+s.) — rise, increase 28
an|stellen (tr.) — employ 15
er stellt sich an (refl.) — *he lines up*
an|stoßen (an+acc.) (intr.+s.) — bump into
stoßen wir auf ihn an — *let's drink to him* 82
an|streichen (tr.) — paint, decorate 31
an|strengen (tr.) — strain 15
sie strengt sich an (refl.) — *she tries hard*
antworten (auf+acc.) (intr.) — answer, reply (to) 12
an|vertrauen (tr.) — entrust 14, 15
er vertraut sich ihr an (refl.) — *he confides in her*

an|wenden (tr.)	apply, use 21
an|zahlen (tr.)	pay a deposit 15
an|zeigen (tr.)	announce, denounce 15
an|ziehen (tr.)	attract, put on 33, 35
sie zieht sich an (refl.)	*she gets dressed*
an|zünden (tr.)	light, set on fire 12, 15
appellieren (an+acc.) (intr.)	appeal (to) 13
applaudieren (dat.) (intr.)	applaud (so.) 13
*arbeiten (an+dat.) (intr.)	work, labor (on) 12
ärgern (tr.)	annoy 11
er ärgert sich über+acc ... (refl.)	*he gets cross about ...*
arrangieren (tr. & intr.)	arrange, fix 13
atmen (tr. & intr.)	breathe 12
ätzen (tr. & intr.)	corrode 11
auf|bauen (tr. & intr.)	put up, construct 15
auf|bäumen (refl.)	rear up 15
auf|bewahren (tr.)	store 15
auf|blasen (tr.)	blow up, inflate 79
auf|blicken (intr.)	look up 15
auf|blitzen (intr.)	flash 15
auf|brechen (tr. & intr.+s.)	break open/up/out 51
er bricht auf (intr.+s.)	*he sets off*
auf|decken (tr.)	uncover 15
auf|drehen (tr.)	turn on/up 15
*auf|essen (tr.)	eat up, consume 69
auf|fahren (intr.+s.)	jump up 76
auf|fallen (intr.+s.)	stand out, notice 79
es fällt mir auf (dat.)	*it strikes me*
auf|fangen (tr.)	catch 85
er fängt den Schock auf	*he cushions the shock*
auf|fassen (tr.)	interpret 15
auf|flackern (intr.+s.)	flare up 15
auf|fordern (tr.)	invite, challenge 15
auf|frischen (tr. & refl.)	freshen up 15
auf|führen (tr.)	perform 15
auf|geben (tr. & intr.)	give up, renounce 61
auf|gehen (intr.+s.)	rise, dawn 88
auf|halten (tr.)	stop, delay 79
er hält sich in ... auf (refl.)	*he is staying in ...*
auf|hängen (tr.)	hang up, suspend 85
auf|häufen (tr. & refl.)	pile up 15
*auf|heben (tr.)	pick up, abolish 38
auf|hören (mit) (intr.)	stop, finish (sth.) 15
ich höre damit auf, ... zu machen	*I stop doing ...*

auf|klären (tr.)	clear up, enlighten 15
auf|knöpfen (tr.)	unbutton 15
auf|laden (tr.)	load 76
er lädt die Batterie auf	*he charges the battery*
auf|lauern (dat.) (intr.)	lie in wait for 15
auf|legen (tr.)	put down 15
er legt auf (intr.)	*he hangs up/he rings off*
auf|liegen (intr.)	be on the table 61
auf|lösen (tr. & refl.)	dissolve, break up 15
auf|machen (tr. & intr.)	open, undo 15
auf|muntern (tr. & refl.)	cheer up 15
auf|nehmen (tr.)	receive, absorb 54
auf|passen (intr.)	watch out, pay attention 15
er passt auf sie auf	*he keeps an eye on them*
auf|räumen (tr. & intr.)	tidy up, clear up 15
auf|regen (tr.)	annoy 15
er regt sich auf (refl.)	*he gets excited*
auf|richten (tr.)	put up 12, 15
sie richtet sich auf (refl.)	*she sits up*
auf|runden (tr.)	even up, round up 12, 15
auf|saugen (tr.)	absorb 15, 38
auf|schlagen (tr.)	open 76
er schlägt das Zelt auf	*he erects the tent*
auf|schließen (tr. & intr.)	unlock 41
auf|schneiden (tr.)	cut up 31
auf|schreiben (tr.)	list, note down 28
auf|schreien (intr.)	exclaim 28
auf|schürfen (tr.)	graze 15
auf sein (intr.+s.)	be on 1
die Tür ist auf	*the door is open*
auf|setzen (tr.)	put on 15
das Flugzeug setzt auf (refl.)	*the plane lands*
*auf|springen (intr.+s.)	jump up, bounce 44
*auf|stehen (intr.+s.)	get up, stand up 91
auf|stellen (tr.)	erect 15
sie stellen sich auf (refl.)	*they line up*
auf|tauchen (intr.+s.)	appear, emerge 15
auf|tauen (tr. & intr.+s.)	defrost, thaw 15
auf|tragen (tr.)	apply 76
auf|treten (intr.+s.)	appear, come on 65
auf|wachen (intr.+s.)	wake up 15
auf|wachsen (intr.+s.)	grow up 76
auf|wärmen (tr.)	warm up 15
auf|wickeln (tr.)	coil, untie 15
auf|zäumen (tr.)	bridle, harness 15
auf|zeichnen (tr.)	draw, record 12, 15

auf|ziehen (tr.)	bring up 33, 35
sie zieht die Uhr auf	*she winds the clock up*
aus|atmen (tr. & intr.)	exhale 12, 15
aus|bauen (tr.)	extend, convert 15
aus|bilden (tr.)	train, develop 12, 15
er bildet sich (als) ... aus	*he is studying/training*
(refl.)	*(to be a...)*
aus|blenden (tr. & intr.)	fade out 12, 15
aus|bomben (tr.)	bomb 15
aus|brechen (intr.+s.)	burst out, break out 51
aus|breiten (tr. & refl.)	spread out 12, 15
aus|dehnen (tr. & refl.)	extend, spread 15
aus|denken (tr.)	think out/up 24
aus|drehen (tr.)	turn off 15
aus|drucken (tr. & intr.)	print out 15
aus|drücken (tr.)	express 15
auseinander nehmen (tr.)	dismantle 54
aus|essen (tr. & intr.)	eat up, finish eating 69
aus|fallen (intr.+s.)	turn out 79
es fällt aus	*it is cancelled*
aus|fragen (tr.)	question, interrogate 15
aus|führen (tr.)	carry out 15
er führt die Waren aus	*he exports the goods*
aus|füllen (tr.)	fill in, complete 15
aus|geben (tr.)	spend, pay out 61
aus|gleichen (tr. & intr. & refl.)	even out, equalize 31
aus|graben (tr.)	dig up, unearth 76
aus|halten (tr. & intr.)	endure 79
aus|hängen (tr. & intr.)	display 15, 85
aus|höhlen (tr.)	hollow out 15
aus|kennen (auf/in+dat.)	know a lot about 18
(refl.)	
aus|kommen (intr.+s.)	get by, manage 58
aus|lassen (tr.)	omit, leave out 10, 79
aus|leihen (tr.)	lend, borrow 28
aus|liegen (intr.)	be displayed 61
aus|löschen (tr.)	extinguish 15
aus|lösen (tr.)	trigger/set off 15
aus|machen (tr.)	turn out/off 15
es macht nichts aus	*it does not matter*
aus|nehmen (tr.)	make an exception of 54
aus|packen (tr. & intr.)	unpack 15
aus|pressen (tr.)	squeeze out 15
aus|probieren (tr.)	try out 13, 15
aus|radieren (tr.)	erase, rub out 13, 15
aus|räumen (tr.)	clear out 15

VERB INDEX

aus|richten (tr.)	line up, organize 12, 15
er richtet mir aus, dass ...	*he sends me a message that ...*
aus|rufen (tr.)	call out 82
aus|ruhen (tr. & refl.)	rest 15
aus|rutschen (intr.+s.)	skid 15
aus|rücken (tr. & intr.+s.)	move out 12, 15
aus|rüsten (tr.)	equip, arm 12, 15
aus|schalten (tr.)	switch off 12, 15
aus|scheiden (tr.)	eliminate 28
er scheidet aus (intr.+s.)	*he retires/drops out*
aus|schlafen (intr.+s./h. & refl.)	have a good sleep 79
aus|schließen (tr.)	bar, exclude 41
aus|schlüpfen (intr.+s.)	hatch out 15
aus|schneiden (tr.)	cut out 29, 31
aus|schreiben (tr.)	write out 28
aus|schütten (tr.)	pour out, empty 12, 15
aus|sehen (wie) (intr.)	look (like) 72
es sieht nach Regen aus	*it looks like rain*
aus sein (intr.+s.)	be out 1
äußern (tr.)	express 11
er äußert sich dazu (refl.)	*he comments on it*
aus|setzen (tr.)	abandon 15
der Motor setzt aus (intr.)	*the engine fails*
aus|spannen (tr. & intr.)	spread out, relax 15
aus|sprechen (tr.)	speak out, pronounce 51
aus|statten (tr.)	equip, fit out 12, 15
aus|stehen (tr. & intr.)	endure, stand 91
*aus|steigen (intr.+s.)	get down 28
er steigt aus	*he drops out*
aus|stellen (tr. & intr.)	display, exhibit 15
aus|sterben (intr.+s.)	to become extinct 51
aus|strahlen (tr.)	radiate, emit 15
aus|strecken (tr. & intr.)	extend, stretch 15
aus|suchen (tr.)	choose, pick 15
aus|tauschen (tr.)	exchange 15
aus|treten (intr.+s.)	come/go out 65
er tritt (die Schuhe) aus (tr.)	*he wears out (his shoes)*
aus|trinken (tr.)	drink up 44
aus|trocknen (tr. & intr.+s.)	dry out 12, 15
aus|üben (tr.)	practice 15
aus|wählen (tr.)	select 15
aus|wandern (intr.+s.)	emigrate 15
aus|waschen (tr.)	wash out, erode 76
aus|weichen (dat.) (intr.+s.)	avoid 31
aus|werten (tr.)	evaluate 12, 15

234

aus|wischen (tr.)	wipe off 15
aus|ziehen (tr.)	take off 33, 35
sie zieht sich aus (refl.)	*she gets undressed*
sie zieht aus (intr.+s.)	*she moves out*
automatisieren (tr.)	automate 13

B

backen (tr. & intr.)	bake, cook 73
baden (tr. & refl.)	take a bath, bathe 12, 15
bannen (tr.)	bewitch, charm 11
basieren (auf+acc.) (tr.)	base (on) 13
es basiert auf+dat ...	*it is based on ...*
basteln (tr.)	make 11
er bastelt gern (intr.)	*he likes doing handicrafts*
bauen (tr. & intr.)	build, construct 11
beabsichtigen (tr.)	intend 14
beachten (tr.)	observe, keep to 12, 14
beantragen (tr.)	apply for 14
beantworten (tr.)	answer 12, 14
bearbeiten (tr.)	arrange, adapt, edit 12, 14
beaufsichtigen (tr.)	supervise 14
beauftragen (tr.)	commission, appoint 14
bebauen (tr.)	build on (land) 14
er bebaut das Land	*he cultivates the land*
beben (intr.)	shake, quiver 11
bedanken (refl.)	say thank you 14
bedauern (tr.)	regret, pity 14
bedecken (tr.)	cover 14
bedenken (tr. & refl.)	think, consider 23
bedeuten (tr.)	mean 12, 14
bedienen (tr.)	serve, wait on 14
er bedient (die Maschine)	*he operates (the machine)*
ich bediene mich (refl.)	*I help myself*
bedrohen (tr.)	threaten 14
bedrücken (tr.)	depress 14
beeilen (refl.)	hurry up, make haste 14
beeindrucken (tr.)	impress 14
beeinflussen (tr.)	influence 14
beeinträchtigen (tr.)	spoil 14
beenden (tr.)	finish, end 12, 14
beerdigen (tr.)	bury 14
befassen (mit) (refl.)	deal with 14
befehlen (dat.) (intr.)	order, tell 49, 50
befestigen (tr.)	fasten, make firm 14
befeuchten (tr.)	moisten, dampen 12, 14

befinden (refl.)	be located 46
beflecken (tr.)	stain 14
befördern (tr.)	transport 14
er befördert sie	*he promotes her*
befragen (tr.)	consult, question 14
befreien (tr.)	free, release 14
befreunden (tr.)	befriend 12, 14
sie befreundet sich mit ... (refl.)	*she makes friends with ...*
befriedigen (tr.)	satisfy 14
befürchten (tr.)	fear 12, 14
begeben (refl.)	make one's way 60
begegnen (dat.) (intr.+s.)	meet, confront 12, 14
***begehen** (tr.)	commit 87
begehren (tr.)	desire 14
begeistern (tr.)	inspire 14
er begeistert sich für+acc ... (refl.)	*he is enthusiastic about ...*
begießen (tr.)	water 40
beginnen (mit) (tr. & intr.)	begin (on) 50
begleiten (tr.)	accompany 12, 14
beglückwünschen (dat.) (tr.)	congratulate 14
begnügen (mit) (refl.)	be content with 14
begraben (tr.)	bury so., 75
begreifen (tr. & intr.)	realize 30
begrenzen (tr.)	border 14
begründen (tr.)	give reasons (for) 12, 14
begrüßen (tr.)	greet 14
begünstigen (tr.)	favor 14
***behalten** (tr.)	keep, retain 79
behandeln (tr.)	treat 14
behaupten (tr.)	maintain 12, 14
er behauptet, dass ...	*he claims that ...*
sie behauptet sich (refl.)	*she holds her own*
behelfen (refl.)	manage, cope 50
beherrschen (tr.)	rule, control 14
behindern (tr.)	hinder 14
bei|bringen (tr.)	tell, teach 24
beichten (tr. & intr.)	confess 12
bei|fügen (dat.) (tr.)	enclose (with) 15
bei|heften (tr.)	attach 12, 15
bei|messen (tr.)	attach value to 69
beißen (tr. & intr.)	bite 29
bei|stehen (dat.) (intr.)	help 91
bei|stimmen (dat.) (intr.)	agree (with) 15

bei|tragen (zu) (tr. & intr.)	contribute (to) 76
bei|treten (dat.) (intr.+s.)	join 65
bei|wohnen (dat.) (intr.)	attend 15
bejahen (tr. & intr.)	affirm, say yes 14
bekannt geben (tr.)	disclose 61
bekennen (tr.)	confess 17
beklagen (tr.)	lament, regret 14
sie beklagt sich	(refl.) *she complains about...*
über+acc ...	
*bekommen (tr.)	get, receive 57
beladen (tr.)	load 75
belagern (tr.)	besiege 14
belasten (tr.)	debit, weigh down 12, 14
belästigen (tr.)	bother, molest 14
belaufen (auf+acc.) (refl.)	amount (to) 81
beleben (tr.)	liven up, revive 14
belegen (tr.)	occupy, cover 14
belehren (tr.)	teach 14
beleidigen (tr.)	offend, insult 14
beleuchten (tr.)	illuminate, light up 12, 14
bellen (intr.)	bark 11
belohnen (tr.)	reward 14
belustigen (tr.)	amuse 14
bemerken (tr.)	remark, note 14
bemühen (um) (refl.)	take trouble (with) 14
benachrichtigen (tr.)	inform 14
benachteiligen (tr.)	handicap 14
*benehmen (refl.)	behave 53
beneiden (tr.)	envy 12, 14
benoten (tr.)	grade 12, 14
benötigen (tr.)	need, require 14
benutzen (tr.)	use 14
benützen (tr.)	use 14
beobachten (tr.)	observe 12, 14
bepflanzen (tr.)	plant 14
beraten (tr.)	advize 78
sie berät sich mit mir (refl.)	*she consults with me*
berauben (tr.)	rob 14
berechnen (tr.)	compute, calculate 12, 14
berechtigen (tr.)	authorize, entitle 14
bereichern (tr.)	enrich 14
bereuen (tr. & intr.)	regret 14
bergen (tr.)	rescue, salvage 48
berichten (über+acc.)(tr. & intr.)	report (on), detail 12, 14
berichtigen (tr.)	correct 14

er besteht auf+dat	*he insists on ...*
sie besteht die Prüfung	*she passes*
(tr.)	*the examination*
bestehlen (tr.)	rob 49, 50
besteigen (tr.)	climb, mount 27
bestellen (tr. & intr.)	order, book 14
besteuern (tr.)	tax 14
bestimmen (tr. & intr.)	determine, decide 14
bestrafen (tr.)	punish 14
bestreichen (tr.)	spread 30
bestreiten (tr.)	dispute 30
bestürzen (tr.)	dismay 14
besuchen (tr.)	visit, attend 14
betätigen (tr.)	operate, work 14
betäuben (tr.)	stupefy, drug 14
beten (intr.)	pray 12
betonen (tr.)	stress, emphasize 14
betonieren (tr.)	pave, concrete over 13
betragen (intr.)	amount to 75
sie beträgt sich gut (refl.)	*she behaves well*
betreffen (tr.)	concern, affect 56, 57
*betreten (tr.)	enter 64
betrinken (refl.)	get drunk 43
betrüben (tr.)	sadden 14
betrügen (tr.)	deceive, cheat 37
betteln (intr.)	beg 11
beugen (tr. & refl.)	bend, stoop 11
beunruhigen (tr. & refl.)	worry 14
beurlauben (tr.)	grant leave 14
beurteilen (tr.)	judge, assess 14
bevorzugen (tr.)	favor 14
bewachen (tr.)	guard 14
bewaffnen (tr.)	arm 12, 14
bewahren (tr.)	preserve, store 14
bewähren (refl.)	prove one's worth 14
bewältigen (tr.)	manage 14
bewässern (tr.)	irrigate 14
bewegen (tr. & refl.)	move 14, 37
beweisen (tr.)	prove, show 27
bewerben (um) (refl.)	apply (for) 50
bewerten (tr.)	evaluate 12, 14
bewilligen (tr.)	authorize 14
bewohnen (tr.)	live in 14
bewölken (refl.)	cloud over 14
bewundern (tr.)	admire 14
bezahlen (tr. & intr.)	pay 14

bezaubern (tr.)	charm 14
bezeichnen (tr.)	mark, indicate 12, 14
bezeugen (tr.)	testify to 14
beziehen (tr.)	cover 33, 34
es bezieht sich auf+	*it refers to ...*
acc ... (refl.)	
bezweifeln (tr.)	doubt 14
***biegen** (tr. & refl.)	bend, curve 32
er biegt um ... (intr.+s.)	*he turns around ...*
bieten (tr. & intr.)	offer, bid 32
bilden (tr.)	form, constitute 12
billigen (tr.)	approve 11
***binden** (tr. & intr.)	tie, bind, bond 45
***bitten** (um) (tr. & intr.)	ask (for), request 63
blasen (tr. & intr.)	blow 77
bleiben (intr.+s.)	remain 26
bleichen (tr. & intr.)	bleach 29
blenden (tr. & intr.)	blind, dazzle 12
blicken (auf+acc.) (intr.)	look (at) 11
blinken (tr. & intr.)	flash, gleam 11
blinzeln (intr.)	wink, blink 11
blitzen (intr.)	flash 11
blöken (intr.)	bleat 11
bluffen (tr. & intr.)	bluff 11
bluten (intr.)	bleed 12
blühen (intr.)	flower, flourish 11
bohren (tr. & intr.)	bore, drill 11
bombardieren (tr.)	bomb 13
borgen (tr. & intr.)	borrow, lend 11
boxen (tr. & intr.)	box 11
boykottieren (tr.)	boycott 13
brach|liegen (intr.)	lie fallow 61
braten (tr. & intr.)	fry, roast 69
brauchen (tr.)	need, take 11
brauen (tr. & intr.)	brew 11
bräunen (tr.)	brown 11
sie bräunt sich (refl.)	*she tans*
brechen (tr. & intr.)	break, beat 48
breiten (tr. & refl.)	stretch 12
bremsen (tr. & intr.)	brake 11
brennen (tr. & intr.)	burn 16
bringen (tr.)	bring 22
er bringt mich um etwas	*he takes something away from me*
bröckeln (tr. & intr.)	crumble 11
brummen (tr. & intr.)	growl, hum, buzz 11

	brüllen (tr. & intr.)	roar, blare, bellow 11
	buchen (tr.)	book 11
	buchstabieren (tr.)	spell 13
	bummeln (intr.+s.)	stroll, dawdle 11
	bücken (refl.)	bend 11
	büffeln (tr. & intr.)	cram (study too much) 11
	bügeln (tr. & intr.)	iron 11
	bürgen (für) (intr.)	guarantee 11
	bürsten (tr.)	brush 12
C	**charakterisieren** (tr.)	characterize 13
	chartern (tr.)	charter 11
D	**dämmern** (impers.)	dawn 11
	dampfen (intr.)	steam 11
	dämpfen (tr.)	muffle, steam 11
	danken (dat.) (intr.)	thank 11
	dar|stellen (tr.)	represent, depict 15
	dauern (intr.)	last, take 11
	davon|kommen (intr.+s.)	escape, get away 58
	davon|laufen (intr.+s.)	run away 82
	dazu|rechnen (tr.)	add on 12, 15
	debattieren (tr. & intr.)	debate 13
	decken (tr.)	cover 11
	ich decke den Tisch	*I set the table*
	definieren (tr.)	define 13
	dehnen (tr. & refl.)	stretch 11
	dekodieren (tr.)	decode 13
	demonstrieren (tr. & intr.)	demonstrate 13
	demütigen (tr.)	humiliate 11
	*denken (tr. & intr.)	think 22
	ich denke an ihn (intr.)	*I think of him*
	was denken Sie von ihm?	*what is your opinion of him?*
	ich denke mir (dat. refl.) (tr.)	*I imagine*
	deponieren (tr.)	deposit 13
	deprimieren (tr.)	depress 13
	desinfizieren (tr.)	disinfect 13
	destillieren (tr.)	distill 13
	deuten (auf+acc.) (tr. & intr.)	point (to) 12
	er deutet den Text	*he interprets the text*
	diagnostizieren (tr.)	diagnose 13
	dienen (dat.) (intr.)	serve 11

VERB INDEX

es dient als/zu	*it serves as/for*
differenzieren (tr. & intr.)	differentiate 13
die Klassen sind differenziert	*the classes are streamed*
diktieren (tr.)	dictate 13
dirigieren (tr.)	conduct 13
diskutieren (über+acc.) (tr. & intr.)	discuss 13
disqualifizieren (tr.)	disqualify 13
disziplinieren (tr.)	discipline 13
dividieren (durch) (tr. & intr.)	divide (by) 13
dolmetschen (tr. & intr.)	interpret 11
donnern (intr.)	rumble 11
es donnert (impers.)	*it thunders*
dopen (tr.)	dope 11
dösen (intr.)	doze 11
dosieren (tr.)	dose 13
drängeln (tr. & intr.)	jostle 11
drängen (tr. & intr.)	push, urge 11
sie drängen sich (refl.)	*they crowd*
drehen (tr. & intr.)	turn 11
er dreht den Film	*he is shooting the film*
dreschen (tr. & intr.)	thresh 39
dringen (intr.+s.)	penetrate 42
drohen (dat.) (intr.)	threaten 11
dröhnen (tr. & intr.)	buzz 11
drucken (tr. & intr.)	print 11
drücken (tr. & intr.)	press, push 11
er drückt sich (refl.)	*he squeezes/skives off*
ducken (tr. & intr.)	duck, cower 11
er duckt sich (refl.)	*he crouches*
duften (nach) (intr.)	smell pleasantly (of) 12
dulden (tr. & intr.)	tolerate, suffer 11
dumpen (tr.)	dump 11
dünsten (tr.)	steam 12
durch|arbeiten (tr. & intr.)	work through 12, 15
durch|blättern (tr.)	leaf through 15
durch|brennen (tr. & intr.+s.)	blow (a fuse), fuse 18
***durch|dringen** (durch)(intr.+s.)	penetrate 44
durchdringen (tr.)	pervade 43
durcheinander bringen (tr.)	confuse, disorganize 24
durch|fallen (intr.+s.)	fail 79
er fällt durch	*he fails (the examination)*
durch|führen (tr.)	carry out 15
durch|geben (tr.)	radio 61
durch|gehen (tr. & intr.+s.)	go through 88

242

durch|halten (tr. & intr.)	hold out 79
durch|lassen (tr.)	let in, leak 10, 79
durch|lesen (tr.)	read through 72
durchleuchten (tr.)	x-ray 12, 14
durchlöchern (tr.)	riddle with 14
durch|machen (tr.)	undergo, experience 15
durchnässen (tr.)	soak 14
durchqueren (tr.)	cross 14
durch|sagen (tr.)	announce 15
durchschauen (tr.)	catch, catch out 14
durch|sehen (tr. & intr.)	look through, check over 72
durch|setzen (tr.)	carry through 15
sie setzt sich durch (refl.)	*she asserts herself*
durchstechen (tr. & intr.)	pierce 50
durchsuchen (tr.)	search through 14
durch|wählen (intr.)	dial direct 15
*dürfen (intr.)	be allowed, may 8
duschen (intr. & refl.)	shower 11
duzen (tr.)	address as "du" 11

E	**ebnen** (tr.)	flatten 12
	eignen (für/zu) (tr. & refl.)	be suitable (for) 12
	eilen (intr.)	rush, hurry 11
	ein|äschern (tr.)	cremate 15
	ein|atmen (tr. & intr.)	breathe in, inhale 12, 15
	ein|bauen (tr.)	build in, install 15
	ein|berufen (tr.)	call up 14, 15
	ein|biegen (in+acc.) (tr. & intr.+s.)	bend in, turn in 35
	ein|bilden (dat. refl.) (tr.)	imagine 12, 15
	ein|blenden (tr.)	fade in 12, 15
	ein|brechen (bei/in+acc./dat.) (intr.+s.)	burglarize, burgle, break into 51
	ein|dämmen (tr.)	dam 15
	ein|ebnen (tr.)	level 12, 15
	ein|fahren (intr.+s.)	come in, drive in 76
	ein|fallen (dat.) (intr.+s.)	occur (to), to have an idea 79
	ein|färben (tr.)	color in 15
	ein|frieren (tr. & intr.+s.)	freeze, deep-freeze 35
	ein|fügen (tr.)	insert 15
	ein|führen (tr.)	introduce, import 15
	ein|gehen (intr.+s.)	die (of a plant) 88
	ein|gravieren (tr.)	engrave 13, 15
	ein|hämmern (tr.)	hammer in 15

ein|setzen (tr.)	put in 15
sie setzt sich dafür ein (refl.)	*she is committed to it*
ein|sperren (tr.)	imprison 15
ein|springen (für) (intr.+s.)	stand in (for) 44
ein|steigen (intr.+s.)	get in/on, board 28
ein|stellen (tr.)	appoint, adjust 15
wir stellen die Arbeit ein	*we stop the work*
er stellt sich auf+acc ... ein (refl.)	*he adapts to ...*
ein|stufen (tr.)	grade, classify 15
ein|stürzen (intr.+s.)	collapse 15
ein|teilen (tr.)	divide up 15
ein|tragen (tr.)	register 76
sie trägt sich ein (refl.)	*she enters her name*
ein|treffen (intr.+s.)	arrive 56, 58
ein|treten (intr.+s.)	enter 65
ein|wandern (intr.+s.)	immigrate 15
ein|weihen (tr.)	initiate 15
ein|wenden (tr.)	object 21
ein|werfen (tr.)	drop off mail 51
ein|willigen (in+acc.) (intr.)	consent (to) 15
ein|zahlen (tr.)	pay in, bank 15
ein|ziehen (tr.)	draft, enlist 33, 35
er zieht ein (intr.+s.)	*he moves in (to a house)*
ekeln (tr.)	disgust 11
es ekelt mich vor+dat ... (impers.)	*I find ... disgusting*
elektrifizieren (tr.)	electrify 13
***empfangen** (tr. & intr.)	receive 84
sie empfängt	*she conceives*
empfehlen (tr.)	recommend 49, 50
empfinden (tr.)	feel 46
empören (tr.)	outrage 14
sie empört sich über+acc ... (refl.)	*she gets angry about ...*
emulgieren (tr. & intr.)	emulsify 13
enden (intr.)	conclude, end 12
engagieren (tr.)	involve 13
er engagiert sich (refl.)	*he gets involved*
entbehren (tr.) (& gen. intr.)	spare, lack 14
entblößen (tr.)	bare 14
entdecken (tr.)	discover, reveal 14
enteisen (tr.)	de-ice 14
enterben (tr.)	disinherit 14
entfernen (tr.)	remove, go away 14

entwickeln (tr. & refl.)	develop, evolve 14
entwirren (tr.)	disentangle 14
entzücken (tr.)	delight 14
entzünden (tr.)	ignite 12, 14
es entzündet sich (refl.)	*it gets inflamed*
erben (tr. & intr.)	inherit 11
erblassen (intr.+s.)	turn pale 14
erblicken (tr.)	catch sight of 14
erbrechen (refl.)	to throw up 50
ereignen (refl.)	occur, happen 12, 14
erfahren (tr.)	find out, hear 75
erfassen (tr.)	seize, comprehend 14
erfinden (tr.)	invent, make up 46
erfreuen (tr.)	please, delight 14
sie erfreut sich	*she enjoys ...*
an+dat ... (refl.)	
erfrischen (tr.)	refresh 14
erfüllen (tr.)	fulfill 14
es erfüllt sich (refl.)	*it is fulfilled*
ergänzen (tr.)	complete, amend 14
ergeben (tr.)	produce, result in 60
er ergibt sich (refl.)	*he surrenders*
ergrauen (intr.+s.)	go gray 14
ergreifen (tr.)	grasp, seize 30
erhalten (tr.)	receive, preserve 78
erheben (tr.)	raise 37
er erhebt sich (refl.)	*he rises up*
erhitzen (refl.)	heat up 14
erhöhen (tr. & refl.)	raise, increase 14
erholen (von) (refl.)	get well, recover (from) 14
erinnern (an+acc.) (tr.)	remind (of) 14
sie erinnert sich an+acc	*she remembers sth.*
etw. (refl.)	
erkälten (refl.)	catch a cold 12, 14
***erkennen** (tr.) (an+dat.)	recognize (from) 17
erklären (tr. & intr.)	explain, declare 14
erklimmen (tr.)	climb 40
erkranken (intr.+s.)	fall ill 14
erkundigen (nach) (refl.)	inquire, ask (about) 14
erlassen (tr.)	pass (law) 10, 78
ich erlasse ihm seine	*I release him from his debts*
Schulden	
erlauben (tr.)	allow 14
erleben (tr.)	experience 14
erledigen (tr.)	deal with, dispose of 14
erleichtern (tr.)	make easier, lighten 14

erleuchten (tr.)	illuminate 12, 14
erlöschen (intr.+s.)	die out 40
erlösen (tr.)	save, deliver 14
ermöglichen (tr.)	make possible 14
ermorden (tr.)	murder 12, 14
ermuntern (tr.)	encourage 14
ermutigen (tr.)	encourage 14
ermüden (tr. & intr.+s.)	tire 12, 14
ernähren (tr. & refl.)	feed, eat 14
ernennen (zu) (tr.)	appoint (to) 17
erneuern (tr.)	renew 14
erniedrigen (tr.)	humiliate 14
ernten (tr.)	harvest 12
erobern (tr.)	conquer 14
eröffnen (tr. & refl.)	open 12, 14
erpressen (tr.)	extort 14
erraten (tr.)	guess 78
erregen (tr.)	excite 14
er erregt sich über+acc ... (refl.)	*he gets worked up about ...*
erreichen (tr.)	reach 14
erröten (intr.+s.)	blush 12, 14
***erscheinen** (intr.+s.)	appear 27
erschießen (tr.)	shoot dead 40
erschlagen (tr.)	murder 75
erschließen (tr.)	open up 40
erschöpfen (tr.)	exhaust, tire 14
erschrecken (tr.)	frighten 14
erschrecken (intr.+s.)	be frightened 50
erschüttern (tr.)	shake, shatter 14
ersetzen (tr.)	replace 14
ersparen (tr.)	save 14
erstarren (intr.+s.)	solidify 14
erstaunen (tr. & intr.)	amaze 14
ersticken (tr. & intr.+s.)	suffocate 14
erstrecken (refl.)	extend 14
ertappen (tr.)	catch/catch out 14
erteilen (tr.)	grant 14
ertönen (intr.+s.)	ring out 14
***ertragen** (tr.)	bear 75
ertränken (tr.)	drown 14
ertrinken (intr.+s.)	drown 43
***erwägen** (tr.)	weigh/weigh up 37
erwähnen (tr.)	mention 14
erwarten (tr.)	expect 12, 14
erwecken (tr.)	arouse 14

erweitern (tr. & refl.)	expand 14
erwerben (tr.)	acquire 50
erwidern (auf+acc.) (intr.)	reply (to) 14
erwischen (tr.)	catch 14
erzählen (tr. & intr.)	tell 14
erzeugen (tr.)	produce, generate 14
erziehen (tr.)	bring up 33, 34
erzielen (tr.)	achieve, score 14
*****essen** (tr. & intr.)	eat 66
existieren (intr.)	exist 13
experimentieren (intr.)	experiment 13
explodieren (intr.+s.)	explode 13
exportieren (tr. & intr.)	export 13

F

*****fahren** (tr. & intr.+s.)	drive, ride, go 73
fallen (intr.+s.)	fall 77
fällen (tr.)	fell 11
sie fällt das Urteil	*she gives judgment*
fallen lassen (tr.)	drop 10, 79
fälschen (tr.)	forge, fake 11
falten (tr.)	fold 12
fangen (tr. & intr.)	capture, catch 83
färben (tr.)	color 11
fassen (tr. & intr.)	grasp 11
fasten (intr.)	fast 12
faulen (intr.+s.)	rot 11
faxen (tr.)	fax 11
fechten (intr.)	fence 39
fegen (tr. & intr.)	sweep 11
fehlen (intr.)	be lacking 11
es fehlt mir an+dat ...	*I lack ...*
(impers.+dat.)	
feiern (tr. & intr.)	celebrate 11
feilen (tr. & intr.)	file 11
feilschen (intr.)	haggle 11
fern halten (tr. & refl.)	keep away 79
fern|sehen (intr.)	watch TV 72
fertig machen (tr.)	finish 15
fertig kriegen (tr.)	get done 15
fesseln (tr.)	tie, grip 11
fest|binden (tr.)	tie up 47
fest|halten (tr. & intr.)	grasp, hold on 79
er hält sich an+dat ...	*he holds on to ...*
fest (refl.)	
fest|klammern (tr.)	fix 15

er klammert sich an+dat ...	*he clings to ...*
fest (refl.)	
fest|legen (tr.)	determine, fix 15
fest|machen (tr.)	fasten 15
fest|nehmen (tr.)	arrest 54
fest|setzen (tr.)	arrange, fix 15
fest|stehen (intr.)	be certain 91
fest|stellen (tr.)	find out, establish 15
feuern (tr. & intr.)	fire, fling 11
filtern (tr. & intr.)	filter 11
finanzieren (tr.)	finance 13
finden (tr. & intr.)	find 45
fischen (tr. & intr.)	fish 11
flackern (intr.)	flicker 11
flattern (intr.)	flutter 11
flechten (tr.)	twine 39
flehen (um) (intr.)	plead (for) 11
flicken (tr.)	mend, darn 11
fliegen (tr. & intr.+s.)	fly 32
fliehen (intr.+s.)	flee 32
fließen (intr.+s.)	flow 39
flimmern (intr.)	flicker 11
flirten (intr.)	flirt 12
flitzen (intr.+s.)	dart out 11
florieren (intr.)	flourish 13
fluchen (intr.)	curse 11
flüchten (intr.+s.)	escape, flee 12
flüstern (tr. & intr.)	whisper 11
folgen (dat.) (intr.+s.)	follow 11
es folgt auf+acc ...	*it comes after ...*
folgern (auf +acc.) (aus)	come after,
(tr. & intr.)	conclude (from) 11
fordern (tr. & intr.)	ask for, demand 11
fördern (tr.)	support 11
formatieren (tr. & intr.)	format 13
formen (tr.)	form, shape 11
forschen (nach) (intr.)	search (for) 11
ich forsche (tr.)	*I research (into) ...*
über+acc ...	
fort|bilden (tr. & refl.)	train 12, 15
fort|fahren (intr.+s.)	go away 76
er fährt mit ... fort	*he continues with ...*
fort|führen (tr. & intr.)	lead away 15
sie führt den Plan fort	*she continues the plan*
fort|setzen (tr.)	continue 15
fotografieren (tr. & intr.)	photograph 13

fotokopieren (tr.)	photocopy 13
fragen (nach) (tr. & intr.)	ask (about) 11
frankieren (tr.)	stamp, frank 13
frei|sprechen (tr.)	acquit 51
frei|lassen (tr.)	free, release 10, 79
frequentieren (tr.)	frequent 13
fressen (tr. & intr.)	eat (of animals), guzzle 66
freuen (tr.)	please 11
es freut mich (impers.)	*I am glad*
ich freue mich auf+acc ... (refl.)	*I look forward to ...*
ich freue mich über+acc ...	*I am pleased about ...*
frieren (intr.+s.)	freeze 32
mich friert (impers.)	*I am cold*
frönen (dat.) (intr.)	be a slave to 11
frühstücken (intr.)	have breakfast 11
fühlen (tr. & intr.)	feel 11
er fühlt sich (krank) (refl.)	*he feels (ill)*
führen (tr. & intr.)	take, lead 11
füllen (tr.)	fill 11
funkeln (intr.)	sparkle 11
funken (tr. & intr.)	radio 11
funktionieren (intr.)	work, function 13
fürchten (tr.)	fear 12
er fürchtet sich vor+dat ... (refl.)	*he is afraid of ...*
fusionieren (tr. & intr.)	merge, amalgamate 13
füttern (tr.)	feed 11

G

gaffen (intr.)	gape 11
gähnen (intr.)	yawn 11
garantieren (tr. & intr.)	guarantee 13
gären (intr+s./h.)	ferment 36
gebären (tr. & intr.)	give birth (to) 49, 50
***geben** (tr.)	give 59
es gibt (impers.)(+acc.) ...	*there is/are ...*
gebrauchen (tr.)	use 14
gedeihen (intr.+s.)	flourish 27
gedenken (gen.) (intr.)	commemorate 23
gedulden (refl.)	be patient 12, 14
gefallen (dat.) (intr.)	please 78
gefangen nehmen (tr.)	take prisoner 54
gegenüber|stehen (dat.) (intr.)	be opposite, face 91
gegenüber|stellen (dat.) (refl.) (tr.)	confront 15

er stellt es (dat.) ... *gegenüber*	*he compares it (with)* ...
*gehen (intr.+s.)	go 86
es geht um ...	*it is a matter of* ...
gehorchen (dat.) (intr.)	obey 14
gehören (dat.) (intr.)	belong to 14
es gehört zu ...	*it belongs to/is part of* ...
gelingen (dat.) (impers.+s.)	succeed 43
es gelingt ihm, ... (zu tun)	*he succeeds in (doing)* ...
gelten (tr. & intr.)	be worth 48
es gilt mir	*it is meant for me*
das gilt für ihn	*that is true of him*
es gilt (zu tun) ...	*the main thing is (to do)* ...
*genießen (tr.)	enjoy 40
genügen (dat.) (intr.)	be enough 14
geraten (in+acc) (an) (intr.+s.)	get (to/into) 79
es gerät ihm gut (intr.+s.)	*he succeeds well with it*
geschehen (mit) (impers.+s.)	happen (to) 71
gestalten (tr.)	form 12, 14
gestatten (tr. & intr.)	permit, allow 12, 14
gestehen (tr. & intr.)	confess 90
gewähren (tr.)	grant 14
*gewinnen (tr. & intr.)	win, obtain 50
gewöhnen (an+acc.) (tr.)	accustom 14
er gewöhnt sich an+acc ... (refl.)	*he gets used to* ...
gießen (tr.)	cast, pour 39
es gießt (impers.)	*it pours (with) rain*
glänzen (intr.)	shine 11
glatt streichen (tr.)	smooth 31
glauben (dat.) (tr. & intr.)	believe (so.) 11
er glaubt an+acc	*he believes in* ...
gleich bleiben (dat. refl.+s.)	remain unchanged 28
gleichen (dat.) (intr.)	resemble 29
gleich|kommen (dat.) (intr.+s.)	equal, match 58
gleich|sehen (dat.) (intr.)	resemble 72
gleiten (intr.+s.)	glide, slide 29
gliedern (tr.)	structure 11
es gliedert sich in+acc ... (refl.)	*it divides into* ...
glimmen (intr.)	glow 39
glühen (intr.)	blaze, glow 11
gönnen (tr.)	not to grudge 11
graben (tr. & intr.)	dig, mine 73
gratulieren (dat.) (intr.)	congratulate 13
grauen (intr.)	dawn 11

mir graut vor ihm (impers.)	*I dread him*
greifen (nach) (tr. & intr.)	grasp, reach (for) 29
grenzen (intr.)	border 11
grillen (tr. & intr.)	grill 11
grinsen (intr.)	grin 11
groß|ziehen (tr.)	bring up, rear 33,35
grunzen (tr. & intr.)	grunt 11
gründen (tr.)	found 12
es gründet sich auf+dat ... (refl.)	*it is based on*
grüßen (tr. & intr.)	greet 11
gucken (intr.)	look, peep 11
gut|schreiben (dat.) (tr.)	credit (to) 28
gut tun (dat.) (intr.)	benefit 92, 91

H

*haben (tr.)	have 2
ich habe Angst vor+dat ...	*I am afraid of ...*
hacken (tr. & intr.)	hack, chop 11
haften (für) (intr.)	be liable (for) 12
haken (tr. & intr.)	hook 11
halten (tr.)	hold 77
er hält mich für einen Idioten	*he takes me for an idiot*
er hält (intr.)	*he stops*
Halt machen (intr.)	stop 15
hämmern (tr. & intr.)	hammer, beat 11
hamstern (tr. & intr.)	hoard 11
handeln (mit) (intr.)	trade (in) 11
er handelt (intr.)	*he acts*
es handelt sich um ... (refl.)	*it concerns/is a matter of ...*
handhaben (tr.)	handle 11
*hängen (tr. intr. & refl.)	hang, suspend 83
harken (tr. & intr.)	rake 11
harmonieren (intr.)	blend 13
harmonisieren (tr.)	harmonize 13
hassen (tr. & intr.)	hate, detest 11
hauen (tr. & intr.)	hew, bash, beat 80
häufen (tr. & refl.)	heap, pile up 11
*heben (tr.)	lift, raise 36
heften (tr.)	staple, fix 12
hegen (tr.)	cherish 11
heilen (tr. & intr.)	heal 11
heim|kehren (intr.+s.)	return home 15
heim|suchen (tr.)	afflict 15
heim|zahlen (tr.)	pay back 15

heiraten (tr.)	marry 12
sie heiraten (intr. & refl.)	*they get married*
heißen (intr.)	be called 80
das heißt auf Deutsch	*in German that means*
heizen (tr. & intr.)	heat 11
helfen (dat.) (bei) (intr.)	help, aid (with) 48
hemmen (tr.)	hamper, inhibit 11
herab|lassen (tr.)	lower 10, 79
er lässt sich herab, ... (zu tun) (refl.)	*he deigns (to do) ...*
herab|setzen (tr.)	lower, reduce 15
heran|treten (intr.+s.)	approach 65
heraus|bekommen (tr.)	get out, work out 58
heraus|bringen (tr.)	bring out 24
***heraus|finden** (tr.)	find out, detect 47
heraus|fordern (tr.)	challenge 15
heraus|geben (tr.)	issue, publish 61
heraus|stellen (tr.)	put out 15
es stellt sich heraus, dass ... (refl.)	*it turns out that ...*
heraus|ziehen (tr.)	pull out, extract 33, 35
herbei|führen (tr.)	bring about 15
herbei|schaffen (tr.)	get hold of 15
herein|kommen (intr.+s.)	enter, come in 58
herein|lassen (tr.)	admit, let in 10
herein|schauen (intr.)	drop in, drop by 15
herein|stürzen (intr.+s.)	burst in 15
her|geben (tr.)	hand over 61
her|kommen (intr.+s.)	come (here) 58
hinterher|rennen (intr.+s.)	chase 18
herrschen (intr.)	rule, reign 11
her|stellen (tr.)	produce, manufacture 15
herüber|kommen (intr.+s.)	come across 58
herum|reichen (tr.)	hand around 15
herum|schlendern (intr.+s.)	putter around/potter about 15
herum|spielen (intr.)	play around, mess about 15
herum|treiben (refl.)	hang around 28
herum|trödeln (intr.)	idle about 15
***herunter|fallen** (intr.+s.)	fall down 79
herunter|klappen (tr.)	let down 15
herunter|kommen (intr.+s.)	come down 58
hervor|brechen (intr.)	burst out 51
hervor|bringen (tr.)	produce 24
hervor|heben (tr.)	highlight 38
hervor|ragen (intr.)	jut out 15

hervor|rufen (tr.)	evoke 82
hervor|stehen (intr.+s.)	stick out; 91
hervor|treten (intr.+s.)	step forward 65
hetzen (tr.)	hound 11
er hetzt; er hetzt sich (intr. & refl.)	*he rushes*
heulen (intr.)	howl, cry 11
hinab|blicken (intr.)	look down 15
hinauf|fahren (intr.+s.)	go up (climb) 76
hinaus|blicken (intr.)	look out 15
hinaus|gehen (intr.+s.)	go out 88
hinaus|laufen (auf.+acc.) (intr.+s.)	amount (to) 82
hinaus|stehlen (intr.+s.)	steal out 49, 51
***hinaus|treten** (intr.+s.)	step out 65
hinaus|ziehen (tr.)	draw out 33, 35
hindern (tr. & intr.)	hinder 11
er hindert mich an+dat ...	*he keeps me from ...*
er hindert mich daran, ... zu tun	*he prevents me from doing ...*
hinein|gehen (intr.+s.)	go in 88
hin|fallen (intr.+s.)	fall down 79
hin|geben (tr.)	give up 61
hinken (intr.)	limp 11
hin|knien (intr. & refl.)	kneel down 15
hin|legen (tr.)	lay down 15
er legt sich hin (refl.)	*he lies down*
hin|reichen (tr.)	hand over 15
hin|richten (tr.)	execute 12, 15
hin|scheiden (intr.+s.)	pass away 28
hin|setzen (tr.)	set down 15
sie setzt sich hin (refl.)	*she sits down*
hin|stellen (intr.)	put down 15
sie stellt sich hin (refl.)	*she goes and stands (there)*
hinter|lassen (tr.)	bequeath, leave 10, 78
hinüber|gehen (intr.+s.)	cross over 88
hinunter|fallen (intr.+s.)	fall down 79
hinunter|gehen (intr.+s.)	go down, descend 88
hinweg|sehen (von) (intr.)	ignore 72
hin|weisen (auf+acc.) (intr.)	point (out) 28
er weist auf+acc ... hin	*he refers to ...*
hinzu|fügen (tr.)	add 15
hoch|heben (tr.)	hoist 38
hocken (intr. & refl.)	squat 11
hoffen (auf+acc.) (tr. & intr.)	hope (for) 11

holen (tr.)	fetch, get 11
horchen (auf+acc.) (intr.)	listen (to) 11
hören (tr. & intr.)	hear, listen 11
hungern (intr.)	starve 11
hupen (intr.)	hoot 11
hüpfen (intr.+s.)	hop 11
husten (intr.)	cough 12
hüten (tr.)	look after 12
sie hütet sich vor+dat ...	*she is on her guard against*
(refl.)	

I	**illustrieren** (tr.)	illustrate 13
	impfen (tr.)	innoculate 11
	imponieren (dat) (intr.)	impress 13
	importieren (tr.)	import 13
	infizieren (tr.)	infect 13
	informieren (über+acc.) (tr.)	inform 13
	sie informiert sich	*she finds out about ...*
	über+acc ... (refl.)	
	inhaftieren (tr.)	imprison 13
	innehalten (intr.)	pause 79
	inserieren (tr. & intr.)	advertise 13
	installieren (tr.)	install 13
	inszenieren (tr.)	stage 13
	integrieren (tr.)	integrate 13
	interessieren (tr.)	interest 13
	ich interessiere mich	*I am interested in ...*
	für ... (refl.)	
	interviewen (tr.)	interview 14
	intrigieren (intr.)	scheme 13
	investieren (tr. & intr.)	invest 13
	ionisieren (tr.)	ionize 13
	irren (intr. & refl.)	be mistaken 11
	er irrt sich	*he is wrong*
	irre|führen (tr)(intr.+s.)	mislead 15

J	**jagen** (tr. & intr.)	hunt, chase 11
	jammern (intr.)	moan, wail 11
	joggen (intr.)	jog 11
	jubeln (intr.)	rejoice 11
	jucken (tr. & intr.)	itch 11

K	**kalkulieren** (tr.)	calculate 13

kämmen (tr. & refl.)	comb 11
kämpfen (um) (tr. & intr.)	fight (for) 11
kapieren (intr.)	understand 13
kapitulieren (intr.)	capitulate 13
kaputt|gehen (intr.+s.)	break, bust 88
karikieren (tr.)	caricature 13
katalogisieren (tr.)	catalogue 13
kauen (tr. & intr.)	chew, gnaw 11
kauern (intr. & refl.)	cower 11
kaufen (tr. & intr.)	buy 11
kehren (tr. & refl.)	turn, return 11
*kennen (tr.)	know 16
kennen lernen (tr.)	get to know, meet 15
kennzeichnen (tr.)	mark, characterize 12, 15
kentern (intr.+s.)	capsize 11
keuchen (intr.)	gasp, pant 11
kichern (intr.)	giggle 11
kitzeln (tr. & intr.)	tickle 11
klagen (tr. & intr.)	moan, complain 11
klappen (tr.)	fold 11
es klappt (intr.)	*it's working out (well)*
klären (tr. & refl.)	clear up, clarify 11
klassifizieren (tr.)	classify 13
klatschen (tr. & intr.)	applaud, clap 11
klauen (tr. & intr.)	nick, steal 11
kleben (tr. & intr.)	stick, bond 11
kleiden (tr. & refl.)	dress, clothe 12
klettern (auf+acc.) (intr.+s.)	climb (up) 11
klingeln (intr.)	ring 11
klingen (intr.)	sound 42
klirren (intr.)	chink, rattle 11
klönen (intr.)	gossip 11
klopfen (tr. & intr.)	knock 11
knabbern (tr. & intr.)	nibble 11
knacken (tr. & intr.)	crack 11
knallen (tr. & intr.)	bang, explode 11
knarren (intr.)	creak 11
kneifen (tr. & intr.)	pinch 29
knien (intr. & refl.)	kneel 11
knipsen (tr. & intr.)	snap, photograph 11
knirschen (intr.)	crunch 11
knistern (intr.)	crackle 11
knittern (tr. & intr.)	crush, crease 11
knurren (tr. & intr.)	growl 11
kochen (tr. & intr.)	cook, boil 11
koexistieren (intr.)	coexist 13

kolorieren (tr.)	color in 13
***kommen** (intr.+s.)	come 55
kommunizieren (intr.)	communicate 13
komplizieren (tr.)	complicate 13
komponieren (tr. & intr.)	compose 13
kompromittieren (tr.)	compromise 13
kondensieren (tr. & intr.)	condense 13
konkurrieren (intr.)	compete 13
***können** (tr. & intr.)	be able to, can 4
konstruieren (tr.)	construct, design 13
kontrollieren (tr.)	control, check, inspect 13
konzentrieren (tr. & refl.)	concentrate 13
kooperieren (intr.)	cooperate 13
koordinieren (tr.)	coordinate 13
kopieren (tr. & intr.)	copy 13
korrespondieren (tr.)	correspond 13
der Winkel korrespondiert mit ...	*the angle corresponds to/with ...*
korrigieren (tr.)	correct 13
kosten (tr. & intr.)	cost, taste 12
kotzen (intr.)	vomit 11
krachen (intr.)	bang, crash 11
krächzen (intr.)	croak 11
kramen (intr.)	rummage 11
kränken (tr.)	hurt, offend 11
kratzen (tr. & intr.)	scratch 11
kräuseln (tr. & intr.)	ruffle, curl 11
kreisen (intr+s./h.)	circle, orbit 11
kreuzen (tr. & refl.)	cross 11
kreuzigen (tr.)	crucify 11
kriechen (intr.+s.)	crawl 39
kriegen (tr.)	get 11
kristallisieren (intr. & refl.)	crystallize 13
kritisieren (tr. & intr.)	criticize 13
kritzeln (tr. & intr.)	scribble 11
krönen (tr.)	crown 11
krümmen (tr. & refl.)	bend 11
kühlen (tr. & intr.)	cool, ice 11
kultivieren (tr.)	cultivate 13
kümmern (um) (refl.)	take care (of), worry (about) 11
kümmere dich nicht um ... *das kümmert mich nicht* (tr.)	*don't worry about ...* *that is no concern of mine*
kündigen (tr. & intr.)	cancel, give notice 11

sie kündigt mir (intr.+dat.)	*she dismisses me*
kürzen (tr.)	cut 11
kurz|schließen (tr. & refl.)	short-circuit 41
küssen (tr. & intr. & refl.)	kiss 11

L

lächeln (intr.)	smile 11
lachen (intr.)	laugh 11
laden (tr. & intr.)	load, charge 73
lagern (tr.)	store 11
lähmen (tr.)	cripple, paralyze 11
landen (tr. & intr.+s.)	land 12
langweilen (tr.)	bore 11
er langweilt sich (refl.)	*he is bored*
***lassen** (tr.)	leave, let, stop 10, 77
laufen (intr.+s.)	run, go 80
laufen lassen (tr.)	let go 10, 79
läuten (tr. & intr.)	chime, ring 12
leben (intr.)	live, exist 11
lecken (tr. & intr.)	lick, lap 11
leeren (tr.)	empty 11
legalisieren (tr.)	legalize 13
legen (tr.)	lay down, put 11
der Wind legt sich	*the wind abates*
lehnen (an+acc.)	lean (up against) 11
(tr. & intr. & refl.)	
er lehnt sich an die Wand	*he leans on the wall*
lehren (tr. & intr.)	teach 11
***leiden** (tr.)	bear 29
sie leidet an+dat ... (intr.)	*she suffers from ...*
leidtun (dat.) (impers)	feel sorry 92
er tut mir leid (intr.)	*I am sorry for him*
leihen (tr.)	lend, borrow 26
leisten (tr.)	accomplish 12
ich leiste es mir (dat. refl.)	*I can afford it/I treat myself*
leiten (tr.)	lead, manage 12
lenken (tr.)	direct, steer 11
lernen (tr. & intr.)	learn, study 11
***lesen** (tr. & intr.)	read 70
leuchten (intr.)	glow, shine 12
leugnen (tr. & intr.)	deny 12
lieben (tr. & intr.)	love 11
sie lieben sich (refl.)	*they are in love*
liebkosen (tr.)	caress 11
liefern (tr. & intr.)	supply, deliver 11

liegen (intr.)	lie, be located 59
es liegt mir viel an+dat	*it is important to me*
lindern (tr.)	ease, soothe 11
loben (tr.)	praise 11
locken (tr.)	tempt, entice 11
lockern (tr.)	slacken 11
lodern (intr.)	blaze 11
lohnen (intr. & impers.) (refl.)	be worthwhile 11
los|binden (tr.)	untie, loosen 47
löschen (tr.)	put out, quench 11
lösen (tr.)	undo, solve 11
er löst die Karte	*he buys the ticket*
es löst sich (refl.)	*it comes undone*
los|fahren (intr.+s.)	set off, get started 76
los|gehen (intr.+s.)	go off, set off 88
los|lassen (tr.)	let loose 10, 79
los|machen (tr.)	unfasten 15
los sein (intr.+s.)	be the matter 1
los|werden (tr.+s.)	get rid of 3
löten (tr. & intr.)	solder 12
lotsen (tr.)	pilot 11
lüften (tr. & intr.)	air, ventilate 12
lügen (intr.)	lie (tell a lie) 36, 11

M

***machen** (tr.)	make, do 11
magnetisieren (tr.)	magnetize 13
mähen (tr. & intr.)	mow, cut 11
mahlen (tr. & intr.)	grind, mill 11
malen (tr. & intr.)	paint 11
mal|nehmen (mit) (tr. & intr.)	multiply (by) 54
mangeln (dat.) (an+dat.) (impers.)	lack 11
markieren (tr.)	highlight 13
marschieren (intr.+s.)	march 13
meckern (intr.)	nag, bleat 11
meiden (tr.)	avoid 26
meinen (tr. & intr.)	think, mean 11
er meint, dass ...	*he says that ..*
melden (tr.)	report 12
sie meldet sich (refl.)	*she checks in/answers*
melken (tr. & intr.)	milk 39
merken (tr.)	note 11
messen (tr. & intr.)	measure 66
miauen (intr.)	mew 14
mieten (tr. & intr.)	rent, hire 12

mildern (tr.)	soothe, calm 11
mimen (tr. & intr.)	mime 11
mindern (tr.)	diminish 11
mischen (tr. & refl.)	mix 11
missbilligen (tr.)	disapprove of 11
missbrauchen (tr.)	misuse 11
missfallen (dat.) (intr.)	displease 78
missglücken (dat.) (intr.+s.)	fail (of so.) 14
misshandeln (tr.)	mistreat 14
misslingen (dat.) (impers.+s)	fail 43
es misslingt ihm	*he fails*
misstrauen (dat.) (intr.)	distrust 14
missverstehen (tr. & intr.)	misunderstand 90
mit|bringen (tr.)	bring along 24
mit|erleben (tr.)	live through 15, 14
mit|fühlen (tr.)	sympathize 15
mit|gehen (intr.+s.)	go along too 88
mit|halten (mit) (intr.)	keep up (with) 79
mit|machen (tr. & intr.)	join in, cooperate 15
mit|nehmen (tr.)	take along 54
mit|rechnen (tr.)	count in 12, 15
mit|teilen (dat.) (tr.)	advise, inform (so.) 15
mit|wirken (intr.)	collaborate 15
mixen (tr.)	blend, mix 11
möblieren (tr.)	furnish 13
modernisieren (tr.)	modernize 13
mogeln (intr.)	cheat 11
*****mögen** (tr. & intr.)	like, want 6
montieren (tr.)	assemble, fit 13
motivieren (tr.)	motivate 13
multiplizieren (tr. & intr.)	multiply 13
murmeln (tr. & intr.)	murmur 11
murren (intr.)	grumble 11
münden (in+acc.) (intr.+s.)	flow (into) 12
*****müssen** (tr. & intr.)	must 7
mustern (tr.)	survey 11

N **nach|ahmen** (tr.)	imitate, copy 15
*****nach|denken** (über+acc.) (intr.)	think (about) 24
nach|geben (intr.)	give way 61
nach|gehen (dat.) (intr.+s.)	follow 88
die Uhr geht nach	*the clock is slow*
nach|grübeln (über+acc.) (intr.)	ponder over 15
nach|holen (tr.)	catch up 15

nach|jagen (dat.) (intr.+s.)	pursue 15
nach|kommen (intr.+s.)	come later 58
er kommt (dat.) *... nach*	*he complies with ...*
nach|lassen (tr. & intr.)	decrease 10, 79
er lässt mir 15% vom Preis nach	*he gives me a 15% discount*
nach|machen (dat.) (tr.)	imitate, copy 15
nach|messen (tr.)	measure again, check 69
nach|prüfen (tr. & intr.)	test 15
nach|schicken (tr.)	forward 15
nach|schlagen (tr. & intr.)	look up 76
nach|sehen (tr. & intr.)	look up 72
nach|sitzen (intr.)	stay after (at school) 67, 69
nach|weisen (tr.)	prove 28
nageln (tr.)	nail 11
nagen (intr.)	gnaw 11
nahe bringen (dat.) (tr.)	bring home to 24
nahe gehen (dat.) (intr.+s.)	grieve, affect 88
nahe liegen (intr.)	suggest itself 61
nähen (tr. & intr.)	sew 11
nahen (dat.) (tr. & refl.)	approach 11
nähern (dat.) (refl.)	approach 11
nähren (tr.)	feed 11
nebeln (impers.)	become misty 11
necken (tr.)	tease 11
***nehmen** (tr.)	take 52
neigen (tr. & refl.)	bend, lean 11
nennen (tr.)	name, call 16
neutralisieren (tr.)	neutralize 13
nicken (intr.)	nod 11
***nieder|brennen** (tr. & intr.+s.)	burn down 18
nieder|lassen (refl.)	settle down 10
nieder|legen (tr.)	lay down 15
sie legt sich nieder (refl.)	*she lies down*
nieder|schlagen (tr.)	knock down 76
nieder|schreiben (tr.)	write down 28
nieseln (impers.)	drizzle 11
niesen (intr.)	sneeze 11
nisten (intr.)	nest 12
nummerieren (tr.)	number 13
nutzen (dat.) (intr.)	be of use (to) 11
nützen (tr.)	use 11
es nützt mir (intr.)	*it is of use to me*

0

öffnen (tr., intr. & refl.)	open 12

operieren (tr. & intr.)	operate (on) 13
opfern (tr. & intr.)	sacrifice 11
ordnen (tr.)	arrange, sort 12
organisieren (tr.)	organize 13
orientieren (tr. & intr.)	orientate 13
oxydieren (tr. & intr.+s.)	oxydize 13

P

paaren (tr. & refl.)	couple, mate 11
packen (tr.)	pack, grip 11
paddeln (tr. & intr.+s./h.)	paddle 11
parken (tr. & intr.)	park 11
passen (dat.) (intr.)	fit 11
es passt zu ...	*it matches ...*
passieren (tr.)	pass 13
es passiert ihm (mit ihm) (intr.+s.)	*it happens to him*
patentieren (tr.)	patent 13
pauken (tr. & intr.)	bone up (on sth.), drill 11
pendeln (intr.+s.)	swing 11
er pendelt	*he commutes*
pennen (intr.)	doze, kip 11
pensionieren (tr.)	pension off 13
pfeffern (tr.)	pepper 11
pfeifen (tr. & intr.)	whistle 29
pflanzen (tr.)	plant 11
pflegen (tr.)	look after 11
er pflegt, ... (zu tun)	*he is in the habit of (doing) ...*
pflücken (tr.)	pick 11
pflügen (tr. & intr.)	plow/plough 11
pfuschen (intr.)	bungle 11
picken (tr. & intr.)	peck 11
pinkeln (intr.)	urinate 11
pissen (intr.)	urinate 11
plagen (tr.)	torment 11
planen (tr. & intr.)	plan, organize 11
plätschern (intr.)	splash, patter 11
platzen (intr.+s.)	blow up, burst 11
plaudern (intr.)	gossip, chat 11
Pleite machen (intr.)	bankrupt 15
plombieren (tr.)	fill (tooth) 13
plumpsen (tr. & intr.+s.)	tumble 11
plündern (tr. & intr.)	rob 11
pochen (intr.)	knock 11
pochieren (tr.)	poach 13

polieren (tr.)	polish 13
poltern (tr.)	crash about 11
potenzieren (mit) (tr.)	raise to the power (of) 13
prägen (tr.)	punch, stamp 11
prahlen (intr.)	boast 11
praktizieren (tr. & intr.)	practice 13
predigen (tr. & intr.)	preach 11
preisen (tr.)	praise 26
pressen (tr.)	press 11
privatisieren (tr.)	privatize 13
proben (tr. & intr.)	rehearse 11
*probieren (tr. & intr.)	try, have a go 13
produzieren (tr.)	produce 13
profitieren (tr. & intr.)	benefit, profit 13
programmieren (tr. & intr.)	program 13
prostituieren (refl.)	prostitute oneself 13
protestieren (intr.)	protest, object 13
protokollieren (tr. & intr.)	record, take minutes 13
prüfen (tr.)	examine, check 11
prügeln (tr. & intr.)	beat 11
sie prügeln sich (refl.)	*they fight*
pudern (tr.)	powder 11
pumpen (tr. & intr.)	pump 11
ich pumpe (mir) Geld bei ihm	*I borrow money from him*
putzen (tr.)	clean 11

Q

quadrieren (tr.)	square 13
quälen (tr.)	torment 11
er quält sich (refl.)	*he struggles*
qualifizieren (tr.)	qualify 13
er qualifiziert sich (refl.)	*he qualifies*
quantifizieren (tr.)	quantify 13
quatschen (tr. & intr.)	talk nonsense 11
quellen (intr.+s.)	well up 39
quetschen (tr.)	crush 11
quittieren (tr. & intr.)	give a receipt 13

R

rächen (tr.)	avenge 11
er rächt sich (refl.)	*he takes revenge*
radeln (intr.+s.)	bike 11
Rad fahren (intr.+s.)	bicycle 76
radieren (tr.)	erase 13
raffen (tr.)	gather 11

raffinieren (tr.)	refine 13
ragen (intr.)	project 11
rahmen (tr.)	frame 11
randalieren (intr.)	rampage about 13
rascheln (intr.)	crackle, rustle 11
rasieren (tr. & refl.)	shave 13
rasten (intr.)	rest 12
raten (dat.) (intr.)	advise 77
sie rät (tr.)	*she guesses*
rationieren (tr.)	ration 13
rauben (dat.) (tr. & intr.)	steal (from) 11
rauchen (tr. & intr.)	smoke 11
räuchern (tr.)	cure, smoke 11
räumen (tr. & intr.)	clear (up) 11
rauschen (intr.)	roar, rustle 11
raus|schmeißen (tr.)	chuck out 31
reagieren (intr.)	react 13
rebellieren (intr.)	revolt 13
rechnen (tr. & intr.)	calculate, count 12
er rechnet auf mich	*he relies on me*
er rechnet mit ihr	*he reckons on/with her*
rechtfertigen (tr.)	explain, justify 11
er rechtfertigt sich (refl.)	*he justifies himself*
reden (tr. & intr.)	speak 12
regeln (tr.)	regulate, direct 11
regieren (tr. & intr.)	rule, govern 13
regnen (impers.)	rain 12
regulieren (tr.)	regulate, adjust 13
reiben (tr. & intr.)	rub, grate 26
reichen (tr.)	hand, reach 11
es reicht bis ... (intr.)	*it stretches as far as ...*
es reicht	*it is enough*
reifen (tr. & intr.+s.)	ripen, age 11
reinigen (tr.)	clean, purify 11
rein|kommen (intr.+s.)	come in 58
reisen (intr.+s.)	travel 11
reißen (tr. & intr.+s.)	tear 29
reiten (tr. & intr.+s.)	ride 29
reizen (tr. & intr.)	irritate, annoy 11
rennen (intr.+s.)	run 16
rentieren (refl.)	be profitable 13
reparieren (tr.)	repair, mend 13
reproduzieren (tr.)	reproduce 13
reservieren (tr.)	reserve, book 13
restaurieren (tr.)	restore, renovate 13
retten (vor+dat.) (tr.)	save, rescue (from) 12

revidieren (tr.)	revise 13
richten (nach) (tr.)	direct, aim (at) 12
ich richte mich nach ... (refl.)	*I conform with ...*
riechen (nach) (tr. & intr.)	smell (of) 39
ich rieche an+dat ...	*I sniff at ...*
rieseln (intr.)	trickle 11
ringeln (tr. & refl.)	twine, curl 11
ringen (tr. & intr.)	ring, wrestle 42
rinnen (intr.+s.)	run, trickle 48
riskieren (tr.)	risk, chance 13
rollen (tr. & intr.+s.)	roll 11
röntgen (tr.)	x-ray 11
rosten (intr.+s./h.)	rust 12
rudern (tr. & intr.+s./h.)	row 11
***rufen** (nach) (tr. & intr.)	call, shout (for) 80
ruhen (intr.)	rest 11
ruinieren (tr.)	ruin 13
rum|kommandieren (tr.)	boss around 13, 15
rutschen (intr.+s.)	slip, slide 11
rücken (intr.+s.)	move 11
rühmen (tr.)	praise 11
er rühmt sich (gen.) (refl.)	*he boasts (of)*
rühren (tr. & intr. & refl.)	stir, move 11

S	**säen** (tr. & intr.)	sow 11
	sagen (tr.)	say, tell 11
	salzen (tr.)	salt 11
	sammeln (tr. & refl.)	collect, gather 11
	satteln (tr.)	saddle 11
	sauber machen (tr.)	clean 15
	säubern (tr.)	clean 11
	saufen (intr.)	drink excessively (alcohol), drink (of animals) 39
	saugen (tr. & intr.)	suck 36
	säumen (tr.)	hem, line 11
	sausen (intr.+s./h.)	dash 11
	schaben (tr.)	scrape 11
	schaden (dat.) (intr.)	damage, harm 12
	***schaffen** (tr.)	get done 11
	schaffen (tr.)	create 74
	ich schaffe es	*I get it done*
	schälen (tr.)	peel, skin, shell 11
	schallen (intr.)	sound, resound 11
	schämen (gen./über+acc.) (refl.)	be ashamed (of) 11

schätzen (tr.)	estimate, value 11
schauen (intr.)	look, glance 11
schaufeln (tr. & intr.)	scoop, shovel 11
schaukeln (tr. & intr.)	rock, swing 11
schäumen (intr.)	foam 11
scheiden (tr. & intr.+s.)	separate, part 26
sie lässt sich scheiden (refl.)	*she gets divorced*
scheinen (intr.)	shine 26
er scheint	*he seems*
scheitern (intr.+s.)	fail, collapse 11
schellen (intr.)	ring 11
schenken (tr.)	give away 11
scheren (tr.)	shear, clip 36
scherzen (intr.)	joke 11
scheuen (vor+dat.) (refl.)	be frightened (of) 11
schicken (nach) (tr. & intr.)	send (for) 11
schieben (tr.)	push, shove 32
schief gehen (intr.+s.)	go wrong 88
schielen (intr.)	squint 11
***schießen** (auf+acc.) (tr. & intr.)	shoot, fire (at) 39
schildern (tr.)	describe, portray 11
schimmern (intr.)	gleam 11
schimpfen (auf+acc.) (intr.)	grumble, curse (at) 11
schirmen (tr.)	shield 11
schlachten (tr. & intr.)	slaughter 12
***schlafen** (intr.)	sleep 77
schlafen gehen (intr.+s.)	go to bed 88
schlafen legen (tr.)	put to bed 15
schlagen (tr. & intr.)	hit, strike 73
er schlägt gegen/auf+ acc... (intr.+s.)	*he crashes against/onto...*
sie schlagen sich (refl.)	*they fight*
schlängeln (refl.)	curl, coil 11
schleichen (intr.+s.)	creep, slip, steal 29
schleifen (tr. & intr.+s.)	sharpen, drag 29
schlendern (intr.+s.)	stroll 11
schleppen (tr. & intr.)	drag, haul 11
schleudern (tr.)	hurl 11
es schleudert (intr.)	*it spins*
das Auto schleudert (intr.+s.)	*the car skids*
schlichten (tr. & intr.)	arbitrate 12
schließen (tr. & intr.)	close, conclude 39
er schließt aus ...	*he concludes from ...*
schluchzen (tr. & intr.)	sob 11
schlucken (tr. & intr.)	swallow, sip 11

schlüpfen (intr.+s.)	slip 11
schmecken (nach) (tr. & intr.)	taste (of) 11
es schmeckt (mir gut) (impers.)	*it tastes good/I like it*
schmeicheln (dat.) (intr.)	flatter 11
schmeißen (tr. & intr.)	throw, chuck 29
schmelzen (tr. & intr.+s.)	melt 39
schmerzen (tr. & intr.)	pain, ache 11
schmieren (tr. & intr.)	grease, smear 11
schminken (refl.)	put on make-up 11
schmökern (tr. & intr.)	browse in a book 11
schmollen (intr.)	sulk 11
schmücken (tr.)	decorate 11
schmuggeln (tr. & intr.)	smuggle 11
schmusen (intr.)	cuddle 11
schnappen (tr. & intr.)	snap 11
schnarchen (intr.)	snore 11
schneiden (tr. & intr.)	cut, slice 29
schneidern (tr. & intr.)	dressmake 11
schneien (impers.)	snow 11
schnitzen (tr. & intr.)	carve 11
schnüffeln (intr.)	sniff 11
schnüren (tr.)	tie up 11
schnurren (intr.)	purr 11
schocken (tr.)	shock 11
schockieren (tr.)	shock 13
schonen (tr.)	spare, save 11
er schont sich (refl.)	*he takes things gently*
schöpfen (tr.)	scoop, draw 11
schrauben (tr. & intr.)	screw (as with a screwdriver) 11
*schreiben (tr. & intr.)	write 26
schreien (tr. & intr.)	scream, call out 26
schreiten (intr.+s.)	stride 29
schrubben (tr. & intr.)	scrub 11
schrumpfen (intr.+s.)	shrink, contract 11
schuften (intr.)	slave, slog 12
schulden (tr.)	owe 12
schütteln (tr.)	shake 11
schütten (tr.)	pour 12
schützen (vor+dat.) (tr.)	shelter (from) 11
schwächen (tr.)	weaken 11
schwanken (intr.)	sway, oscillate 11
schwänzen (tr. & intr.)	play truant 11
schwärmen (für) (intr.)	rave (about) 11
schwarz|arbeiten (intr.)	moonlight 12, 15

schwärzen (tr.)	blacken 11
schwarz|fahren (intr.+s.)	travel with no ticket 76
schwatzen (tr. & intr.)	gossip 11
schweben (intr.+s./h.)	hover, glide 11
schweigen (intr.+s./h.)	be silent 26
schweißen (tr. & intr.)	weld 11
schwellen (intr.+s.)	swell 39, 11
schwimmen (tr. & intr.+s./h.)	swim, float 48
schwindeln (intr.)	lie, cheat 11
schwinden (intr.+s.)	dwindle, fade 45
schwingen (tr.& intr. & refl.)	swing, oscillate 42
schwirren (intr.+s.)	whizz, buzz 11
schwitzen (intr.)	sweat 11
schwören (tr. & intr.)	swear 36
scrollen (tr. & intr.)	scroll 11
segeln (tr & intr.+s./h.)	sail 11
segnen (tr.)	bless 12
sehen (tr. & intr.)	see, glance 70
sehnen (nach) (refl.)	long (for) 11
*sein (intr.+s.)	be 1
senden (nach) (tr. & intr.)	send (for) 19
sie sendet das Signal	*she broadcasts the signal*
senken (tr. & refl.)	lower, sink 11
setzen (tr.)	put, place 11
er setzt sich (refl.)	*he sits down*
seufzen (tr. & intr.)	sigh 11
sichern (tr.)	secure 11
sicher|stellen (tr.)	make safe 15
sichten (tr.)	sight 12
sickern (intr.+s.)	seep 11
sieben (tr.)	sieve 11
siedeln (intr.)	settle (down) 11
sieden (tr. & intr.)	simmer 12
siegen (intr.)	overcome 11
siezen (tr.)	address as "Sie" 11
singen (tr. & intr.)	sing 42
sinken (intr.+s.)	sink, fall 42
sinnen (intr.)	ponder 48
*sitzen (intr.)	sit 67
sitzen lassen (tr.)	abandon 10, 79
skizzieren (tr.)	sketch out 13
*sollen (tr. & intr.)	shall, be obliged to 9
sonnen (refl.)	sunbathe 11
sorgen (für) (intr.)	look (after) 11
er sorgt sich um ... (refl.)	*he worries about ...*
spalten (tr. & refl.)	split 12

spannen (tr.)	tighten 11
sparen (tr. & intr.)	save 11
spazieren führen (tr.)	take for a walk 15
spazieren gehen (intr.+s.)	go for a walk 88
speichern (tr.)	store, fill 11
speisen (tr. & intr.)	dine 11
spekulieren (intr.)	speculate 13
spenden (tr. & intr.)	donate 12
spendieren (tr.)	buy (for so.) 13
sperren (tr.)	close, bar 11
spezialisieren (auf+acc.) (refl.)	specialize (in) 13
spiegeln (tr. & intr.)	mirror 11
es spiegelt sich (refl.)	*it is reflected*
spielen (tr. & intr.)	play, act 11
spinnen (tr. & intr.)	spin 48
er spinnt	*he's crazy*
spionieren (intr.)	spy 13
spotten (über+acc.) (intr.)	mock 12
*sprechen (intr.)	speak 48
er spricht von ...	*he is talking of ...*
er spricht über+acc ...	*he is talking about ...*
sprengen (tr.)	blow up 11
sprießen (intr.+s.)	sprout 39
springen (intr.+s.)	jump 42
spritzen (tr. & intr.)	spray, splash 11
sprudeln (intr.)	bubble, fizz 11
sprühen (tr. & intr.+s./h.)	spray 11
spucken (tr. & intr.)	spit 11
spuken (intr.)	haunt 11
spulen (tr.)	wind 11
spülen (tr. & intr.)	rinse, wash up 11
er spült	*he washes up*
spüren (tr.)	feel, sense 11
stabilisieren (tr. & refl.)	stabilize 13
stammen (aus) (intr.)	come (from) 11
stampfen (intr.+s./h.)	stamp 11
stapeln (tr. & refl.)	pile (up) 11
stärken (tr. & intr.)	strengthen 11
starren (auf.+acc.) (intr.)	stare, gaze (at) 11
starten (tr. & intr.+s.)	start, take off 12
statt|finden (intr.)	take place 47
Staub saugen (intr.)	vacuum 15
stauen (tr.)	dam 11
es staut sich (refl.)	*it piles up*
staunen (über+acc.) (intr.)	be amazed (at) 11
stechen (tr. & intr.)	sting, stab, bite 48

stecken (tr. & intr.)	put, be stuck 11
stecken bleiben (intr.+s.)	get stuck 28
*stehen (intr.)	stand 89
stehen bleiben (intr.+s.)	stop, pause 28
*stehlen (dat.) (tr. & intr.)	steal (from) 49
er stiehlt sich davon (refl.)	*he creeps away*
steigen (intr.+s.)	climb, go up 26
steigern (tr. & refl.)	increase 11
stellen (tr.)	place, put 11
er stellt eine Frage	*he asks a question*
er stellt es auf den Kopf	*he turns it upside down*
er stellt sich (refl.)	*he turns himself in*
stempeln (tr.)	stamp, frank 11
sterben (an+dat.) (intr.+s.)	die (of) 48
sticken (tr. & intr.)	embroider 11
stiften (tr.)	found, donate 12
stillen (tr.)	ease, suckle 11
still|halten (intr.)	keep still 79
stimmen (tr. & intr.)	tune 11
ich stimme für ihn	*I vote for him*
das stimmt	*that's right*
stinken (intr.)	stink 42
stocken (intr.)	falter 11
stöhnen (intr.)	moan, groan 11
stolpern (intr.+s.)	stumble, trip 11
stopfen (tr. & intr.)	stuff, darn 11
stoppen (tr. & intr.)	stop, block 11
stören (tr. & intr.)	disturb, bother 11
er stört (mich)	*he interrupts (me)*
stornieren (tr. & intr.)	cancel 13
stoßen (tr. & intr.+s.)	bump 80
er stößt auf+acc ...(intr.+s.)	*he comes upon ...*
stottern (tr. & intr.)	stammer 11
strafen (tr. & intr.)	punish 11
strahlen (intr.)	shine, glow 11
strapazieren (tr.)	strain 13
sträuben (gegen) (refl.)	resist 11
streben (nach) (intr.)	strive (for) 11
strecken (tr. & refl.)	stretch 11
es streckt sich	*it sticks out*
streicheln (tr.)	stroke 11
streichen (tr.)	stroke, paint 29
er streicht die Wand	*he paints the wall*
er streicht das Wort	*he deletes the word*
er streicht (intr.+s.)	*he wanders*
streifen (tr.)	touch 11

sie streift (intr.+s.)	*she roams*
streiken (intr.)	strike 11
streiten (intr. & refl.)	argue, quarrel 29
streuen (tr.)	scatter 11
stricken (tr. & intr.)	knit 11
strömen (intr.+s.)	pour, stream 11
studieren (tr. & intr.)	study 13
stutzen (tr.)	trim 11
er stutzt (intr.)	*he falters*
stürmen (tr. & intr.)	storm, rage 11
stürzen (intr.+s.)	fall 11
sie stürzt sich (refl.)	*she rushes*
er stürzt (tr.)	*he flings*
stützen (auf+acc.) (tr. & refl.)	support, lean (on) 11
subventionieren (tr.)	subsidize 13
suchen (tr.)	look for 11
er sucht nach ... (intr.)	*he searches for ...*
summen (tr. & intr.)	buzz, hum 11
sündigen (intr.)	sin 11

T

tadeln (tr.)	censure 11
tagen (intr.)	sit, confer 11
tanken (tr. & intr.)	fill up 11
tanzen (tr & intr.+s./h.)	dance 11
tapezieren (tr.)	wallpaper 13
tätscheln (tr.)	pat 11
tauchen (tr.)	dip 11
er taucht ins Wasser (intr.+s.)	*he dives into the water*
tauen (tr. & intr.)	thaw 11
taufen (tr.)	baptize 11
taugen (für.) (intr.)	be suitable for 11
täuschen (tr.& intr.)	deceive 11
er täuscht sich	*he is mistaken*
tauschen (gegen) (tr. & intr.)	exchange, barter (for) 11
teilen (tr. & intr.)	share, part, divide 11
teil‖nehmen (an+dat.) (intr.)	take part (in) 54
telefonieren (nach) (intr.)	telephone (for) 13
terrorisieren (tr.)	terrorize 13
testen (tr. & intr.)	test 12
tippen (tr. & intr.)	type 11
tönen (intr.)	resound 11
töten (tr. & intr.)	kill 12
trachten (nach) (intr.)	yearn (for) 12
tragen (tr.)	carry 73

er trägt einen Anzug	*he wears a suit*
trainieren (tr. & intr.)	train, exercise 13
trampen (intr.+s.)	hitchhike 11
tränken (tr.)	water 11
trauen (dat.) (tr. & intr.)	trust 11
wir lassen uns trauen (refl.)	*we get married*
ich traue mich, zu ...	*I dare to ...*
trauern (um) (intr.)	mourn (for) 11
träumen (von) (tr. & intr.)	dream (about) 11
***treffen** (tr. & intr.)	hit 56
er trifft mich (tr. & refl.)	*he meets me*
sie treffen sich	*they meet*
treiben (tr.)	drive 26
er treibt Sport	*he goes in for sport*
wir treiben Werbung	*we advertise*
er treibt (intr.+s.)	*he drifts*
trennen (tr. & refl.)	separate, divide 11
***treten** (intr.+s.)	tread, step 62
er tritt gegen die Tür	*he kicks the door*
triefen (intr.)	drip 11, 39
trimmen (refl.)	train, get fit 11
***trinken** (tr. & intr.)	drink 42
er trinkt auf mich/auf mein Wohl	*he toasts me*
trocknen (tr. & intr.+s.)	dry 12
trödeln (intr.)	dawdle 11
trommeln (tr. & intr.)	drum, beat 11
tropfen (tr. & intr.)	drip 11
trösten (tr.)	comfort, console 12
trotzen (dat.) (intr.)	defy 11
trüben (tr.)	make dull 11
trügen (tr. & intr.)	deceive 36
***tun** (tr. & intr.)	do, pretend 92
er tut, (als ob)	*he pretends (to be)*
turnen (tr. & intr.)	do gymnastics 11
tyrannisieren (tr.)	bully 13
U **übel nehmen** (tr.)	take amiss 54
üben (tr. & intr.)	practice, exercise 11
überblicken (tr.)	overlook 14
überbrücken (tr.)	bridge 14
überein|stimmen (intr.)	agree 15
ich stimme mit ihm in+dat ... überein	*I agree with him about ...*
überfahren (tr.)	run over 75

VERB INDEX

überfallen (tr.)	attack 78
überfluten (tr. & intr.+s.)	flood 12, 14
übergeben (tr.)	hand over 60
er übergibt sich (refl.)	*he vomits/is sick*
überholen (tr. & intr.)	overtake 14
überhören (tr.)	not to hear 14
überlaufen (tr.)	overrun 81
über|laufen (intr.+s.)	overflow 82
überleben (tr. & intr.)	survive 14
überlegen (tr. & intr.)	reflect, think over 14
übermitteln (tr.)	convey 14
übernachten (intr.)	spend the night 12, 14
übernehmen (tr. & refl.)	take over 53
überprüfen (tr.)	check 14
überqueren (tr.)	cross, go across 14
überraschen (tr.)	surprise 14
überreden (tr.)	persuade, coax 12, 14
ich überrede sie zu ...	*I talk her into ...*
überreichen (tr.)	hand over 14
überschlagen (tr.)	skip, pass over (pages) 75
er überschlägt sich (refl.)	*he somersaults*
über|schlagen (tr.)	cross, fold over 76
überschreiten (tr.)	cross, exceed 30
überschwemmen (tr.)	flood 14
übersehen (tr.)	overlook 71
er übersieht es	*he overlooks it*
übersetzen (tr.)	translate 14
überspringen (tr.)	jump over 43
übersteigen (tr.)	exceed 27
übertragen (tr.)	transmit 75
sie übersetzt aus dem Deutschen	*she translates from German*
übertreffen (tr.)	surpass 56, 57
übertreiben (tr. & intr.)	exaggerate 27
überwachen (tr.)	supervise 14
überwältigen (tr.)	overcome 14
überwiegen (tr. & intr.)	outweigh, predominate 34
überwinden (tr.)	overcome 46
überzeugen (tr.)	persuade, convince 14
umarmen (tr.)	embrace 14
um|bauen (tr. & intr.)	adapt, convert 15
um|bringen (tr.)	kill 24
um|drehen (tr. & refl.)	turn around, turn over 15
um|fahren (tr.)	run down 76
umfassen (tr.)	comprise, encircle 14
umgeben (tr.)	surround 60

um|gehen (intr.+s.)	go around 88
ein Gespenst geht im Haus um	*a ghost haunts the house*
er weiß mit Kindern umzugehen	*he knows how to handle children*
umgehen (tr.)	avoid, bypass 87
um|kehren (tr. & refl.)	turn back 15
um|kippen (tr.)	tip over 15
er kippt um (intr.+s.)	*he passes out*
um|kommen (intr.+s.)	perish 58
um|leiten (tr.)	bypass, divert 15
um|rahmen (tr.)	frame 15
umreißen (tr.)	outline 30
um|schalten (tr. & intr.)	switch over, change 15
umschließen (tr.)	border, enclose 40
um|sehen (nach) (refl.)	look around (at) 72
um|steigen (intr.+s.)	change (trains) 28
um|stellen (tr. & intr.)	rearrange, retune 15
sie stellt sich auf+acc ... um (refl.)	*she adapts to ...*
um|stoßen (tr.)	upset, turn upside down 82
um|tauschen (tr.)	exchange 15
um|wandeln (in+acc.) (tr. & refl.)	change (into) 15
um|werfen (tr.)	knock over, down 51
um|ziehen (intr.)	move house 33, 35
er zieht sich um (refl.)	*he changes his clothes*
unterbrechen (tr.)	break off, interrupt 50
unter|bringen (tr.)	house, accommodate 24
unterdrücken (tr.)	suppress 14
unter|gehen (intr.+s.)	set, sink 88
unterhalten (tr.)	support 78
er unterhält mich	*he entertains me*
sie unterhält sich mit ... (refl.)	*she talks with ...*
unterrichten (tr. & intr.)	teach, instruct 12, 14
untersagen (tr.)	forbid 14
unterscheiden (tr. & intr.)	distinguish 27
sie unterscheiden sich (refl.)	*they differ*
unterschlagen (tr.)	embezzle 75
unterschreiben (tr. & intr.)	sign 27
unterstellen (tr.)	keep, store 15
unterstreichen (tr.)	underline 30
unterstützen (tr.)	support, back 14
untersuchen (tr.)	examine, check 14
unterwerfen (tr.)	subject 50

er unterwirft sich (dat.) (refl.)   *he submits (to)*
unterzeichnen (tr.)   endorse 12, 14
urteilen (intr.)   judge 11

V   **verabreden** (tr.)   arrange 12, 14
   sie verabredet sich mit ...   *she arranges to meet ...*
   (refl.)
verabscheuen (tr.)   hate, detest 14
verabschieden (tr.)   say good-bye to 12, 14
   er verabschiedet sich (refl.)   *he says good-bye*
verachten (tr.)   scorn 12, 14
verändern (tr. & refl.)   change 14
veranlassen (tr.)   arrange for 14
veranstalten (tr.)   organize 12, 14
verantworten (tr.)   be responsible for 12, 14
verarbeiten (tr.)   process 12, 14
verärgern (tr.)   annoy 14
   er ist verärgert über+acc ...
   (refl.)   *he is cross about ...*
verbannen (tr.)   banish 14
verbarrikadieren (tr.)   barricade 13
verbergen (vor+dat.) (tr. & refl.)   conceal (from) 50
verbessern (tr. & refl.)   improve 14
verbieten (tr.)   forbid 34
verbinden (mit) (tr. & refl.)   bind, connect (with) 46
   er verbindet die Wunde   *he bandages the wound*
verbitten (dat. refl.)   refuse to tolerate 63, 64
   das verbitte ich mir   *I will not tolerate that*
verblassen (intr.+s.)   fade 14
verbleiben (tr.)   remain 27
verbleichen (intr.+s.)   fade 30
verbluten (intr.+s.)   bleed 12, 14
verblüffen (tr.)   dumbfound 14
verbrauchen (tr.)   spend, consume 14
verbreiten (tr. & refl.)   disperse, spread 12, 14
verbrennen (tr. & intr.+s.)   burn up 17
***verbringen** (tr.)   spend (time) 23
verdächtigen (gen.) (tr.)   suspect (of) 14
verdammen (tr.)   condemn, damn 14
verdampfen (tr. & intr.+s.)   evaporate 14
verdanken (dat.) (tr.)   owe, be indebted (to) 14
verdauen (tr.)   digest 14
verderben (tr. & intr.+s.)   spoil 50
verdeutlichen (tr.)   make clear 14
verdichten (tr. & refl.)   compress 12, 14

verdienen (tr. & intr.)	deserve, earn 14
verdoppeln (tr. & refl.)	double 14
verdrängen (tr.)	displace 14
verdrehen (tr.)	distort 14
verdrießen (tr.)	annoy 40
verdunkeln (tr. & refl.)	darken 14
verdünnen (tr.)	dilute 14
verehren (tr.)	respect 14
vereinbaren (tr.)	arrange, agree 14
vereinen (tr. & refl.)	unite 14
vereinfachen (tr.)	simplify 14
vereinigen (tr. & refl.)	reunite, combine 14
verengen (tr. & refl.)	narrow 14
verfahren (refl.)	lose one's way 75
verfallen (intr.+s.)	decay, deteriorate 78
verfassen (tr.)	compile, write 14
verfilmen (tr.)	film 14
verflüssigen (tr. & refl.)	liquify 14
verfolgen (tr.)	pursue 14
verformen (tr. & refl.)	deform 14
verfrachten (tr.)	transport 12, 14
verfremden (tr.)	alienate 12, 14
verfügen (über+acc.) (intr.)	have at one's disposal 14
verführen (tr.)	seduce 14
***vergeben** (tr.)	forgive, give away 60
vergehen (intr.+s.)	pass 87
***vergessen** (tr. & intr.)	forget 68
vergewaltigen (tr.)	rape 14
vergießen (tr.)	spill 40
vergiften (tr.)	poison, contaminate 12, 14
vergleichen (tr.)	compare 30
vergnügen (tr.)	satisfy 14
sie vergnügt sich mit ... (refl.)	*she amuses herself with ...*
vergraben (tr.)	bury 75
vergrößern (tr. & refl.)	enlarge 14
verhaften (tr.)	arrest 12, 14
verhalten (refl.)	behave 78
verhandeln (über+acc.) (tr. & intr.)	negotiate (about) 14
verhauen (tr.)	bash 14
verheiraten (mit) (refl.)	get married (to) 12, 14
verhindern (tr.)	prevent, thwart 14
verhören (tr.)	interrogate 14
verhungern (intr.+s.)	starve 14
verhüten (tr.)	prevent 12, 14
verirren (refl.)	lose one's way 14

*verkaufen (tr. & intr.)	sell 14
verkehren (mit) (intr.)	associate (with) 14
der Bus verkehrt zwischen A und B	the bus runs between A and B
verkennen (tr.)	misjudge 17
verkleiden (tr.)	disguise, box in 12, 14
er verkleidet sich als ... (refl.)	he is disguised as ...
verklingen (intr.+s.)	fade 43
verkommen (intr.+s.)	go to pieces 57
verkörpern (tr.)	embody 14
verkümmern (intr.+s.)	waste away 14
verkürzen (tr. & refl.)	shorten 14
verlangen (tr. & intr.)	demand 14
er verlangt nach ...	he asks for ...
verlängern (tr. & refl.)	extend 14
verlassen (tr.)	leave, desert 10, 78
er verlässt sich auf+acc ... (refl.)	he relies on ...
verlaufen (intr.+s./h.)	smudge 81
er verläuft sich (refl.)	he loses his way
verlegen (tr.)	transfer, move 14
verleihen (tr.)	lend 27
verleiten (tr.)	lead astray 12, 14
verlesen (tr.)	read out 71
er hat sich verlesen (refl.)	he misread
verletzen (tr.)	wound, contravene 14
verleugnen (tr.)	deny 12, 14
verleumden (tr.)	slander 12, 14
verlieben (in+acc.) (refl.)	fall in love (with) 14
*verlieren (tr. & intr.)	lose 34
verloben (mit) (refl.)	get engaged (to) 14
vermachen (tr.)	bequeath 14
vermarkten (tr.)	market 12, 14
vermehren (tr. & refl.)	increase 14
vermeiden (tr.)	avoid 27
vermessen (tr.)	survey 68
vermieten (tr.)	let, hire out 12, 14
vermischen (tr. & refl.)	blend, mix up 14
vermissen (tr.)	miss 14
vermitteln (tr. & intr.)	arrange, arbitrate 14
vermögen (tr.)	be capable of 6
vernachlässigen (tr.)	neglect 14
vernehmen (tr.)	hear, perceive 53
er vernimmt die Zeugen	he interrogates the witnesses

verneigen (refl.)	bow 14
verneinen (tr. & intr.)	answer with'"no"14
vernichten (tr.)	destroy 12, 14
veröffentlichen (tr. & intr.)	publish 14
verordnen (tr.)	prescribe, decree 12, 14
verpacken (tr.)	wrap up, package 14
verpassen (tr.)	miss 14
verpflegen (tr.)	feed 14
verpflichten (tr.)	oblige 12, 14
er verpflichtet sich (refl.)	*he commits himself*
verprügeln (tr.)	beat, thrash 14
verraten (tr.)	betray 78
verreisen (intr.+s.)	go away 14
verrenken (tr.)	dislocate 14
verrichten (tr.)	carry out 12, 14
verriegeln (tr.)	bar, bolt down 14
verringern (tr.)	reduce 14
verrühren (tr.)	mix 14
versagen (intr.)	fail, break down 14
versammeln (tr. & refl.)	assemble 14
versäumen (tr.)	miss 14
verschärfen (tr.)	intensify 14
verschieben (auf+acc.) (tr.)	postpone (until) 34
verschiffen (tr.)	ship 14
verschimmeln (intr.+s.)	go moldy 14
verschlafen (intr. & refl.)	oversleep 78
verschlechtern (tr. & refl.)	worsen 14
verschleiern (tr.)	veil 14
verschließen (tr.)	lock, seal 40
verschlingen (tr.)	devour, gobble 43
verschmutzen (tr.)	pollute 14
verschonen (tr.)	spare 14
verschöne(r)n	brighten up 14
verschrauben (tr.)	screw together 14
verschreiben (tr.)	prescribe 27
verschrotten (tr.)	scrap 12, 14
verschweigen (tr.)	keep quiet about 27
verschwenden (tr.)	waste 12, 14
verschwimmen (intr.+s.)	become blurred 50
***verschwinden** (intr.+s.)	disappear 46
verschwören (refl.)	conspire 37
***versehen** (mit) (tr.)	provide (with) 71
versenden (tr.)	send out 20
versengen (tr.)	scorch 14
versetzen (tr.)	move 14

vervollständigen (tr.)	complete 14
verwalten (tr.)	manage 12, 14
verwandeln (in+acc.) (tr. & refl.)	transform, change (into) 14
verwanzen (tr.)	bug 14
verwechseln (tr.)	confuse, mix up 14
verweigern (tr.)	refuse 14
verweisen (tr.)	expel 27
er verweist auf+acc ... (intr.)	*he refers to ...*
***verwenden** (tr.)	use 20
verwickeln (tr.)	tangle up, involve 14
er verwickelt sich in+ acc ...(refl.)	*he gets involved in ...*
verwirklichen (tr.)	fulfill 14
verwirren (tr.)	confuse 14
verwischen (tr.)	blur 14
verwöhnen (tr.)	spoil 14
verwunden (tr.)	wound 12, 14
verwundern (tr.)	astonish 14
verwüsten (tr.)	devastate 12, 14
verzehren (tr.)	consume 14
verzeichnen (tr.)	record, note 12, 14
verzeihen (dat.) (tr. & intr.)	forgive (so.) 27
verzerren (tr.)	distort 14
verzichten (auf+acc.) (intr.)	do without 12, 14
verzieren (tr.)	decorate 14
verzögern (tr.)	delay 14
verzollen (tr.)	pay duty on 14
verzweifeln (an+dat.) (intr.+s.)	despair (of) 14
vibrieren (intr.)	vibrate 13
vollbringen (tr.)	accomplish 23
vollenden (tr.)	complete 12, 14
voll stopfen (tr.)	stuff, cram 15
vollstrecken (tr.)	execute 14
vollziehen (tr.)	carry out 33, 34
voran|gehen (dat.) (intr.+s.)	go ahead (of) 88
voraus|sagen (tr.)	forecast 15
voraus|setzen (tr.)	presuppose 15
vorbei|fahren (an+dat.) (intr.+s.)	drive past 76
vorbei|gehen (an+dat.) (intr.+s.)	go past 88
vorbei|kommen (intr.+s.)	come by, call in 58
vorbei|schauen (intr.)	call in 15
vor|bereiten (tr.)	prepare, get ready 12, 15
vor|beugen (dat.) (intr.)	forestall 15
vor|führen (tr.)	present 15
vor|gehen (intr.+s.)	proceed 88
die Uhr geht vor	*the clock is fast*

vor|haben (tr.)	intend 2
vorher|sehen (tr.)	foresee 72
vor|kommen (intr.+s.)	occur 58
vor|lesen (tr. & intr.)	read aloud 72
vor|liegen (intr.)	be available 61
vor|merken (tr.)	note down, reserve 15
vor|nehmen (tr.) (dat. refl.)	intend to do sth. 54
vor|rücken (tr. & intr.+s.)	advance, move forward 15
vor|schlagen (tr.)	suggest, propose 76
vor|schreiben (tr.)	specify 28
vor|spielen (tr. & intr.)	play, audition 15
vor|stellen (tr.)	introduce 15
sie stellt sich vor (refl.)	*she introduces herself*
ich stelle es mir vor (dat. refl.)	*I imagine it*
vor|täuschen (tr.)	fake 15
vor|tragen (tr.)	carry forward 76
vor|werfen (dat.) (tr.)	reproach (so.) with 51
vor|zeigen (tr.)	show 15
vor|ziehen (dat.) (tr.)	prefer (to) 33, 35

W

wachen (intr.)	be awake 11
wachsen (intr.+s.)	grow 73
wagen (tr.)	dare 11
er wagt sich (refl.)	*he ventures*
wählen (tr. & intr.)	choose, vote for 11
er wählt die Nummer	*he dials the number*
wir wählen (intr.)	*we vote/hold an election*
wahren (tr.)	protect 11
wahr|nehmen (tr.)	perceive 54
wandeln (tr. & refl.)	change 11
wandern (intr.+s.)	walk, hike 11
wärmen (tr.)	warm 11
warnen (vor+dat.) (tr. & intr.)	warn (of), alert 11
warten (auf+acc.) (intr.)	wait (for) 12
waschen (tr. & refl.)	wash 73
weben (tr. & intr.)	weave 36
wechseln (intr.)	change 11
wecken (tr.)	wake 11
wedeln (mit) (intr.)	wag 11
weg|geben (tr.)	give away 61
weg|gehen (intr.+s.)	go away, depart 88
***weg|laufen** (intr.+s.)	run away 82
weg|nehmen (dat.) (tr.)	take away (from) 54
weg|räumen (tr. & intr.)	clear away 15

weg|tragen (tr.)	carry off 76
weg|werfen (tr.)	throw away 51
wehen (tr. & intr.+s/h)	blow 11
wehren (refl.)	resist 11
weh|tun (dat.) (intr.)	hurt 92
weichen (dat.) (intr.+s.)	yield (to) 29
weiden (intr.)	browse 12
weigern (refl.)	refuse 11
weihen (tr.)	dedicate 11
weinen (intr.)	weep 11
weiter|gehen (intr.+s.)	go on 88
weiter|machen (tr. & intr.)	carry on 15
welken (intr.+s.)	wilt 11
*wenden (tr. & refl.)	turn 19
ich wende mich an ihn	*I consult him*
werben für (intr.)	recruit, advertise 48
*werden (intr.+s.)	become 3
werfen (tr. & intr.)	throw, cast 48
wetten (tr. & intr.)	bet, gamble 12
wickeln (tr.)	bind, wrap 11
widerlegen (tr.)	refute 14
widersetzen (dat.) (refl.)	oppose 14
widersprechen (dat.) (intr.)	contradict 50
wider|hallen (tr.)	resound, echo 15
wider|spiegeln (tr.)	reflect 15
widmen (tr.)	dedicate 12
sie widmet sich (dat.) (refl.)	*she devotes herself (to)*
wieder|finden (tr.)	find again 47
er findet sich wieder (refl.)	*he recovers, finds himself*
wieder|geben (tr.)	give back, resound 61
wiederholen (tr. & intr.)	repeat 14
wieder|verwerten (tr.)	recycle 12, 14, 15
wieder|herstellen (tr.)	restore 15
wiegen (tr. & intr.)	weigh 11, 32
sie wiegt das Kind	*she rocks the child*
wiehern (intr.)	neigh 11
wimmeln (von) (impers.)	teem (with) 11
winden (tr. & refl.)	curl, wind 45
winken (tr. & intr.)	wave, sign 11
wirken (intr.)	work, be effective 11
er wirkt (nervös)	*he seems (nervous)*
wischen (tr. & intr.)	wipe 11
*wissen (über/von+acc.) (tr. & intr.)	know (about) 25
wittern (tr. & intr.)	scent 11

wohnen (intr.)	reside, live, stay 11
wölben (tr. & refl.)	curve, bulge 11
***wollen** (tr. & intr.)	want, will 5
wringen (tr. & intr.)	wring 42
wundern (über+acc.) (refl.)	be surprised (at) 11
es wundert mich, (dass) ... (impers.)	*I am surprised (that) ...*
wühlen (intr.)	dig 11
wünschen (tr. & intr.)	wish 11
ich wünsche mir etw. (dat. refl.)	*I desire something*
würgen (tr.)	strangle, choke 11

Z

zahlen (tr. & intr.)	pay 11
zählen (tr. & intr.)	count 11
er zählt zu der Gruppe	*he belongs to the group*
ich zähle auf ihn	*I am counting on him*
zähmen (tr.)	tame 11
zanken (intr. & refl.)	argue 11
zaubern (tr. & intr.)	conjure 11
zeichnen (tr. & intr.)	draw 12
zeigen (tr. & intr.)	show 11
er zeigt auf+acc ...	*he points to ...*
zelten (intr.)	camp 12
zensieren (tr. & intr.)	censor 13
er zensiert die Arbeiten	*he marks the work*
zentralisieren (tr.)	centralize 13
zerbrechen (tr. & intr.+s.)	break, smash 50
zerdrücken (tr.)	crush, squash 14
zerfallen (intr.+s.)	disintegrate 78
zerfressen (tr.)	corrode 68
zerkrümeln (tr.)	crumble 14
zerlegen (tr.)	take apart, analyze 14
***zerreißen** (tr.)	tear up 30
zerren (tr. & intr.)	pull 11
zerschlagen (tr.)	smash 75
zersetzen (tr. & refl.)	decompose, corrode 14
zerstäuben (tr.)	spray 14
zerstören (tr. & intr.)	ruin, destroy 14
zerstoßen (tr.)	crush 81
zerstreuen (tr. & refl.)	scatter, disperse 14
zertreten (tr.)	trample 64
zeugen (tr. & intr.)	generate, testify 11
***ziehen** (tr.)	pull 33
er zieht nach ... (intr.+s.)	*he moves to ...*

zielen (auf+acc.) (intr.)	aim (at) 11
zieren (tr.)	adorn 11
zirkulieren (intr.)	circulate 13
zischen (tr. & intr.)	hiss 11
zitieren (tr.)	quote 13
zittern (intr.)	tremble, shiver 11
zögern (intr.)	hesitate 11
zoomen (tr. & intr.)	zoom 11
zucken (tr. & intr.)	twitch 11
er zuckt mit den Schultern	*he shrugs his shoulders*
zu|decken (tr.)	cover up 15
zu|drehen (tr.)	turn off 15
zufrieden stellen (tr.)	satisfy 15
zu|geben (tr.)	admit, concede 61
zu|gehen (auf+acc.) (intr.+s.)	approach (so., sth.) 88
zu|greifen (intr.)	help oneself 31
zugute kommen (dat.) (intr.+s.)	benefit 58
zuhaben (tr.)	be closed 2
zu|haken (tr.)	hook up/on 15
zu|hören (dat.) (intr.)	listen (to) 15
zu|knöpfen (tr.)	button 15
zu|korken (tr.)	cork up 15
zu|lassen (tr.)	allow, authorize 10, 79
zu|machen (tr. & intr.)	shut, close down 15
zu|messen (tr.)	measure out, apportion, 69
zu|muten (dat.) (tr.)	expect (of so.) 12, 15
zunichte machen (tr.)	wreck, shatter 15
zurecht|finden (refl.)	cope, find one's way 47
zurecht|kommen (mit) (intr.+s.)	cope (with) 58
zurück|bringen (tr.)	bring back 24
zurück|fahren (tr. & intr.+s.)	drive back 76
zurück|fallen (intr.+s.)	fall back 79
*****zurück|geben** (tr.)	give back 61
zurück|gehen (intr.+s.)	go back 88
zurück|halten (tr. & refl.)	hold back 79
zurück|kehren (intr.+s.)	return 15
zurück|kommen (intr.+s.)	come back, get back 58
zurück|lassen (tr.)	leave behind 10, 79
zurück|prallen (intr.)	bounce back 15
zurück|rufen (tr. & intr.)	call back 82
zurück|schicken (tr.)	send back 15
zurück|schrauben (tr.)	cut back 15
zurück|setzen (tr. & intr.)	reverse, back up 15
zurück|treten (intr.+s.)	resign, step back 65
zurück|weisen (tr.)	turn down, refuse 28

zurück|werfen (tr.)	reflect, throw back 51
zurück|zahlen (tr.)	pay back 15
zurück|ziehen (tr. & intr. & refl.)	draw back, move back 33, 35
zu|rufen (dat.) (tr. & intr.)	shout (at so.), hail 82
*zusammen|brechen (intr.+s.)	break down, collapse 51
zusammen|drängen (tr. & refl.)	crowd together 15
zusammen|fahren (tr. & intr.+s.)	crash 76
er fährt zusammen	*he gives a start*
zusammen|fallen (intr.+s.)	collapse, coincide 79
zusammen|fassen (tr. & intr.)	sum up, summarize 15
zusammen|hängen (mit) (tr. & intr.)	link, relate (to) 85
zusammen|klappen (tr. & intr.+s.)	collapse, fold up 15
zusammen|kommen (intr.+s.)	link up 58
zusammen|laufen (intr.+s.)	merge, run together 82
zusammen|leben (intr.)	live together 15
zusammen|legen (tr.)	combine 15
wir legen zusammen (intr.)	*we pool our money*
zusammen|nehmen (refl.)	pull oneself together 54
zusammen|passen (intr.)	suit one another 15
die Farben passen zusammen	*the colors match*
zusammen|pressen (tr.)	compress 15
zusammen|raffen (tr.)	bundle up 15
zusammen|rufen (tr.)	summon 82
zusammen|rücken (tr. & intr.+s.)	move together 15
zusammen|schließen (refl.)	join together 41
zusammen|schrumpfen (intr.+s.)	shrivel up, shrink 15
zusammen|setzen (tr.)	assemble 15
es setzt sich aus ... zusammen (refl.)	*it consists of ...*
zusammen|stellen (tr.)	compile, put together 15
zusammen|stoßen (tr. & intr.+s.)	crash 82
zusammen|tun (tr. & refl.)	put/get together 92
zusammen|zählen (tr.)	add up 15
zusammen|ziehen (tr. & intr.)	move together 33, 35
es zieht sich zusammen (refl.)	*it contracts*
zusammen|arbeiten (intr.)	cooperate 12, 15
zu|schauen (dat.) (intr.)	watch 15
zu|schlagen (tr. & intr.)	slam, bang 76
zu|schreiben (dat.) (tr.)	credit, ascribe (to) 28

zu|**sehen** (dat.) (intr.)	watch, look on 72
zu|**sprechen** (tr.)	award 51
zu|**stimmen** (dat.) (intr.)	agree (to) 15
zu|**teilen** (dat.) (tr.)	allocate (to) 15
zu|**trauen** (dat.) (tr.)	credit (so.) with 15
ich traue mir nichts zu (dat. refl.)	*I have no confidence in myself*
zu|**treffen** (intr.)	apply 56, 58
zuvor|**kommen** (dat.) (intr.+s.)	anticipate 58
zu|**weisen** (tr.)	assign 28
zu|**ziehen** (tr. & intr.)	close 33, 35
ich ziehe mir ... zu (dat. refl.)	*I incur ...*
zu|**bereiten** (tr.)	prepare 12, 15
zu|**gestehen** (tr.)	confess 91, 90
zu|**nehmen** (tr. & intr.)	increase, grow 54
züchten (tr.)	rear 12
zünden (tr.)	light 12
zweifeln (an+dat.) (intr.)	doubt 11
zwingen (zu) (tr.)	force (into), compel 42
zwitschern (tr. & intr.)	twitter 11

NOTES

288